Bucket Showers & Baby Goats

Volunteering in West Africa
Volta Region, Ghana

CHRISTINE BROWN

DEDICATION

This book is dedicated to the people of Saviefe. I think about you every day and I am honored to call you my friends. Thank you for welcoming me into your homes and your hearts.

And especially to the Anyo Group:

Semanu (Sema), Rose Anku-Ateletsa (Mama), Walter, Richard, Emil, Hans, Tony, and Beatrice, I want to say,

akpe, ka ka ka (thank you very much).

ACKNOWLEDGEMENTS

To my family, thank you for your continued support throughout my endeavors around the world, for watching after my dog while I'm away, and for meeting me at airports with fresh vegetables.

To my Uncle Jimmy, thank you for encouraging me to compile my stories into this book.

I also want to give a BIG "thank you" to my dear friends and travel companions, Denise and Samantha. Thank you for your strength, your humor, your sense of adventure, and your willingness to deal with unforeseen complications. Together we learned a lot about life, community, and farm animals… and I'm grateful for your friendship.

INTRODUCTION

During the summer of 2008, I came to a realization. My first three years of post-college professional experience had turned me into another cog of Corporate America. I was a project coordinator at a management and IT training company in the Dulles Tech Corridor of Northern Virginia. I shared an apartment in downtown Silver Spring with a college friend, and day-in and day-out, I went about my life. All around me I watched as young people settled for lackluster suburban lives with monotonous routines. They didn't seem interested in expanding their horizons in the same way I was. As long as they had a 401K and were in line to becoming homeowners and VIP shoppers of Crate and Barrel, they were satisfied. I, on the other hand, was getting restless.

I wanted to do something with my life that would help others, help communities, and mean something to someone. I had taken a course in college, *The Sociology of Poverty*, where I learned (largely for the first time) about the hard reality of life for migrant workers throughout the U.S. I never realized just how many people lived in poverty in the U.S. In fact, when I took the course in 2004, the number of Americans living below the poverty line in the U.S. (about 37 million people) exceeded that of the entire population of Canada. According to 2012 Census data, the number of Americans living in poverty had risen to 46.5 million.

But this book is not the story of poverty in the United States. I was interested in poverty and health issues experienced by vulnerable communities around the world. I wanted to know why those communities experienced such hardship, whether for environmental reasons, a lack of resources, political unrest, etc. I wanted to see firsthand what vulnerable really meant, and how ideas could be translated into policy and development.

People would ask me why I was so interested in development issues, and they would say things like, "Africa is such a big problem; you can't fix it." I was so frustrated, "Africa is a *continent*, not a *problem*." In my mind, small scale projects in small communities would be the best way to address a community's needs, depending on the country, the political climate, the environment, the people, and what those people wanted for themselves.

Knowing that my uninspiring career at the time had reached a plateau, I resigned, and started the application process to graduate programs in international development. I then began searching for volunteer opportunities that would not only provide me with necessary field experience on which I thought I could build my career, but as it turns it out, it would also serve to inspire the rest of my life.

Part 1

2008

Volunteer Plans

The *Global Volunteer Network*, a New Zealand based NGO, offered a community development volunteer opportunity to Ghana, and I signed up. The *Global Volunteer Network* sent a program guide as a brief introduction to Ghana and the challenges Ghanaian people face:

- A high percentage of Ghanaian people are subsistence farmers, only growing enough for their own family and at times perhaps a little extra for trading or cash sales.
- Life expectancy is less than 57 years.
- Ghana was the second largest producer of cocoa in the world at one time. In the early 1990s gold become their number one leading export, but as global prices fell, it hit the economy hard.
- Tourism and timber have become a significant generator of income.
- Many Ghanaians do not attend school past the primary level. School fees and uniform prices prevent many children from attending school altogether. Poorer families will keep their children at home to work in the fields or send them off to work to bring back money for the family.
- There aren't enough teachers to cope with large class sizes. In some areas there will be morning and afternoon sessions of school to accommodate up to 100 students per teacher.

This endeavor would last for the month of October, working with *BRIDGE* – a non-profit organization in Ghana founded by two Peace Corps veterans. Operating in the Volta Region of

Ghana, the aim of BRIDGE was to help build sustainable village-based organizations in Ghana to better equip communities with methods to reduce poverty. By partnering with village-based organizations, BRIDGE was able to help fund and support projects like creating educational and vocational opportunities for youth, and encouraging grassroots research. Cultural immersion is an important piece of the puzzle as well for creating partnership and trust, ideally contributing to lasting impact.

As volunteers, we could expect to be tasked with anything from consulting community members in leadership skills, helping the CBO to create an effective accounting system, training them in computer and English skills, and assisting them in writing proposals for development projects they may want to plan.

We will be staying in Saviefe Gbogame (pronounced *Sav-ee-eff-ay Bo-gah-may*), a rural village about 45 minutes outside of Ho, the capital city of the Volta Region. The village farms mostly corn and cassava. The mission of our partner organization is to alleviate poverty through education. The community-based organization (CBO), Anyo Group, is educating the community on the importance of child education, especially for female children. They began building a library in the village but they lack funding for completion. We are tasked with conducting meetings with Anyo Group to develop an organizational profile and action plan so they can complete the library construction, which will eventually be run with the help of an income-generating farming project.

The logistics for the trip came together piece by piece. In July, I received my yellow fever vaccine, followed by the rest of the vaccines a few weeks later. The flight dates were approved by the organization, so once I booked my flight, I visited the Ghanaian Embassy (conveniently located in DC) to apply for my visa. My good friend Denise has volunteered with me as well, and I couldn't ask for a better travel companion. Of course, when Denise visited the Ghanaian embassy for her visa application, who should appear but the President of Ghana!

I moved in with my father, for a rent-free living situation, but I still needed to pay for my flights (roundtrip airfare to Ghana was about $1500) and my vaccines (which run up to $500 – just Yellow Fever is $145) and a small program fee which covered the homestay and meals. This went directly to Anyo Group, and to the Asafu family that would be hosting us.

September 27, 2008
The Journey

I woke this morning, surprisingly headache-free, after a night of send-off drinking and only three hours of sleep. My room was cluttered and boxes were strewn about from my recent move from my cozy 2-bedroom apartment with Laura to my new *bachelorette pad*, as it were, in my father's basement. With Laura now living in Boston, I had lost my voice of reason and only began packing last night. Of course, I went into panic mode when I couldn't find the box with the red puma shoebox, in which lay my trusty iPod.

My father was away on business in Kuala Lumpur, completely unaware of the inevitable disaster zone I created in his living room. Alas! Finally, I discovered the red shoebox and breathed a sigh of relief as I stuffed the iPod into my backpack. I should mention, the "backpack" I speak of is a large pack, almost as big as I am, extremely heavy and more top-heavy than

I had anticipated. Clearly, you need such a backpack to fit your month's supply of clothing, soap, and extras when you need to carry everything yourself over fairly long distances on dirt roads... where luggage on wheels would prove more difficult.

I also packed books: three novels and two guidebooks on Ghana and West Africa. I'm a slow reader so I figured three books for pleasure might be a little ambitious, the same way I ambitiously purchased a dresser for clothing organization yet still leave piles of clean laundry on the floor instead for easy access. I have surprised myself though. The first book I chose, Bad Monkeys, is a fast read and keeps me curiously turning the page to find out if this woman who was arrested for murder, is crazy or telling the truth about her involvement in a secret organization fighting evil, or as quoted "the Final Disposition of Irredeemable Persons," aka Bad Monkeys. Very engaging, I recommend it especially for those with attention spans that resemble that of a goldfish, like me. At any rate, after we'd been in flight for about an hour, I was already finished with 40% of the book. Opting for a reading break, I began my first journal entry to document this trip:

I was just handed dry-roasted peanuts. Obviously, this is common on airplanes, or was before everyone became allergic to peanuts, but it reminds me of my mother. I have memories of her wandering around the house, constantly holding a jar of peanuts, and she always had peanut-breath when she said goodnight to me.

We have ten hours left of our flight before we arrive in Accra and we've just hit some fairly significant turbulence. I'd rather not think of the vast ocean beneath me. Something tells me if the plane goes down, the water will be cold, and someone might accidentally take my life vest and I'll be left with a freaking seat cushion to cling for dear life. I wonder if Denise has seen

Shark Week. I'll ignore the turbulence and go back to the peanuts.

I'm always intrigued by the tininess of airplane food. The fork and knife are 3 inches long, which would go over well on flights to the North Pole. We had a small cup of salad, 2 crackers with a slice of cheese, which was in a wrapper with a red pull-tab but mine was broken and you'd require MacGyver skills to open it. Luckily, Denise has that exact skill set, so problem averted. We also got a piece of bread with butter, tortellini with a resemblance of Chef Boyardee, and a brownie which I skipped since I don't like chocolate.

September 28, 2008
First Day

Once we de-boarded the plane we were met outside the airport by Joy, a young man (mid 20s I think) with short braids and linen pants, and a gold band cuffed around his right wrist. He led us to a taxi, which we took to the tro-tro stop. A tro-tro is a full-size van, used as a bus. Our tro-tro held fifteen adults and a lot of stuff in the nonexistent trunk- our bags, two other large bags, a smaller bag, and two tires. Vendors swarmed the tro-tro, pulling open the windows and trying to sell everything from fruit to water to books and watches. When they wanted your attention, they would make hissing noises.

Joy purchased three packets of water for us to have for the tro-tro trip. You bite off a corner of a sealed plastic bag, and suck the filtered water that way. It costs about five cents per pouch, or one cedi (almost a dollar) for a giant bag of them. Each pouch is 500 ml. It was a three-hour ride on the tro-tro to Ho, where we jumped out to get into another taxi to take us to the Bridge Volta Office, a few minutes down the road located in what was referred to as "KK House." We met Bismark (head of the office) and used the facilities, which lacked toilet paper. I left mine in the taxi by accident. Coincidentally, I did smack my head against the car door, so that's my excuse for forgetting. Bismark and Joy then drove us the forty-five minutes to our village, Saviefe Gbogame. The orange dirt road was riddled with giant potholes that Bismark skillfully weaved through at four miles per hour.

Once we arrived in the village of Saviefe, it was a whirlwind of welcoming and introductions. As the taxi approached the village, children would point and smile at us. The car had not even fully stopped yet and men from the village leaned into the windows, welcoming us with "woezo", opening the doors, taking our bags and telling us to "follow, follow." Anyone nearby would stop whatever they were doing to come and greet us, and there were so many children that appeared. We were led to our compound and our bags had already been carried ahead. Apparently, everyone had expected us to be a couple, rather than two friends. Though they did refer to Denise as *Dennis* throughout the trip.

We were introduced to *everyone,* beginning with some men in Anyo Group. Someone appeared with plastic lawn chairs and we were seated with Tony, Emil and Hans, along with Bismark and Joy. Tony was a teacher in the village, and our assigned counterpart in Anyo Group. He served as our point person if we had any concerns, and was also the primary contact between Anyo Group and Bismark. Plastic chairs suddenly appeared (carried by some older boys) and we sat for formal introductions and a quick lesson on Ewe greetings. Ewe is the local language spoken. Most people know English in Ho, but only some can speak English in the villages.

Tony, Emil, and Hans escorted us to greet our landlord within our host family's compound. Traditionally, when a visitor is received in Ghana, the host is meant to wash the guests' feet of mud from their long travels. This roughly translated into our landlord pouring us each a double shot of whiskey. I took it down (two tries though) and could barely hold my own with the four men sitting with us. After one round, cups were passed around again for a second pour. Denise and I exchanged glances, took a breath, and downed the second cup. After not having much sleep, and it being about fifteen hours since my last real meal, I was giggly to say the least... definitely feeling it.

After our welcome beverages, Denise and I were excused to our part of the house within the compound to rest. The cement walls of the family compound were painted white, with an open doorway into a dirt courtyard with several wooden posts holding up a thatched canopy for shade. The yard, which had little vegetation except a few large aloe plants along the wall, was bordered by several cement rooms. The bright blue doors were propped open and each entrance marked with a knee length piece of fabric hanging as a curtain.

Denise and I entered a doorway into what would be our home for the next five weeks. A small front room (probably eight by ten feet) boasted a plastic table with two chairs for meals and workspace. Next to the table, a second door connected to a bedroom with a small table and two full-size beds beneath mosquito nets. The windows (one in the bedroom and one in the front area) had a screen with large glass shades, usually slanted open to let in fresh air. The windows and both doors were draped with a piece of fabric that swayed with the breeze most of the day, but lay still at night. Semanu (Sema for short), our caretaker and a female representative of Anyo Group, provided lunch of rice and some type of spicy meat which was incredibly delicious.

I was exhausted, and couldn't wait to just lay down. After approximately forty-five seconds of rest, I opened my eyes and directed them to some loud giggles, which belonged to the three sets of feet standing on the other side of our curtain-door. Curious about their new visitors, Fida (12), Grace (12, but looks 9), and Jessica (3), stuck their heads under the curtain to get a better look. This is a foreshadowing as to how all children would pop in over the coming weeks.

Denise and I left our beds to follow the girls through the village to the unfinished library and the schools. There were animals everywhere - cats, goats, sheep, chickens, roosters, baby chicks, kittens, just absolutely everywhere I turned I needed to be careful to not walk right into them. The Primary and Junior Secondary schools consisted of a string of plots joined together by a wall on each end, and a roof. Each plot had some desks and a chalkboard. It looked like a picnic area - completely open except for the wall at each end, and shorter waist-high walls to separate each room. Tony and Emil caught up with us and began explaining plans for the library, and how the books will help the kids to become better students and go further with their education. Tony is also trying to organize a football team in his village to help the young boys stay clear of the wrong people and wrong influences.

We walked through the village and met the co-chairman of Anyo and an elder in the village, Walter. He offered us hot nuts that he picked from a local tree and boiled over a fire. He didn't know the name of the nut, but it's similar to a brazil nut, and you peel off the skin to eat it. He also gave us Malta Guinness (non-alcoholic) which was really good. There were so many signs and vendors for Guinness in this country. The men asked questions about the United States: the weather, the violence, the upcoming election, whether or not we had mosquitoes... We were excused and told to rest, as they were planning a welcome ceremony for us. Denise and I walked back to our room with a multiplying trail of curious children behind us. Jessica soon joined us in our room, and played with my hand as I closed my eyes. Grace walked in to join her, and the two of them played with Denise's camera while I drifted off to sleep.

I woke to the sound of loud roosters, goats crying out what sounded like a rooster impression shortly after, and then the drums. I heard chanting. We went outside to see the whole village (what looked like eighty people) had gathered in our compound's courtyard, singing, dancing, and chanting to the drums. It was amazing! We joined in the dancing, which was easy since it was just girls going around in a circle while the boys beat the drums in the center. Jessica popped out in front of me to join the dance. The feisty three-year-old waved her little arms in the air and swung her hips, imitating the older women.

After a while, Denise and I sat down to watch the rest of the ceremony in awe. Jessica soon found herself a good seat to view the festivities - on my lap! Pretty soon we were surrounded by all the children, ages two to twelve. They would say their name, or just smile and nod to whatever I asked them. It was truly a very welcoming experience, and wonderful to see the ceremony they hold for special occasions.

When it was over, Denise and I shared an omelet and a couple slices of bread, and brushed our teeth with a bucket and a bag of water. Tucked away under our mosquito nets (which were heroically hung by Sema after she realized we tried to fasten them to the ceiling with dental floss and medical tape), we fell asleep listening to the singing of a church service being conducted in the courtyard outside our room. The acapella hymns, more traditional Protestant rather than Gospel, were beautiful. They also lasted for four hours until just past midnight, which made it a bit awkward every time we needed to venture to the outhouse in our pajamas.

Everyone is so friendly. Tomorrow, we travel back to Ho for an orientation and to meet other volunteers. We will begin to sort donated books for distribution to area villages. I'm dirty and sweaty but couldn't be happier to finally be here. Tomorrow I also get to try bucket showers.

September 29, 2008
Day Two

In case you were wondering, the actual crack of dawn began at 5:15 AM. People were yelling and children were squealing and running all over the place. The roosters and goats were making noise too. We got up and brushed our teeth. We use just toothpaste and a toothbrush and spit into a bucket we found. We walked to the toilet which is in a sort of cement outhouse with a wooden door. Just inside the door there are two cement stalls, each with wooden doors that don't actually close. There's no sink but there is a small light bulb hanging from the ceiling, giving off as much light as a small flashlight, but often the most light comes through a small concrete window (hole) in the wall just above the toilet. There is no running water and no function to the toilet tank, so it requires a bucket flush. A water barrel sits in the corner of the outhouse with a bucket on top. You scoop the water and pour it into the toilet bowl after you're done, and that's your "flush." We emptied our toothbrushing spit at this time.

On to the shower area, a cement square enclosure about six feet high, with no roof, and a spigot on the wall (for aesthetics only). Our landlord walked from the shower back toward his rooms with a blue towel wrapped around his waist. A small boy saw us loitering by the shower area and brought over two buckets of water from the well. We recognized the black bucket from our room (we didn't realize its purpose until now) but wondered where the second gray bucket came from. I took the black bucket and Denise took the gray.

A little unnerving at first, showering in an open-air space with no roof or door was actually quite refreshing. I splashed myself, washed my face, and dunked my hair. I tried to splash-rinse the shampoo out but I don't think I did a very good job. For the rest of me, it was splash-soap, splash-soap, splash. Not bad! I definitely felt very clean compared to the rest of the day with layers of sunscreen, insect repellent, dirt and grime. After scratching one mosquito bite, my fingernails would be black. When we finished our shower, we asked the boy where we should return the gray bucket to. He took it and replied, "I will take it back to the toilet." Denise and I shot each other a look and just started laughing.

We got dressed and went to the roadside of the village to wait for the bus to Ho. The bus comes between 7:30 and 8 AM, just 1 bus per day, except for Market Day when the bus will come 3 times. Market Day happens every five days - this week it's on Wednesday. The bus stopped at every village along the way to pick up more people. In some villages, the driver would get out and we'd have to wait up to twenty minutes before he returned to drive us to the next village! The bus was extremely hot and humid. Everyone (except me and Denise) had handkerchiefs to wipe the sweat from their necks and faces - making a mental note to bring one for the next bus ride. Some windows were open so when the bus began to move again, even ever so slowly, you caught a very small, but very refreshing breeze.

Riding along, many people on the bus welcomed us. Children pointed from the road and people would call out "white ladies" or "obruni," describing an outsider or foreigner. Literally "those who come from over the horizon," the term is often used as "white person". The air smelled like corn, trees, and the strong scent of oranges, which came from a woman a few seats behind us with a basket of them to sell at the Market in Ho. Oranges here are not orange, by the way. They're green on the outside, and white on the inside. Just like oranges, only a little more bitter. They should be called Greenges. And no one eats the pulp - you're meant to spit it out and folks will look at you funny if you don't.

After two hours (remember it should only take 45 minutes), we arrived in Ho and walked to the second KK House where other volunteers were sorting donated books to distribute to 18 area schools. Some were primary and others were junior (JSS) or senior (SSS) secondary schools. First, we sorted by primary or junior level, then by subject. We had piles for each school and once the books were sorted, we tried to distribute each set evenly between the different school piles. Many boxes that were donated contained sets of textbooks but some books we received only had a set of five books. We left those for the end to decide which school had a greater need. After about three hours of sorting, it was lunch time.

We walked with Bismark and Joy and the other volunteers to a small covered seating area. A man came out from behind a curtain carrying cokes! That was a nice treat. They were in skinny glass bottles and tasted a little different than they do back home. We were given rice and a chicken wing. The chicken was so tough it was difficult to pull apart, but the rice was good, as always.

We stopped in the Bridge Volta Office with Tony and Sema. They had accompanied us to Ho and followed us around, I guess as any caretaker (or bodyguard) would do. Bismark said the orientation would have to wait until Thursday, but mentioned other initiatives with the JSS students he'd like us to work on, including encouraging higher education, and discussing the risk and danger of teenage pregnancy and the spread of HIV/AIDS.

After our meeting with Bismark, Tony took us through the market, mazes of thatched roofs and wooden stands where all kinds of goods were being sold. Walking along dirt paths between the vendors and brushing away hanging fabric of the brightest colors, we tried to keep up with Tony. He introduced us to his mother who was selling candy and cigarettes. A small weaving again through the back side of the market led us to his sister who was selling vegetables. The produce smelled so fresh! The market was loud and bustling. We walked over to the taxis to wait for Sema who had split off to pick up a few things earlier. Children ran up, tugged on my shirt and asked in English, "How are you?" I said, "I'm fine, how are you?" but they just smiled and repeated the question. They wanted to shake hands, hold hands, high-five, the whole deal.

Over by the taxis we entered a bar (shack) where one man sat behind a counter and you could purchase shots. Five shot glasses sat on the counter, though I wondered how he would clean them between uses. He gave us change for 1 cedi so we could buy a sack of water pouches. You have to get those in Ho, they don't have water for sale in the villages.

The road in Ho is as I've described, orange dirt. Pedestrians do NOT have the right of way. A ditch runs along the side of the road for drainage. Storefronts are right over the ditch and since there is no sidewalk, you have to jump over the drainage ditch, but sometimes there are boards laying across you can step on. These drainage ditches are not cute little streams, by the way. They are opaque green, and littered with trash. Some parts of the city smell of trash and sewage, but most of Ho smells like the combination of Malta Guinness, sweet bread, and dirt. This is supplemented in the villages with the smell of goat meat. Sema appeared with 2 trays of fresh eggs and a large pink printed back full of something. We climbed into a taxi and headed home.

Taxis and busses honk more in one day than I honk in an entire year back home. The roads are narrow, so coming around a bend, the honk warns people and animals to get out of the way. We did clip the leg of a baby goat on our way, and shortly thereafter hit another goat who just stood in awe as we headed straight for it, honking the horn. We hit that one harder than the first, but both goats seemed ok. I don't know... they hobbled off the road, so they weren't dead. Denise had a hard time with that.

When we drove up to the village, several children ran up to greet us. Denise practiced carrying the sack of water on her head, and the children walked us back to our room. While Sema prepared our dinner (noodles with peppers and small pieces of fish), the children gathered on our front steps and in our room. A boy shined our flashlight at Jessica and she tried to blow it out. We practiced Ewe and they practiced English. One boy brought over a book to show us. He began reading Denise's notebook while Jessica was enthralled with the flashlight (especially on the blinking red setting). Soon, I broke out the crayons I brought and ripped some paper from my notebook, and a bunch of them gathered on the floor with me to color.

Sema shooed the children away when she brought in our food, but they just waited patiently outside until we were finished and then came back in to play. A few small boys, about 4 years old, crawled under our door curtain to appease their curiosity. They really liked the crayons. Grace lay down on the floor and Jessica soon followed. We said goodnight around 8:30 PM. About an hour later, it was time to wash up, change and climb under my mosquito net. When I went outside to the toilet I saw Jessica (3), Grace (12), their brother Kosi (15) and Selom (6) sleeping with a blanket on a wooden platform usually used to lay out and dry corn for the mill. It was really hot that night, so they dragged a yellow foam mattress outside for more air flow. They looked so peaceful.

Returning to the room, I could hear something scurrying around on the roof. Denise suggested a lizard, but the sounds were too big to be a lizard. Maybe a chicken? They don't fly though... a rat? Then a large bump came from above us and I changed my mind. I think it's a goat. I don't know how he'd get up there but I'd rather think it's a goat than a chicken-sized rat. Lying in my bed, I watch a really big mosquito try really hard to get in. Ha! Can't get me! I'm in my fancy net.

September 30, 2008
Life Goes On

So, I did get a few mosquito bites last night. The repellent I am using has 40% DEET. Strong stuff. It takes the ink off my sandals, which leaves a greenish teal print on my feet. I also noticed the label on my pen is now practically gone!

I would like to mention something about roosters. It's not like the cartoons where they do their cock-a-doodle-doo thing once in the morning and everyone wakes up and starts their day. These things scream for over an hour, straight, beginning at 5 AM. I checked the time.

Today and tomorrow, Denise and I will be staying in the village to work. After breakfast and another bucket-splash session, we'll just be living among everyone else and playing with the children, once they're finished school. Sema said she'd teach us to carry things on our heads (yesterday I saw a woman carrying a basket of dishes on her head!) and how to wash our clothes, which is probably just more buckets. Pretty straightforward.

Well I must say, I'm becoming very efficient with the bucket-splash system for bathing. This morning we walked around the village and met Tony's mother-in-law, and his 2 children, Richmond (8) and Dina (2). Dina was scared of us. His mother-in-law offered us pieces of a yam she was peeling. It's not like ours back home; they're white, textured potatoes. Tony's wife had gone to the farm, which is apparently very far. We learned that Tony is a teacher at the Junior Secondary school in the village. He teaches technical skills, for wood and metal.

Saviefe is a township with 3 villages—Agorkpo (the capital of Saviefe), Deme, and Gbogame (where we are). We met the chief of Gbogame today. He is the head teacher at the primary school in Agorkpo. His wife is also a teacher at the same school.

We walked fifteen minutes to the next town, Deme. There, we came to a bar (small shack with 2 chairs, a counter, and a bartender named Erickson). We also met a very talkative, slightly crazy man named Roka who wanted to show off his English skills by quizzing us on American history. Erickson gave us Guinness, joked about Roka, and tried to get him to leave us alone. Tony had to distract him and take him outside.

We walked with Tony and Erickson around Deme, and we met more villagers who invited us to their wedding the weekend after next! That'll be really fun to take part in. We went to a house with pink baby chicks (literally fuzzy baby chickens that are painted bright pink so the hawks won't snatch them). Inside we were offered shots - more of that washing feet tradition! This time it was a liquor distilled from palm wine, and we began discussing the upcoming election. All three men (Tony included) are for Nana because the NPP (New Patriotic Party) has apparently done a good job so far in getting rid of school fees for primary and junior secondary schools. We arrived back in Gbogame and watched some children play soccer. They didn't have school today because it's a Muslim holiday. We had lunch and soon Jessica, Grace, and Selom showed up to play.

Anyo Group

At 4 PM we walked to Sema's house to meet with the seven-member executive committee of the community-based organization, Anyo Group. In Ewe, "anyo" means "it will be better." We sat under a thatched covering and looked out across the palm trees to the mountains and dark gray skies. It looked like a storm was nearby, but you wouldn't guess it from the still air. Clothes were hanging to dry on a line. As I looked more closely, a shirt looked familiar and I realized they were my clothes! Sema must have gathered them from our room when we went to Deme, and washed them for me! Honestly, we are so well taken care of here.

We introduced ourselves to the group and discussed what we'd like to accomplish. In essence, we have three goals, first of which is the library. We asked them to speak to vendors about pricing more material so we'd have an estimated budget by the end of the week. We'll also do some research on potential donors. Our second goal is to conduct computer training for the committee members on a Dell Toughbook laptop donated from a past volunteer. None of the members have previous training or experience with computers. However, the few donated computers will be kept in the library once it's finished. Once we train the committee members, we'll give them training material so they will be able to train the children and others in the village. We will conduct ongoing training for the next 4 weeks for the members. Our third goal for this trip is something I'm really looking forward to. We will implement and begin a health education program and talk to the JSS students about the importance of education and encourage them to go to senior secondary school and college.

Kids are allowed to marry at age 18, but Tony thinks if they are encouraged and believe they can go to college, that they won't rush into marriage. Teenage pregnancy is rampant in Saviefe, and there is no health education taught in schools. The only way kids learn about sex is from their parents, but many parents don't talk to them about sex or other health issues. Bismark said that Bridge has never done this before, but he wants us to talk to the JSS students about health, disease, sex, the spread of HIV, the problems with teenage pregnancy, and encourage higher education. The hope is that once we hold some health education sessions and develop sex education materials, the teachers can take over once we leave. Tony is going to speak with the school authorities about the current curriculum and find out where we can fit in the health program. It helps that Tony is on the board of the school authority!

The meeting was very productive and the committee seemed very excited about our plans, and extremely pleased to have two volunteers. Many villages get only one volunteer at a time, and even then, it can be a year between when one volunteer leaves and another arrives to continue the work. This is a big reason we want to start training the committee members on computer skills, and on methods of health education, so they can continue to impart that knowledge to the rest of the village once we leave. We have a lot to do in such a short visit.

Life Goes On (Continued...)

After the meeting we went home to play with the children (who were waiting patiently on our stoop) before dinner. Jessica climbed into my lap and Grace began singing a church song for us, which prompted Jessica to leap up and bounce and dance around. Their brother, Kosi (15), joined us and showed me papers from his Ewe class at school. In Ewe class they learn about the Ewe language and about Ghana. Selom (6) also showed up.

I learned that Sema was married before but did not have any children so her husband left her. This is not common and he does still live in this village. After her sister died 6 years ago, Sema adopted her baby nephew, Selom, and raises him as her own son. Selom is very shy and gets upset when he doesn't feel included. I've been trying to reassure him and encourage him, especially with his drawing and counting. Jessica can be distracting with her dramatic attention-seeking spunk, but I do hope Selom comes out of his shell a bit. Kosi and Grace are very mature but probably also used to competing for attention with Jessica, and they have about a month before their 5th sibling arrives.

The family dynamics are really interesting. It's as if there are "village children," no one introduces themselves and children as their son or daughter. The older kids care for and watch over the younger ones, and some adults are also involved (if they are nearby) in watching over them and disciplining them if they have to. It definitely puts a very literal spin on "it takes a village to raise a child."

October 1, 2008

Back home I have a slight phobia of farm animals. I mean, they're great and all, but chickens especially, I don't like them near me, let alone touching me. Never in my life have I walked so close to chickens and roosters. Roosters are very aggressive animals! Ok, I know some of you are thinking - big deal, you walk next to chickens. I don't think you realize how intimately I am living with chickens, goats, sheep, and cats. Everywhere! The cats and kittens look skinny and their fur is patchy, which makes me think they carry disease (along with chickens eating and pecking trash from the drainage ditch).

I've gotten used to it though. You shoo away goats and chickens that start to go in your house, or start to eat the corn that's laying out to dry before taking it the mill for grinding. I barely even notice the cats and chickens under my chair when I sit outside. At any rate, I *do* notice the roosters. They are unaware they should only cry out in the morning so wherever you are, whatever time of day, they are pretty hard to ignore. It just occurred to me that I have no idea how a chicken and a rooster have sex. I would say maybe chickens can lay eggs anyway, without… bird sex… but then if you have a chicken coup for eggs… why in the hell would you ever *choose* to have a rooster?

Today began with a chicken in the outhouse. The door is typically open unless the outhouse is in use, and one thing I've learned is that chickens like to walk through all open doors. We've already had to shoo them out of our bedroom a few times. I entered the outhouse, closed the door behind me, and a giant chicken started flapping and squawking at my feet, so obviously I fell back against the door screaming. At least Denise, Sema, and Beatrice all had a good laugh.

We walked to the JSS school to meet up with Tony and meet all the children. The unfinished library lacks any more materials to build with, so without funding for additional materials, the Anyo Group is at a standstill, leaving a partially painted open air structure to sit and wait. Proposals for funding have been written and sent out, but it's been over a year and they've received no response.

The children in the classrooms were very enthusiastic when we walked up. We'd enter a classroom and the children would immediately stand and in unison greet us, "mia woezo!" We saw Jessica's class outside but didn't see Grace when we went to the JSS classes. Later we learned she didn't go to school today because, since her mother was going to Market Day in Ho, Grace was needed on the farm. We came to the Primary 1 class and I spotted Selom at the first table. I waved, and he bashfully waved back and then slowly stood, walked over, and gave me a hug. He looked at the floor but you could still see his smile, then he tucked his head under my ribs.

Later we spoke more with Tony about our plans. He asked how soon we could meet with the students to discuss higher education and sex education, and we agreed to start next week. The headmaster wants to meet with us to discuss in more detail as well. Tony talked to us about the challenges he faces as a teacher, and how he thinks the kids don't actually retain the information they are taught. He could lecture all day and ask questions about the material the following day, and the children will just stare at him. They are given homework but some children just don't complete it. When they do not complete their homework, children are punished either by addressing the entire class, or with a cane. Using a cane is illegal, but the teachers think it's the only way to get the children to obey, and complete their assignments.

There are no methods of positive reinforcement, and children don't seem to care if they are held back two or three years. There is no remorse or embarrassment, or attempt to improve. The parents aren't involved at all either, and don't encourage studying. Like Grace today, if they find it necessary, they'll pull the child from school to work on the farm instead. Her older brother was in school, so I wonder if because she's the oldest daughter she is required to do farming instead of school more often than Kosi. I suggested having an after-school program where teachers could take turns staying an hour or so after classes end to encourage students to start on their homework, and answer any questions they may have. Tony said they did have something like that, but it fell apart. He didn't give much detail.

All classes (except Ewe class) are taught in English, but most of the children we've spoken to do not speak it or understand it very well. Grace is an exception; her English is amazing. Though English is the national language of Ghana, many people in the villages speak indigenous languages depending on the region. I imagine English provides a learning barrier, if the children don't understand the language in which the subjects are being taught. It seems that the education is mostly lecture, without many activities throughout the day to reinforce what they've learned. It's not a very interactive environment. When the kids return home, there are many distractions and they need to do work around the home. The hope is that when the library is complete, the kids will have a place to go to study and complete their homework.

The benefits of the library are two-fold. A boy we met yesterday named Divine (20) thinks that the finished library (with electricity), will provide teenagers with a place to go after dinner to study. He thinks this will give them something to do, a safe place to go, and he believes this will help prevent teenage pregnancy. Divine told us that it is best to teach abstinence "because condoms kill sperm, so they kill the chance of making life." And this goes against the law of God, as the bible says "go forth and have children," not "go forth and use condoms to have sex a lot." People we've come across in this village are under the impression that since condoms aren't 100% effective, it doesn't make any difference and you may as well not use them at all. Denise and I are assuming this was taught to them as if to say, "well, it's not going to 100% prevent a pregnancy, so really you just shouldn't have sex." But kids are going to have sex. Now, they're just choosing not to use condoms at all since they're not 100% effective anyway.

Divine also shared that even though there is no sex education, people think they know all there is to know already. The primary concern right now (in their minds) is teenage pregnancy. The only sexually transmitted disease they know about, or hear about, is AIDS. No one even mentions other possibilities like syphilis or gonorrhea. Divine also mentioned that even here in the village, girls will prostitute themselves for a small amount of money for food - the equivalent of 50 or 75 cents. It's a vicious cycle: lack of education → more poverty → prostitution and teenage pregnancy → more children with less involved and less educated parents encouraging them to work on the farm.

Thunder rolled in once we were back at our rooms. Some children fell asleep on our floor. Kosi loves to read so he watches us intently as we write, and he likes to read over our shoulders. We gave him *Gulliver's Travels* to read so hopefully that will occupy him for a while. The children are so curious and pay close attention to everything! For certain subjects not appropriate for their young ears, Denise and I began to communicate with each other in Spanish. The kids are always around, leaving privacy as a vague and faraway concept. The kids also have no problem taking your water pouch or glass and helping themselves, which is fine, but good lord these are some thirsty children! No one knocks either, not even adults, even if your door is closed. Though, our doors are kept open most of the time to keep the air flowing, and we just have a curtain hanging to block some sun.

Tony came and took us to a field next to the school where nine boys (18 to early 20s) were playing soccer. We watched them practice for about an hour. The sky turned dark gray behind them, almost black. We headed home before the rain came, stopping briefly to meet with the headmaster of the JSS. He was very welcoming and said he was very happy about our goals to develop programs for the school. The thunder and lightning were getting stronger.

I learned more about Grace and Jessica's family today. The mother is from Liberia and came to Ghana (without her husband—I'm not sure if he died or if she just left him) with Kosi (3 at the time) and Grace (just a baby). There are nine years between Grace and Jessica, another baby about 1 ½ years old, and another one on the way who will arrive in probably a month or so. I don't think the father is around though. I've only seen their mother twice, and she lives in this same family house, across the courtyard.

Jessica is surely proof that American children are babied and fussed over much more than necessary. She smacks into more cement floors and steps than you could imagine but without a concerned adult to make a fuss, she pops back up, laughs, and goes about whatever she was doing. She spins in circles near the steps, and climbs on top of chairs, but you really don't worry about her. Kids are tough, resilient. They'll be fine. I think she and Selom are getting sick though. They're coughing up mucus.

We heard pounding from a room across the courtyard so naturally we went to investigate. Kosi had what looked like a double ended baseball bat and was pounding boiled yams into a wooden bucket. He would wet the bat with water and continue to pound. The yams were slowly transformed into dough, which will be used in a fufu soup for us on Friday, a traditional Ghanaian dish.

October 2, 2008

It rained last night and became quite chilly in our room. With only a bottom sheet on each bed, I wrapped myself in a thin scarf I brought to add a bit of warmth. The rain made the morning air colder than usual, so Beatrice added hot water she had boiled to our shower buckets of well water. The hot shower was really nice. Steam was actually coming off our bodies!

Without being escorted by Tony, we walked to the bus stop where more people came to greet us and test our knowledge of Ewe. A few seemed concerned that we were going to Ho alone, but were satisfied when we were able to say, "Meyi Ho mava," meaning, "we are going to Ho and coming back." Hans and Emil came up to say hello as well as the vice chief, Dick, and our new friend Divine. Denise identified a waterfall nearby she wants to visit, and Divine offered to accompany us to the waterfall next week. It's nice to have someone close to our age to hang out with, who also speaks English fairly well and has useful input for our projects. He comes to visit with us at the compound almost every day.

Once we got to Ho, we finished sorting the donated books. Saviefe Gbogame is one of the 18 villages that get these books! Yay! Score 1 for the home team! Now the books are packed (in 16 or 17 boxes) and ready to be picked up. Tony will have to coordinate this on his own, and will solicit some help from other villagers to collect enough money to pay for a tro-tro to drive the books from Ho to the village, which is an endeavor costing about 20 cedi (approximately $20, but that's a lot of money to them). They're going to wait for next week's Market Day, when tro-tros can be considerably easier to hire for maybe a little less money. The sorting task took 4 hours, which meant that we had already missed the bus back to Ho, so we decided to take our time and figure out a ride later.

We went to a restaurant called White House for lunch, which is kind of funny because the few expats (i.e. white people) in town go there to eat. I got chicken and rice—again, the rice was really good and the chicken was like leather. I did find out some other things they had on the menu so next time I'm getting vegetable pizza and vegetable salad! There's not really cheese on the pizza, but it's close enough, and I'm craving vegetables now. Lunch took forever, so by the time we got to the office it was already 3 PM! The last bus leaves Ho at 1:30 PM, which doesn't leave much time to get things done.

After our orientation with Bismark, we attempted to use the internet café, but there was a virus on some of the computers so it wouldn't recognize our flash drive, and the computers were so slow, even typing required an extra three second response time. If I opened up more than one window, whether it was internet and Word, or two internet windows, I was doomed. By the time I checked a few emails, and finally was able to upload my blog entries, it was 5:45 PM! It was getting dark, and started to thunder very loudly again. We caught a taxi back to the village, arriving in the dark at 6:30. We felt bad, we knew that Tony, Sema, and Beatrice would be worried, and sure enough, Beatrice and Sema joked something in Ewe, meaning "very, very bad girls."

Divine came over after dinner and asked if we could give him computer training as well. We talked about the school system here, and his goals, and firmed up plans for the waterfall excursion next week. It took a long time for him to ask for training… I could tell he wasn't sure if the training was just for Anyo or if he could ask for some too. He was very pleased when we said "of course," and put him on the training schedule for Thursday at 7 PM. This pushes our bedtime back a bit, but that's ok.

October 3, 2008
The Slowness

People here move very slowly. Tony's strides seem to be in slow motion, one foot down… then the other, to create a lethargic mosey. People linger with nothing to say, after a meeting or a visit, and just stare, and wait for something unknown. The language barrier sometimes provides very little to be said after the initial greetings we know in Ewe. It's announced, "Ok I think I will leave you now," and then people sit and stare for a few minutes, then say "ok" and finally get up. If you say you're going to leave, and they reply with "so soon?" that means you're supposed to stay and look at each other some more. The general lack of urgency about everything is different, running on a much slower pace than I'm used to. I had so many goals to accomplish in such a short amount of time, so I wanted to get started right away. Coming to this village from a society obsessed with time, obligation, and schedules, the slow pace of life here put an abrupt halt on that mindset.

At first, it sometimes left me pacing around, feeling unproductive, but now I only get frustrated when we try to do work in Ho. It takes an hour and a half to two hours to get there in the morning, putting you in Ho around 10 AM. The last bus from Ho leaves at 1 PM, so you only have 3 hours to do work, which is simply not enough time. If we stay later to complete our work, the consequence is a taxi back to the village, costing 15 cedi (very expensive, considering the bus only costs 80 pesewas - about 75 cents). Now though, it seems I've slipped into the slowness and the relaxed way of life with ease. Denise is having some difficulty adjusting, but I find it refreshing to be disconnected from the obsession with time. Here, you can just breathe, take it all in, and let your mind wander.

The days are slow and the heat is strong. We get up at 5:30 AM with the goats and roosters, get our buckets from the well to shower, and after bathing, Sema makes breakfast—eggs and sometimes eggs with porridge. We finish breakfast by 6:45 and the kids come to say good morning. They go to school at 8, leaving the family compound very quiet and still, with only the chickens and goats to disrupt the peace. We do some planning for our projects and help around the house. Today we helped carry buckets from the well and helped Sema and Beatrice pound some yams and plantains for our fufu lunch. The heat and carb-rich food force you to consider a nap. Afterwards you may have an hour or so before the children arrive home from school. That is, if they go to school. Grace and Kosi are home today, I'm not sure why. Grace has only been to school 2 days this week- Monday and Thursday. Tuesday was a holiday, but she was needed on the farm on Wednesday. The afternoons are spent planning the school presentations and mapping out training sessions. Dinner is served around 6:30 PM, after which the children crawl back under our curtain to play, making subsequent work more difficult. By 9 PM I try to relax, and read, stretched out under my net before falling asleep to the sound of nature outside my window, i.e. the bleating of our goats.

Our Children

The relationship between Selom (6) and the other children is one of jealousy and anger. It turns out that when he "comes out of his shell," he becomes a brat, refusing to listen or obey. He hits Jessica when he gets jealous of whatever she is playing with, whether it be a crayon or a water pouch or us. If we tell him "no," he goes around us to get to Jessica and smacks her again. She doesn't cry or anything, but does her best to hit back. Being an only child, he doesn't seem to play well with others, or know how to share. One-on-one, he can be very sweet but even then, he tries to forcibly take things he wants, even after we've said "no" and put it away, like a camera, flashlight, or orange. (We gave him one already.) Even when we're holding the camera, you can feel the strength and determination in his little body as he grabs it and pulls hard, looking at you with stubborn disregard for authority. I wonder what his older years will look like. I hope he gets the right guidance. He chimed in when Denise started singing, "Jesus loves me, this I know, for the bible tells me so. Little ones to him belong, they are weak but he is strong… Yes, Jesus loves me, the bible tells me so…"

Kosi (15) seems eager to learn and his English is impressive. He's quiet, mature, and gentle with the younger ones. He finds Bob Marley on my iPod and flips through books left on the table. He is very mindful and always willing to translate for us.

Grace (12) has a very mature disposition, but every now and then she'll act childish to either get attention, or when she lets her guard down and remembers how to be a kid. Sometimes she'll fall asleep in our room, or on a chair in our seating area. Other times she may just pretend to sleep, especially when we start to shoo them out. She's like our junior caretaker. She follows us around, and brings us chairs wherever we go. During the rain we went to a storage/plumbing room to watch Beatrice and Kosi pound fufu; Grace disappeared and returned with 2 chairs for us! When we went to the soccer practice on the field behind the schools, Grace followed, went into a school, and returned carrying a 5-foot wooden bench on her head. She is very concerned when she notices any cuts on my hand, and is very watchful over Jessica in a gentle, but authoritative manner. Sometimes though, she doesn't smile. She'll come in and sit silently, even if there are other people with us, like Divine or Kosi. I can't tell if something's wrong but she'll look at you, and then look away, not making any expression. But she likes to stay in our room as long as possible, even when she's tired enough to fall asleep in a chair.

Jessica (3) is the life of the party with dramatic attitude and expressive eyes. She'll run up ahead through a curtained doorway, hold the curtain back and cock her head, and her face just says it all: *Helloooo! You're supposed to follow me!* From our speaking with her, she's learned, "come on, come on." She's bold for such a young child, the first child to run up and greet us when we arrived. She dances and climbs all over us, singing songs she learned in Sunday school or from her brother and sister, and is always waiting around the corner for us. Last night she cried as Kosi carried her back to their room. She's so sweet and picking up so much English. She'll say "it's MY glass," or "it's MY paper," and repeat almost anything you say with matching enthusiasm and inflection. She's not afraid of anything, and is bold enough to hit older children much bigger than she is. They hit her back but she holds her own. We try to discourage hitting between the children, but it's difficult since that's the form of discipline used here. Other volunteers asked me if I've seen a beating yet, and said it's pretty hard to watch. I hope I don't have to see one here. They also described another form of punishment used, when a young girl was down on her knees, holding stones above her head. Back to Jessica though, honestly, I would be glad to take her home with me! She's so smart, always laughing, and full of constant energy (except when you turn around and she's passed out on the floor or in one of our beds). She's up before we are, waiting patiently until she sees our curtain blowing in a small breeze, (indicating we must be awake since our door is open) then trots in to say good morning. Yesterday she was so tired when we returned to the village, she couldn't even say hello. She just looked at us. She was tired because she went to the farm with her mother, who told us Jessica wanted to follow us but needed a bath first. Jessica's voice is a little raspy, which almost makes everything she says that much more adorable. I wake up from naps often to the sound of her giggling. This is especially true when she's standing next to my bed because it's play time, not nap time, apparently. I'll miss her when I go back to the States.

The others are very curious and friendly, though the extent of the conversation is me asking "mia foa?" to which they smile and reply, "eh." Babies are ok and just look at us, wide-eyed. Toddlers, like Jessica, are eager to play, as are the older children. To a one or two-year-old though, we are monsters! They scream and cry or try to run away. Yesterday a mother brought her screaming child closer to demonstrate we were NOT monsters, and forced her child's hand to touch Denise's hand. The child went silent and just looked at the hands, then back up to Denise, then to her mother, and back at the hands.

No matter where we go, we accumulate a trail of wandering children, sometimes fifteen or twenty of them! We also have child paparazzi crowds at our bedroom window (sans the cameras). The window is open but the curtain is down. As I stand by the window at night, taking out my contacts, or brushing my teeth, I hear small footsteps (in groups) and whispers. I say in English, "Goodnight," which they repeat, then

I have to say "Mia dogu," (to say I'll see you tomorrow) and they giggle and run off.

Notes

In speaking with some people closer to my age (in their 20s), it's confirmed that kids definitely don't understand much of what they're taught when taught in English. Therefore, they are reluctant to speak up or participate in class, and don't understand their homework. There is little opportunity for participation though, as I've mentioned before. For example, there is a computer class, taught by lecture in English, but they don't even have a computer! So, they can't be actually learning, interactively, about how to use one. The kids can recite pages from their text, in English, but have no idea what the pages mean. The Primary 2 kids can recite the entire Primary 2 text. That's what they're taught to do—just recite the text and maybe one day when they understand English, they'll remember what they recited and it'll all make sense. Great plan.

I asked Bismark about something I'd heard—that men cheat on their wives while the women are told to simply turn their heads, and are not protecting themselves from disease. He agreed that is the way many handle it, adding that it is common for men to take girlfriends after they are married, but women are expected to stay faithful. If a woman asks the man to use a condom, that would be disrespectful… so they don't. I suggested we should convince the men that it would be a good idea to protect themselves against disease (via condom use) if they are going to sleep with more than one person. Bismark gave me a look and informed me, "We don't want the men to be unfaithful." I acknowledged and said, "yes, but if they are going to cheat, they should know that condoms are a good thing." Again, Bismarck shook his head. It's so frustrating. As grown men, Bismark and Joy were chuckling as I was asking questions on the subject. It's like… a baby holding a live grenade. Maybe we should take it away? No, maybe instead, we should convince the baby that letting go of the grenade would be a bad thing, so they should just keep holding it. ARGH!

A 14-year-old in Bismark's village just became pregnant. After he spoke with her, it was clear she didn't know that what she was doing with the boy was indeed the act of sex. She thought they were just "messing around." We're going to have to start from square one for our presentations for the JSS students…

There are two funerals this week (different villages, but both nearby) for two teenage mothers who both died during labor. No one is trained as a midwife, and no one in the villages have a car. One girl went into labor and began to experience some complications, so she tried to walk to the hospital. I think there's a clinic two or three villages away from Saviefe Gbogame, but I don't know how far she was trying to walk. She died on the road, before reaching the hospital. The baby didn't survive.

For the younger children, our school presentations will address hygiene as well as education. We will be teaching the importance of washing hands with soap before you eat, and after you use the toilet, as well as brushing your teeth twice a day. As far as teaching health and hygiene though, I'm at a loss of how to teach much more than this. Even the basics, I'm not sure how effective our teaching will be, since some parents don't brush their own teeth, and many people "wash" their hands by simply pouring water over them. I had to ask Tony if every family has soap and use it on a regular basis. He says they have it, but doesn't know how often they wash their hands. Also, it's not going to be very helpful to educate them on a balanced diet with 5 food groups… their food groups consist of 1) yams and cassava, 2) rice and porridge, 3) bananas, plantains, oranges, and 4) meat. Boiled carbs, stewed carbs, mashed carbs, raw carbs, and meat. Really, they don't eat enough vegetables here, and I've only seen them in the markets in Ho. The only vegetables they have here in the village are cassava and yam.

October 4, 2008
Adventure Day

Denise and I decided to break from the calmness of the village for a little sightseeing adventure today. Denise had read in her guidebook about a town nearby called Kpando. A German mission was established there in 1904, so some of the old buildings would be interesting to look at. Also, just further down the road is a small town, Fesi, which is supposedly well known for their pottery. We figured while we were in Kpando, we could buy another sack of water (we were carrying our last 3 pouches) and some toilet paper since we were almost out of that as well.

At seven in the morning we stood by the roadside of the village and waited for a car to drive by. A couple cars drove by, and finally a bright orange car stopped as we waved them down to hitch a ride to Bame (pronounced *bah-may*), a half hour away. Tony and Hans stood by, protectively, and spoke to the three men inside in Ewe, as if to tell them to make sure we got to Bame ok. The ride was bumpy and pretty quiet at first. The guy next to me had headphones on. I couldn't help but look over a few times to see if he had an iPod or something. He caught me looking and revealed it was played from his cell phone. He took out the headphones and the music came through the phone, breaking the ice. He asked if I liked the music, and we began talking about all sorts of things. His name was Prince, and he was 28 years old. His brothers were Bright and Sena (which means gift from God), both older than him I think. They live in Bame but were in Accra for a funeral. Prince asked me how I liked Ghana and if I could see how they suffer. Then we started talking about the schools and the poverty, and why Denise and I were there, what we were trying to accomplish. We got to Bame in one piece, hopped out, and they refused to take any money for the ride. Prince, however, did say he wanted to marry me. Luckily, a hospital van (an ambulance, but really just a van with an "H" on the side) was driving by, so we flagged him down with Prince and Bright's help, and hitched a ride, yet again, only this time to Kpeve. The plan was to then catch a tro-tro to Kpando. It turns out that the driver lives in Kpando, so he took us straight there. He dropped us in the middle of town at 9:15 AM. We hadn't expected to arrive so early, and some vendors weren't out yet. We walked around and looked at a music stand. We also were on the lookout for any small things we could get the kids, like a soccer ball, or some colored pencils and paper.

We did see an old German church with a giant bell tower. Crossing onto a side street, we tried to go near it, but a large block wall was built around it so you couldn't even attempt to get on the grounds. In this process, we were swarmed with children, but not in a good way. They were pulling on us, asking us to buy them things and give them things, following us down the entire road. We got back to the main road and I told Denise, "no more side streets…".

Since many vendors weren't out yet, we decided to take a walk, so we broke out a water pouch and walked the 5 km to Fesi. On the way a few groups of men stopped and talked to us, many of whom were very confused as to why we were walking to Fesi… why we were going there in the first place, or what we were even doing in Kpando. The second group of five or six guys including the most social trio, Enoch, Philipe, and Bozi. Enoch shook my hand but wouldn't let go, and just kept talking. We don't have a phone which makes it easy when people ask for our phone number, but he was determined and gave us his email and said he wanted to marry me. Geez Louise. Anyway, we got to Fesi, all ready to go see some pottery and lo and behold, a funeral was taking place right in front of the pottery shed. Hmm. So, we walked to the end of Fesi, which wasn't far, and then came back. I should mention this particular Saturday seems to be funeral day. Divine also went to a funeral today.

When we reached Kpando, it was lunch time so we found the Justice Club, also suggested in Denise's guidebook. They weren't serving food, just beer. We were really hungry so we asked a guy on the street where we should eat, which prompted him to lead us off the beaten path, through two more side streets to Rosas. We never would have found it on our own, but inside beaded curtains we found a small seating area with wooden chairs and cushions, ceiling fans, and on the back wall rested a big mirror and a sink with running water! Yay! I ordered a coke, and we ate rice and chicken. We left and asked if there was a toilet we could use. We were led to a small cement enclosure about 2 feet square, no roof, and nothing on the ground… no toilet, no drain, nothing. We looked at each other and just walked back to the side street. We wandered through the market, and having asked for a bathroom, we were led to an area for men to bathe… we clarified "toilet" and were led to a small building that looked like the bathrooms at a pool back home. Denise paid 10 pesewas to use the facilities and emerged some moments later with a look of absolute disgust. She informed me that there were a few stalls, but all were dark. One was cobwebby and extremely dirty to say the least, which is the one she used. Another toilet had part of the bowl broken off and was lying on the ground. The final toilet had shit sprayed everywhere, literally. By this time, I think we were both more than ready to go back to our village.

We walked through town, bought toilet paper, colored pencils, and finally came across a sack of water: my main objective for the trip. It was open at the top, but we didn't care. We were all out of water at this point and had none back in the village. I carried it, but the opening stretched and soon I was struggling to keep water from falling out. All in all, it had been an exhausting day without much pay-off. Kpando was just a busier town with more people, more trash, and more poverty. As I struggled to hold the giant sack of water, Denise asked if I wanted to find an internet café. I just looked at her. "No," I told her, "I don't. I just want to go home."

I was craving Saviefe Gbogame at this point and the peaceful quiet and the friendly people and our normal outhouse. She asked someone anyway where the internet café was, and we were then led to someone else who then told us it was closed on the weekend. We walked (I hobbled with the water) over to the tro-tros and a man on a bicycle with a cooler on the front stopped us and asked where we were going, and pointed us to the tro-tro that was driving back to Kpeve. He too, asked me to marry him. A nice ego boost, but he settled for Denise buying a chocolate ice cream bar from his cooler.

A note on the transportation system: As Denise so eloquently states, it sucks. Cars and tro-tros are barely held together, with upholstery ripped out exposing the springs and skeleton of the seats, if there are any. Mirrors aren't attached, and sometimes the horns don't work. It reminds me of an old army jeep, but held together by the passengers inside. People and things are stuffed inside, exceeding capacity by at least six people. You are crammed between a door you hope stays shut on the pothole ridden road, and four other people, across a seat made for three. Children and babies are held on anyone's lap that has room, and you just pray your stop is coming soon.

Our tro-tro to Kpeve was a full-size van, meant to hold eleven people. We crammed sixteen people and one baby into that thing. The ride wasn't exactly pleasant. I was in the middle of our row, and another row of people were facing me. There are no seat belts, and even if there were, clearly there wouldn't be enough for everyone. That said, the tro-tro swerved and hit the brakes suddenly which sent me flying into the people in front of me, one woman in particular was clearly in a foul mood, even before I fell into her. You swerve on the roads to avoid hitting goats and potholes, and to pass other vehicles, and in doing so, you're squished between people while trying to get even a hint of a breeze from the open window. It's so stuffy though, it's rare you get any relief until you actually exit the tro-tro.

When we got to Kpeve, we got out to catch another tro-tro going back to Saviefe. Some men were trying to tell us there were no more cars going to Saviefe and we'd have to pay 15 cedi to get a tro-tro back. I replied, "hell no," and crossed the street where I recognized a man in a robe from our ambulance ride. He pointed us to the Saviefe tro-tro. It was purple. We climbed in, and waited for them to fill the rest of the tro-tro before they drove us all away from Kpeve. I wish we had stayed in the first tro-tro, because in this second one, were crammed twenty adults, one child, and one baby. Denise's feet were on top of a battery with heat scorching through her sandals. I held my backpack and the sack of water on my lap, which was leaking. We were in the first row behind the driver, yet believe it or not, four people were between us and the driver.

Finally, we got to Saviefe, and Denise and I climbed out of the tro-tro. I can't tell you how happy I was to be back home. Selom ran up and gave me a big hug, and then carried my backpack back to the house, so I could carry the water, holding the sack together so more didn't fall out. When we arrived at our house, Selom ran to the oranges, picked one up and showed me, and asked something in Ewe. I said, "Yes, you can have one. Because you asked, would you like 2 oranges?" He picked up another, and then shook his head, smiled and put it back. I turned to put down the sack of water, and saw that Sema had placed 2 brand new sacks of water on the floor for us. I totally could have just stayed in the village today!

We walked over to Sema's house to let her know we had returned and found her eating bananas with her brothers who had just come back from the farm. Selom turned up shortly thereafter, along with Jessica. The roosters were pacing around crowing, and some chickens kept going into Sema's house and she would chase them out. The roosters honestly wouldn't shut up and I was holding a water pouch, debating on whether or not to squirt one next time he crowed. It was 4 PM! They're supposed to only do that in the morning! Denise asked me if I would go to someone else's house and squirt their alarm clock with water just because it went off in the afternoon. I had to laugh. We walked back to our house and played with the children for a while. As Grace listened to my iPod, we taught Jessica how to say "uh oh spaghettios" and she tried on my sunglasses and hat. We also taught her "yo yo yo, what up G." We're such bad influences.

Tony stopped in to say he really didn't think we would make it back to the village, and also told us he enjoys our company. He didn't get a chance to speak with the two previous volunteers about serious topics like he has with us about health education.

When it was time for bed, the children were outside the bedroom window again, giggling and whispering. Only this time when we said goodnight, and "mia dogu," the children didn't leave. They continued to stand there and giggle outside our window, which then made me and Denise start to laugh. We've noticed a girl hanging around Grace lately. She's younger, maybe seven or eight, and seems fascinated with us. We'll go make friends tomorrow.

Food

The food here is mostly good, but it is so carb heavy, it makes your body feel full and slow. We don't exercise much (which is not outside my norm anyway) but it would probably do me some good to exchange one of my two daily naps for a walk to the next village.

We've had eggs every day (sometimes twice a day). I've been so thankful on days the eggs are accompanied by porridge. I've never been so happy to see porridge in my life! The porridge is made from corn, tastes like grits, and has the consistency of watery oatmeal. We do have jam so I added some of that, and yesterday Sema gave me a banana, which I saved to add to porridge this morning. Delish! The only condiments we have are jam, mayonnaise, a margarine-like substance, condensed milk and powdered milk (both of which I can't have). We don't have salt or pepper, which can leave certain dishes quite bland. I've also learned that if I am served something at lunch time that I like, I need to eat a lot of it, because I may not be so lucky come dinner time.

Fufu is interesting. It's like a giant dumpling made of mashed yam and plantains, about 5 inches in diameter. You pour a soup over it, which is really good with plenty of spices. The soup we had contained pieces of a chicken. Which pieces, I couldn't even tell you. I picked around those because I'm a little picky with my meat, and ate the soup, and a few bites of fufu, which was so rich, you really couldn't eat half of what was in your bowl. Apparently, fufu can make some people's stomachs upset. We had it at lunch time, so for dinner we were served very watery white rice. That was it. No spices, no salt, no meat… just the watery rice. I thought it was probably because they were cautious, wanting to cater to our sensitive stomachs. So, I had three pieces of bread, and a little bit of the watery rice. I added jam, thinking it might taste like porridge, but it actually reminded me of when you get duck sauce in your Chinese food rice. I finished with some hot tea.

Today, lunch was fried plantains and white beans with spices and sauce—very good! I should have eaten more of it. Dinner tonight was the same watery rice. *sigh* Some food is very good and has lots of spices, but all the food is pretty mushy. I need a crunch. I would love to have some cold vegetables right now. I think I'll see if I can recognize any vegetables at the market and try to make something. I want meat. There are goats around. I wonder if there's a taxi available to hit one for me that we could cook. Just joking. Getting delirious from lack of protein and vegetables. I'm glad Denise brought Clif bars.

Ghanaians tend to give a guest a lot of food and if you eat all of it, it means you're not full. But if you leave some, you're full. I hope they eat what we don't, or give it to someone instead of just throwing it away. When I was little, I always heard, "eat all your vegetables, there are starving children in Africa." And I always wondered, "yea but are you going to send my leftovers to Africa?" But I really am in Africa now, so I hope whatever I don't eat is given to someone.

October 5, 2008
Church

We were invited to church with Walter, one of the village elders who is also one of the executive members of Anyo Group. I borrowed a long skirt from Sema—green and purple. It was too big so I rolled the waist 3 times and held it up as I walked, which was hard to do because the fabric was surprisingly heavy and thick. Walter, wearing a traditional African robe, met us outside the church, located next to the schools.

Global Evangelical Church is made of stone and cement with a stage-like area set one step above the rest to house the altar, a wooden table draped with a white cloth. Ten village elders wearing brightly colored robes sat in front. We sat with Walter on the right side of the altar (facing the congregation) with three other elders. Facing us in the front two pews (lined up plastic lawn chairs) were the other six elders. I consider these men extra-elders because they sat most of the service and when they did get up for the offering dance, they moved extremely slowly. Across the altar, to the left, sat the choir decked out in black graduation robes, complete with caps and tassels.

The church was very intricate, especially considering that every building in the village is built by the people in the village, with their own tools, their own hands, their own skills. There were three sets of giant wooden double doors, each with biblical carvings. I counted three hundred and two small square holes, tiny window holes, at the top of the walls stretching to the rafters. A large intricate stone cross sat beyond the rafters, above the main entrance to the church.

The service in total lasted three hours, and by the end I was so hot wearing Sema's skirt, I could barely breathe. The first hour was dedicated to singing and dancing, which was amazing to watch. They had drums that played in the choir or would be placed between the pews to accompany the congregation. The center of the church was designated for dancing, where people would get up and dance in circles, or in a conga line fashion, or as they made their way to the collection box.

The rest of the service consisted of prayers and readings in Ewe, where Emil did much of the preaching as the catechist of the church, and this concluded with more singing and dancing. Walter did a short reading in English for us, which was really nice. The rest of the service we just sat and listened to the prayers and readings in Ewe. It was almost meditating. I let my mind wander as I watched the congregation. One of the elders facing me was down on his hands and knees over his bible. Other women were walking around the church with their arms stretched up, singing and swaying to the songs and prayers. Sunday school was being conducted in one of the schools next to the church, for ages 2-17. Some women in church had their babies resting on their backs, wrapped with a giant piece of fabric. With all of the women dancing, I wondered about the head support, as I watched the babies bounce in their wraps like bobble-heads.

All in all, it was a wonderful experience to watch so many of the community come together and worship in this way.

October 6, 2008
Bad Day

I need to preface this entry by saying this is the worst *case of the Mondays* ever.

Being Monday, we planned to go to Ho to work in the Bridge office. We needed to access some files so we could find out where the past proposals were sent on Anyo Group's behalf. We also needed to make worksheets for our student presentations, and print them at the office. Some personal priorities were on the list as well: we needed to exchange money, get a phone, and get more toilet paper. We also planned on getting some vegetable pizza from White House.

The day began like any other day—we were up at 5:30, showered, and finished breakfast by 6:45. We played with Jessica for a little bit, and began to get ready for our trip. We packed our backpacks, but I conveniently forgot to pack the rest of our toilet paper, or our ponchos. At 7:30, we walked to the roadside to wait for the bus to Ho.

On Monday and Thursday last week, a bus arrived and continued up the mountain. Shortly thereafter, maybe five minutes later, the second bus arrived, which then takes you on to Ho. Along the roadside, we sat there with the chief, who was going up the mountain, to teach at his primary school in Agorkpo. Again, the bus is supposed to come between 7:30 and 8. We waited, reading our books next to the chief, until finally the first bus came at 9:15. We waited a few more minutes, and

Tony came by, surprised we were still there. He informed us that there is only one bus that goes to Ho today, and that we should have boarded the bus that goes up the mountain, and then found a tro-tro to Ho. This would have been nice to know, so I asked him how you know when only 1 bus is coming. He shrugged and replied, "It depends."

Divine was with us so he suggested we just "catch a car," i.e. hitchhike, to Ho. As you may imagine, not many cars come through our village. Finally, a car came by, and with Divine doing all the talking and negotiating, they agreed to drive us to Ho for 3 cedi, as soon as they picked up another person in our village they were waiting for. They were waiting for that person for a very long time.

At 9:45, the bus came back down the mountain, and was actually headed for Ho so it seemed to work out that we'd be able to ride the bus as planned. As we stood in line to board the bus, people (adults) yelled "yavoo, yavoo!" in an extremely disrespectful manner. They repeated, "Yavoo! There's no room. You have to stand." We acknowledged and said that's ok, that we have legs, we can stand. Again, they would repeat it. All the while, people were laughing and yelling "yavoo," and other things in Ewe.

I paid our fare, but the conductor owed me 8.40 in change, which he wrote on my ticket. We stood, packed between people, for the hour and 45-minute bumpy ride to Ho. About 10 minutes into the journey, the conductor passed me 8 cedi, and said we would get the 40 pesewas later. I asked to confirm, "Ok, you'll give me the 40 pesewas later," and a bunch of people roared up in laughter, yelling, "Yavoo, don't you understand English? Yavoo!" Everything else was in Ewe but this was the first time I felt uncomfortable in Ghana because of my skin. Kids will shout "yavoo," but always in a cheerful, curious way. You never hear adults saying it.

The bus had rows of three seats, then a narrow aisle, and another row of 2 seats, which was packed as we stood in a single file line in the isle. I have bruises from bracing myself between the two rows of seats, so as not to fall into anyone, or fall forward which would have created a domino effect, when the giant mass bus swerved around potholes and goats. The woman sitting to my left was incredibly rude. We had to hold on to her headrest to stable ourselves and she would push Denise's arm away, over and over. She would bang her head against my hand as well, clearly wanting us to know we were in her way, as her large hips spilled over the seat into the aisle. Denise and I spoke our frustrations in Spanish, and endured the next 90 minutes in silence, listening to the radio personality speak in Ewe urging listeners to do something. The forceful tone was reminiscent of old communist propaganda.

To cheer us up, we opted to make our first task in Ho getting the vegetable pizza. On the way, we thought we'd stop at a bank to exchange some currency, but both banks we stopped in were filled with people waiting. I mean, it looked like the DMV on a Saturday morning. We figured we'd eat first, and then maybe less people would be at the bank later in the day.

We arrived at White House, went out back to the open-air patio, and saw that some of our volunteer friends were already there, so it was nice to sit and chat with them. They informed us that the office was closed for some reason and no one could get a hold of Bismark or Joy. With the office closed, our options for work were severely limited. Without the files, we couldn't get anything else done on the library project until Thursday, and without the printer, we couldn't prepare worksheets for the student presentations. This was really frustrating.

As we considered our possible back-up plans, a girl came over to take our order. She was expressionless as we spoke to her and slowly took the menu away, scuffing her feet all the way back to the kitchen. Denise and I were the only ones left at the table, along with an older British guy we met, when our food arrived. Alas, they were out of vegetable pizza. I did order a vegetable salad, but this came drenched in mayonnaise. I hate mayonnaise. I think Ghanaians assume all expats really like it. I ordered chicken with potato chips. The chips are French fries, so that was a nice treat. I tasted the chicken but opted to stick with the fries. As I finished my last French fry, the clouds became dark and the wind shifted.

The ensuing rain storm came up very quickly, leaving us dashing from the patio thatched umbrella to the covered restaurant fifty feet away. By this time, it was getting late and we had so much work to do. We couldn't go to the office, since it was locked for no reason, so we needed to get to the internet café to use the computers. It was just a block and a half away, around the corner, but the rain fell like buckets from the sky, leaving us reluctant to leave the dry restaurant. The Brit gave us a black plastic bag that we draped over our backpacks containing our cameras and important papers. My flip flops are very slippery when wet, so I couldn't run. We braced ourselves, and stepped out from under the beaded curtain of White House, into the monsoon.

I gasped as I stepped into the cold shower. The rain hit hard and after a few seconds in the storm, we were soaked through. I stepped very carefully over the drainage ditch along the road. My feet were slipping already so each step was a miracle if I didn't fall into the road or the ditch of trash and sewage, now moving quickly with the extra precipitation. The drainage ditch is lined with cement on either side, and large cement blocks waited to be set over the ditch to form a sidewalk. Some blocks were in place; others were broken and fallen through. Most of the ditch however, was not covered yet, and the blocks lay stacked unevenly or lean from the road next to the ditch. These uneven blocks were my stepping stones. Water resembling rust-orange paint rushed beneath me, almost overflowing the ditch (which is two feet deep). Crossing the street was just as nerve-racking. Cars sped around the corner and I couldn't run over the rivers of orange lining the street, so it was like Russian roulette trying to cross without slipping.

We finally made it to the internet café, every ounce of our clothing was dripping on the floor. We sat down at the computers, paid our 20 pesewas for 25 minutes of use, and began working. Not 4 minutes later, the lights went dark and every computer shut down. We later realized it wasn't a power outage, but rather the internet café didn't pay their electric bill. The guy running the place said he had to make a call, but that the electricity would be back soon, in the next hour or two. Just then, Bismarck and Joy pulled up in a car, it was 2 PM. They unlocked the office, which was great, but the computers with the Anyo Group files were still corrupt from a virus so we couldn't access them. The printer was also out of commission.

To kill some time we figured we should stop by the bank to exchange some currency, as it was surely not going to be crowded in this weather. We were already soaked, so we figured another jaunt in the rain couldn't hurt, though I did leave my backpack in the Bridge office just in case.

We walked to the nearby bank, about a block away, which was by far the most developed building I'd seen in Ghana yet. This bank was fancier than the airport, and (drumroll please) it had air conditioning! The floor was white tile resembling marble slabs, and the carpet (carpet!) and décor had a very modern feel. Pendant lights hung from the ceiling and the leather furniture in the waiting area looked brand new. Walking in, Denise and I looked like disheveled homeless kids. A police officer opened the door, looked us over, and directed us to the glass enclosed tellers. We each walked up to a window and asked to exchange money.

The teller asked for my passport. I said I didn't have it with me. He asked for any picture I.D. but I didn't have anything with me, I had left everything in my backpack at the Bridge office. He asked my name, to which I said, "Christine Brown."

He said, "No, my name is Christian Brown!"

Glancing at his name tag he was trying to hide, I knew he (Frank) was lying, so I replied, "Well you know what? My cousin is Chris Brown, you know, the singer? Pretty cool, huh?"

He smiled and asked if I was kidding, which I admitted. Obviously, do I look like I'm related to Chris Brown? After this, he smiled and agreed to exchange my money this time, but next time I needed to bring an I.D. I agreed, and passed him a sopping wet $100 bill I had in my pocket. It was raining!

He held it up and scoffed, "THIS is how you people handle your MONEY?!"

Gee, I'm sorry sir. I didn't know I had to protect my pockets from today's monsoon in West Africa! I kept that part to myself, but inevitably, he gave me a really hard time about exchanging it.

Denise had an equally hard time, as one of her bills had a small tear the size of a splinter, and they wouldn't take it. She was getting very frustrated and started explaining our horrible day to the teller, who clearly couldn't give two shits about our day. I looked at her as if to say, "Stop. Breathe. Calm down." She looked at me and said, "I know I have to calm down." They finally exchanged the rest of our money and we headed back to the office.

There was nothing more we could do since the printer wasn't working and we couldn't get to the files. By this point, the internet café had power again so we checked our email with our remaining 21 minutes we had from before, and did some research or our upcoming sex education talk for the JSS students. Our patience was nonexistent at this point, so we left, and opting to forego another public transit experience for the day, we caught a taxi next to the orange river of rain and dirt along the road.

The driver, Gideon, recognized us from driving us back to the village last week, so we started to make some small conversation. I zoned out, looking out the window at the lushness of the land around us. The mountains were covered in green, with trees and vegetation everywhere. The rain had created an intensely thick mist that draped over the mountaintop like hot fudge on a sundae. Gideon had the windows open to let in the cool air the rain brought. I wasn't completely dry yet, so I was shivering a little in my wet tank top and cotton capris. My flip flops were mostly dry but still a little slippery. I ignored the cold, and was thankful we weren't in a stuffy bus full of unfriendly people.

When we arrived back to the village, we bid goodbye to Gideon and saw Divine waiting at the roadside. We waved, and quickly went to our room to change into dryer clothes. I wore jeans for the first time here, along with my old softball t-shirt. Jessica ran up to greet us, and we decided to go on a walk by the schools, just to stretch our legs and breathe some of the cool dusk air before it got too dark. Divine joined us, along with Beatrice's daughter, Praise, and with Jessica on Denise's shoulders, the five of us trekked off through the village.

We got to the schools and were just moseying around when we saw a path going off into the woods. We asked if we could follow it, and Divine told us it went to the cemetery, and began to lead the way. It was really interesting, and the walk was nice. The evening air was misty and cool, which was easy to enjoy now that I was nice and dry. The cemetery was lined with trees that twisted at the trunk. Burial plots were six feet deep, but a stone or marble slab the size of the coffin sits on the ground.

Divine explained who the people in the first row were, including their late headmaster who died in 2005, another man who brought electricity with a generator to the village in the 1960s, all men who made a significant contribution to the village. Leaving the cemetery, we took a different path leading us past a villa. Yes, a *villa*, at the edge of our village that we had never noticed before. The daughter who grew up there was actually named Miss Ghana in 1995. Now she is an actress on television, but I'm not sure if she acts in Ghana or the UK or the US. Standing in the middle of the road (something you don't have to really worry about here), we said goodnight, and Divine invited us to watch a movie sometime while we're here. Denise and I looked at each other with surprise, and asked, "Do you have a TV with a movie player?" He nodded, and we began to think that maybe everyone else had a fan and a TV except us!

We went back home and dinner was waiting for us—fried rice and boiled down cassava leaves (you may think you're getting spinach, but really, you can't escape the cassava). It was good, but really oily. After dinner, we held our first computer training lesson for Tony and Emil. Both had a little bit of experience on a computer before, so we didn't need to show them the concept of the hardware. We went over minimizing and maximizing a window, how to open Word, how to save a document, how to make a folder, how to find the folder, and open up a document from it. This took about an hour, but we did make some progress.

By the end of the training session, we were exhausted and headed off to the toilet, one last time for the night. I should mention here, that several times in the last few days, Denise has screamed or freaked out in a hyperventilating manner, over a spider in the bathroom. Returning to the room, Denise started to have another freak out when she opened the door to our room. I walked in behind her, and gave her a hard time for gasping over a silly spider. She gave me a look. "No Christine. It's not a spider. It's a giant rat that just scurried across the floor, and under YOUR bed."

After jumping on top of our chair, I apologized for doubting her freak out reasons, and I waited patiently while she went into the room and chased it out from under my bed. I have now decided that under our circumstances, being squeamish about spiders (and rats) is perfectly acceptable.

We finished getting ready for bed, and we went outside to "make toothpaste spit on the ground," as we were told. I stood on the very top step, behind Denise, accidentally squirting her with water. She laughed since she knew there was no way I was getting off that top step, for fear the rat might come back and decide to attack my feet for some reason. We went to sleep, but I didn't sleep for long. My stomach was upset from the oily dinner, so I proceeded to get sick several times, all through the night. Yay, Monday.

October 7, 2008
Missing some "me" time

I'm sitting here listening to Damien Rice on the laptop, trying to ignore the ten children in our room. Kids definitely don't ask for anything, they just take. I noticed Kosi and Grace watching music videos on my iPod. I don't mind, but I wanted to make sure they weren't watching anything inappropriate. You can hardly blame them though. No one here has personal possessions. Clothes and food are all shared. It's life in a village community. Everything is communal, almost. At least, everything they know. When I come in with an iPod, why shouldn't they get to play with it whenever they want? Why should they have to ask? They don't have to ask to use anything else in the village like the shared bedrooms, toilets, showers, wells, etc. The other children that followed Selom into our room are just lurking everywhere. Having manners is an absent concept and they never go home. They're always here. Jessica just ran in and sat on my lap. Oh well. We are the after-school program. I don't mind having Jessica around, she's always so cheery. I'll admit though, some of the other children are brats, and others are just annoying how they always stand outside our window, trying to look in, or crawl under our curtain to see what we're doing. Honestly, we've been here long enough now, I wish they would just see us as normal people.

Separately, I sometimes get the feeling that people here worry about us even more, because of our skin. They tell us to not go out in the sun, and they get nervous when we get a cut. It's almost like they think we'll break more easily, or we're more delicate. We spoke with one of the other volunteers about it and she shared how she explained it for her village.

"See those chickens? There are brown chickens, and there are white chickens, but they all have feathers, they all lay eggs, and they all squawk just the same. I'm the white chicken."

I'll be glad to go for a walk back home without being stopped by five people along the way to ask where I'm going, why I'm going, am I coming back, when I will be back, should they come with me. They like to chaperone us, but sometimes you just wish you could do something on your own, without being escorted around.

Corporal Punishment

Today at lunch time, we saw Grace standing at the wall of our compound. We wondered why she was home and not in school. She had her uniform on, and a woman was standing behind her, talking to her, and doing something to Grace's back. I'm not sure if she was putting something on her back, or brushing off dirt from the uniform. You couldn't tell from where we were. Later, we walked by her, in the same spot by the wall, only this time she was sitting down, and you could tell she had been crying.

I did find out who Jessica's father is—the son of our landlord. He came around the corner and just as he passed us, we saw him pick up a giant stick, the size of sugar cane, from the ground, and head straight for Grace. I turned to see him smack her a few times with it as she wailed in pain and surprise. I couldn't watch any further, my stomach sank. Denise and I walked back to our room silently. We could still hear Grace with every strike for a few more minutes while we were inside. We didn't have to say anything to understand how the other felt. I wonder what warranted that punishment… I wonder what Grace did.

Later this afternoon we walked by the schools, right as kids were getting out of class for the day. All of the JSS kids, however, were standing at attention in the school yard. A closer look revealed that several students were getting beat with the cane as punishment for being late to class earlier in the day. This punishment, for whatever the kids may have done, always takes place in front of the entire school at the end of the day.

Grace

Something seems off with Grace. You can tell there's something missing… psychologically, she's not where she should be. She throws tantrums at like the switch of a light, she lashes out at another child, or completely shuts down. You can't tell if she can even hear you, she just stares, making no facial expression, and won't acknowledge anyone speaking to her. Her mood can change so quickly from being stable and carrying herself in a mature fashion, to acting overly childish. I realize she is still a child, but it's such a stark change as she almost transforms into the mindset of a child 6 years her junior. We did find out today that she and Jessica and Kosi have a sister, age 6, who lives in Ho with her grandmother. I'm not sure why, but the mother said they don't see the child very often.

October 8, 2008
Lazy Day

Tomorrow, our day is jam-packed, and we'll be rushing around, without our daily naps that we've become so accustomed to. We'll get up at 5:30 AM as usual, and then at 8 AM we have our first presentation for the JSS students. Hopefully we will be done by 9:45, and we're going to *catch a car* into Ho, for Market Day. While in Ho, we'll of course be attempting to use the office to find where those proposals were sent, and the internet to do more research for the presentations. After we return home, we'll have dinner, then we have Divine's computer lesson at 7 PM for an hour. At 8 PM we'll be planning the presentation for the Primary classes, which we will present Friday morning at 8 AM.

So, we've decided to take advantage of a lazy day today. After breakfast, Jessica came over. I don't think the pre-K students attended school today. She colored and climbed all over me while I tried to read, but finally I put down the book and I was looking at some photos on my camera. Jessica saw it, her eyes widened, and she started making all kinds of faces at me, then jumping toward me to look at the funny face picture she thought I'd just taken. It was adorable so I decided that it would be fun to watch her reaction, and I can delete any pictures later to save room on the memory card. What ensued was actually really fun. Jessica is certainly no camera shy, and was acting like a model. She would pose, hands on her hips with such sass you wouldn't believe. But after a few goofy pictures, she would make an expression so laced with emotion, hold for the camera, and as soon as I clicked she turned into the bouncy 3-year-old again, looking at her photo. This continued for a while, and at this point, I can actually put together a small photo project when I get home: a day in the life of Jessica. Some of the pictures are absolutely amazing, others are just so damn cute. I concluded with a most appropriate photo, when I saw her passed out later in the afternoon, halfway on the dirt, halfway on a mattress someone had pulled out onto the ground, sleeping soundly. She just goes, goes, goes, and then bam! She's out like a light.

Denise and I took a walk down the road towards Bame before lunch to get some sun and some exercise. It was a peaceful walk. We talked about the day-to-day life here, what could change, what could improve. When you look at the village, and ask yourself where to start, it can be overwhelming. It does come down to education, even though the repercussions of it won't be visible for another generation or two (given the pace they reproduce here). There is no tax system, almost everything is a bartering deal. No taxes mean no money for fixing the roads, or organizing a trash pick-up. Trash cans are nonexistent here, and litter is everywhere. People here go about their days, just getting by. And that's how they live.

As we ate lunch, we looked at each other with concern when we heard a screaming chicken right outside our door, screaming over and over. We looked out the window and immediately sat back down and stared at the wall. A man was plucking the chicken. He was only plucking out the big feathers, I guess to prevent the chicken from flying, but it was awful to witness.

Lunch was especially good with fried plantains, stewed white beans, finished with fresh pineapple. The pineapple is my favorite, so sweet and juicy, and almost has a hint of coconut flavor. After lunch, I finished my book. We walked over to the schoolyard (after school let out to avoid the massive stampede of children whenever we go over here) and met Tony to do his organizational scorecard survey we have from Bridge. He wasn't teaching this week, he's manning a booth for the NPP, for people to come up and check their voter registrations.

At 4 PM we walked to Walter's house, and outside we conducted a computer training session for Walter and Richard. Richard is the village tailor, but also has a wooden counter that serves as a bar. Hans showed up 40 minutes later. The training went well. We had to start with the basics, explaining the concept of the mouse, and finally we ended with the shift key to make upper case letters. The mouse concept was kind of funny though. We told them that cursor on the screen can be called an "arrow," to which they acknowledged, "oh… aerial." We drew a picture of an arrow, and again, "oh ok, aerial." We spelled it on paper. Again, "Ok, aerial." It was a very productive session though. We went over a lot of material. As we sat, baby chicks were at my feet. One walked over my foot, and by accident, I moved my foot back and shoved another chick in the process. After the training we went back to our room to work on the JSS presentations, had dinner, and worked until we went to sleep. Hopefully the presentations will go over well.

October 9, 2008
JSS Presentation #1

We gave our first presentation to the JSS students today. It was pretty basic to start things off. We introduced ourselves, and explained why we were there. We talked about school and asked what their favorite and least favorite subjects are. We talked about furthering their education, going to university, and finding a career. Going around the room, we asked each student what they wanted to be when they grow up. Answers varied: nurse, doctor, lawyer, broadcaster, journalist, writer, teacher, soldier, pilot, engineer, bank manager, football player. After a class discussion, the students agreed that university was important for having a career.

We talked about how to do well in school, touching on time management skills, and stressing how important it is to study and do their homework every day. We asked what problems they might come across in school. Students raised their hands, or called out answers: have to go to the farm after school, don't understand the homework/lesson, have to care for younger siblings, etc. After talking with the students about these issues, we asked them what they could do to fix these problems. The teachers had previously asked us to stress the teacher's role as the students' biggest resource, which we of course relayed to the students.

We really tried to get across to them how important it is to:

a) Look at the assignment as soon as they receive it, instead of waiting until they get home to realize they're confused.

b) Ask for help from the teacher right away if they don't understand something.

c) Set aside time every day to study their notes and complete assignments.

We conveyed that the teachers are there to help them learn, and want them to understand. We also said that if they need more time at home for schoolwork, they can politely explain to their parents how important school is, and ask if they can work something out, where they can have more time for assignments every evening.

We asked each student to answer some questions on a sheet of paper for us to learn from them. Questions included: favorite and least favorite subject in school and why; do they plan to go to university; what problems do they face in school; and a space to write down questions about anything "for Christine and Denise to answer." Reading their answers was really interesting. Problems they listed were "don't understand the subjects" or "money" or "don't have school bag or school sandals or pen" or "I want to go to senior secondary school but my father doesn't have enough money." Other problems were "I don't understand when the teacher uses a big word," or "I don't want to repeat or get pregnant."

All in all, I think the presentation went over very well. I think we got through to most of the kids about the importance of education, what they can do to improve, how to solve problems they might have, and to use their teachers for help and guidance. We'll be speaking with the Primary School students tomorrow on the same subject, but less detailed. Tony translated for us in the first two classes, and supervised the third class. He was very pleased with our material and told us it was "perfect."

October 9, 2008
A Ghanaian Field Trip

Thursday was Market Day in Ho, so after our JSS presentations, we packed our backpacks with the essentials (ponchos and toilet paper included this time), and headed over to Sema's house. As we waited outside for Sema to change, I noticed more of our laundry hanging to dry on the line. Sema appeared, all decked out in a fancy black glittery top, a long fitted denim skirt, and denim brim hat with the silhouette of Michael Jordan on the front. The three of us walked to the roadside of the village to *catch a car* to Ho. This is the equivalent of hitchhiking, but it's part of the norm here. It's very safe, everyone does it.

Luckily for us, a tro-tro came through the village on its way to Ho, which sometimes happens on Market Days. This tro-tro had five rows of five people, plus two people next to the driver. The middle person in a row would sit on a folding chair in the aisle, very cozy. Still, this is a better tro-tro than the usual ones we get. At least on this one, everyone had a seat. A few times, the tro-tro attempted to ascend a hill, and was clearly struggling like it didn't have enough power.

We had several things on the agenda for Ho: make photocopies for Tony for some voter registration forms, try to finally get vegetable pizza, get a phone, and get the computer files from Bridge about the Anyo Group's proposals. Of course, this was our plan, but as history may predict, we haven't had a great track record for getting things done in Ho. Almost every time we go to Ho, something goes wrong.

We got off the tro-tro in the middle of Ho, and started walking toward White House. On the way, we noticed a place to get photocopies. We stopped, and copied Tony's registration form. One task, done! We kept walking to White House, and after a long, hot walk up a hill, we were there. What do you know, they actually had vegetable pizza available! Task 2, done! Denise and I each ordered one, and I got a coke. Sema ordered banku, a traditional Ghanaian dish that she wants to make for us soon. It's like fufu, but it has more texture and you eat it with your hands. I finished my pizza in record time, and after we finished eating, the clouds started to move in very quickly. I could smell it in the air that it was about to rain. We quickly paid, and walked very quickly further up the hill. On the way, we stopped at an MTN store (a cell phone service) and bought a phone for 34 cedis. Task 3, done!

We walked to the Bridge office, and the rain began to move in. It started sprinkling and then just a light rain, but it was getting worse. We got under the roof of the office building just in time. The rain began to pour in buckets and we headed up the stairs. The office looked closed at first, but then two other volunteers emerged. We entered and luckily, the computer with the Anyo Group files on it was actually functional! The printer was still broken, but we did find the files. We copied them onto our flash drive, but in reading over them, we realized there was no indication that the proposals were actually sent, or where they were sent to. There was a contact list, including the name, email, and phone number of the previous counterpart (like Bismark), who has since left Anyo Group. I copied the information down, and went to the internet café downstairs. I emailed him, asking for more information on the proposals, so hopefully I'll get a response by Monday. Task 4, sort of done!

By this time, the rain had stopped, and the streets were actually dry again, as the heat pressed down over the town. Sema led us to the big market, and we found a small street shop where we bought toilet paper, jam, mouth wash, and some other essentials. Task 5, done! We were in good shape, I couldn't believe it! We actually did everything we came to do!

We walked through the market, weaving through wooden stands, stepping over people on the ground, ducking under fabric and beads hanging above, and quickly getting out of the way when someone with a very large basket balancing on their head came our way. Sema stopped and bought some canned tuna, peppers and cabbage. We went into a small stand with fabric displayed. Denise and I each bought a few yards to make skirts and bags out of. We went to another street stand shortly thereafter and saw some other fabric that I just couldn't pass up. It was gorgeous and perfect to make bags as gifts for a few friends and family back home.

After we were loaded up on fabric (that was incredibly inexpensive), we wandered to a woman sitting on the ground over a tray displaying assorted strings of beads. Women and girls (even toddlers) wear several strands of beads around their hips, under their clothes, for decoration. As silly as it may be, we got some strands for ourselves so now I can have beads for decoration under my clothes too! We found another woman who was selling beads and bracelets that she'd made. Some bracelets were strands with a single large bead. One would cost you 20 pesewas, but she let us have six for 1 cedi. I also got a couple bracelets that she had made, with lots of beads on them. One was just 50 pesewas! By this time, we were very satisfied and exhausted, and my endorphins were in a good place since I essentially got to play at the Ho shopping mall. We were ready to leave Ho and find a ride back to the village. Keep in mind, every other time we've been to Ho, something has gone wrong and so far, today was perfect...

Sema led us through the maze of market people once more, straight to a tro-tro, headed for the village. It was the same type as the morning, with five rows of five seats each. The front passenger seat sits two people, and it folds forward for you to access the only door. We climbed in, straight to the back seat. I sat by the window. We waited for a while to fill the entire tro-tro, and I watched the sky as clouds began to move in again. The back seat is not where you should be if you're tall, which works out well for me (I'm almost 5'3"). My head was very close to the top, and glancing into the corner, about 4 inches from my head was a metal rod that stuck out, from where the top roof rack was attached. I ducked down, and laid my head and my arms over my backpack on my lap and watched the people outside. The windows span 2 ½ rows, and slide open. My window was wide open, and started just above the seat, right under my hips, and stretched behind me to the end of my seat. To spell it out, if I wasn't holding on, I would fall out of the window, but I viewed it as a bonus to help me not feel claustrophobic in the back of this packed vehicle. We jammed everyone in the tro-tro, and began our journey home.

The Volta Region of Ghana is really the only mountainous area. There are lots of hills. Denise and I took a picture of how stuffed our tro-tro was with people, and sure enough, it started to struggle going up the first major hill after leaving Ho. It sputtered and began to slow to a stop, at which point, 4 guys who were hanging off the back jumped off, and 2 guys jumped off the roof. This was surprising, since we didn't know they were up there, but it was too late, the tro-tro died.

We all got out with our stuff and stood on the side of the road. We were too far from Ho to walk back to where we could get a taxi, or another tro-tro. It was getting dark, and the clouds were moving in faster now. It was going to rain any minute. After a short while, the tro-tro was revived, and started up the hill, ever so slowly. Everyone ran up the hill after it, to climb back in after it overcame the hill. We climbed in, and the tro-tro began again. A slow start, but finally we were on our way! The guys ran alongside us, grabbed the backside of the tro-tro, and pulled themselves on, very manly.

My window was still open and since I was in the back seat, one guy accidentally grabbed my waist instead of the tro-tro. After a second attempt, he finally got on, and then a couple of them climbed onto the roof. As soon as we were going, it got darker, we heard a crack of lightning, and the sky opened up, dumping buckets of rain. I couldn't figure out how to close my window—it was stuck open. The guy hanging on behind me reached around, grabbed my arm and very quickly said, "Sista, please, take my phone and bible." He handed me his cell phone and pocket-size bible so they wouldn't get wet (of course, who wants their bible to get wet?) and then he closed the window! It wasn't closed all the way, but at least this way only a small part of me would be soaked. For some reason, the woman in front of me kept trying to open the window but I was holding it closed. Finally, she succeeded and rain poured in on me, but at least she got the nice breeze she was seeking.

With all of the bumps in the road, I hit my head against the sharp metal opening of the window more than a few times. It wasn't the most pleasant thing ever. The rain had mostly stopped, but driving on a narrow dirt road through the African brush presented other surprises. Trees and branches would smack into me or scrape my arm. I wasn't paying attention when one branch smacked me and I yelled something like "ack." The guy hanging on behind me started laughing, which caused me to start laughing too! I stuck my head out the window and joked with him, which apparently made the guys on the roof looking down at me start laughing too. I guess you're not supposed to stick your head out the window, which was a lesson reiterated with the next branch.

The entire right side of my body was wet and the wind was cold. The sky was a blanket of dark gray, and you could see black silhouettes of the open trees. I could see some of the brush illuminated from the headlights, and looking down, the moonlight shined on my arm and backpack. The air was cool, and I was beginning to reach that meditative state again… Then the tro-tro died, for the second time.

This time, we were near a grouping of homes, not big enough to be a village, but at least we were near some civilization, kind of. People jumped off the roof and the back again, only this time we all stayed inside. It was a little while of just waiting for something. For what, I'm not sure. I began to notice that the guys from the roof weren't helping anymore—they were sprawled out on the ground with their hands behind their heads, looking at the sky! Perfect time to chill out, I suppose. Finally, the tro-tro was yet again revived. I'm not sure how long we were stopped there.

Shortly after we got going again, we stopped (deliberately this time) to pick up four large sacks of corn that were left by the roadside. Someone is probably going to get a fairly intense beating for leaving it there, but I guess it's up for grabs. We loaded them up, and continued. Sometimes it looked like we were going off the road into the cornfield, but the road would reappear again. Throughout the ride, if the tro-tro swayed to avoid a pothole, a stream of cold rain run-off from the roof would run down my arm. From this, I was getting pretty wet again. We stopped to let some people off under a lone street lamp. Looking out, I could see our shadow, including the men braced on the roof, which was kind of cool. Under the light I also realized the stream of cold rain I was experiencing, that now covered my entire right side, was actually mud. Brown, watery mud, all over me.

We got going once more, and further down the road, the tro-tro died, for a third time. This time, we were in the middle of the African brush, and our prospects at a solution were not looking promising. We waited again, for quite a while. I asked Sema how far we were from the village, and she said maybe a mile. I stuck my head all the way out the window, which prompted the guy on the roof above me to say "hi." I looked around and thought I recognized a particular large tree that Denise and I had seen on our walk the other day. I suggested we get out and walk, which Denise was all about. Sema hesitated so we stayed in the tro-tro for a while longer. Finally, we were going once more, and a woman yelled "Agorkpo! No Stop!" meaning, "do not stop, go all the way to Agorkpo," so I yelled back, "Yes stop! Saviefe Gbogame!"

After a little while, we entered our village. When the tro-tro came to a stop in our village, it was sputtering again. We got out and I called to one of the guys on the roof to return his phone and bible. He thanked me, and we stood there, wondering if the tro-tro would start again. The chief, along with about 20 people from the village were standing there. The chief welcomed us back, and said we would go on a walk to Agorkpo the next day.

We walked home, and had eggs for dinner. We had missed our computer training lesson for Divine, but figured we'd apologize and reschedule for tomorrow. After we got ready for bed, like clockwork, children showed up at our window. My patience was running low and I was exhausted. This time, after saying goodnight with a pronounced and lingering inflection as "good -niiiiight," and giggling a few times through the window, the children didn't go home. They ran around the front, into our compound, and straight through our front door curtain. We had six children in our room- Happy, Wisdom, Gideon, Sabrina, Millicent, and a small one whose name I can't remember.

I greeted them, and told them I was glad to meet them in person, instead of only through a window. I was about to say, now that we've met, they don't need to hang around the window, and that we can talk more tomorrow. The older girl (Happy) was in one of the JSS classes that day for our presentation. She started, "You said we could come to you with questions and problems." I sighed, pulled up a chair, and invited her to continue.

She had plenty of questions for us. What is the U.S. like? If I go to university here, can I get a job as a seamstress in U.S.? Do you miss it when you're here or do you like Ghana? I like English, do you like Ewe? Were you born with hair, or do you have a hairdresser? Are Americans just as friendly and welcoming as Ghanaians are? What is the weather like in U.S.?

It went on for quite a while, and I addressed each question carefully. Part of it felt like I was telling a fantasy story. Rain falls from the sky and freezes because it's so cold, and lays a blanket of fluffy white over the ground. You can pick it up and make a man made of snow, and throw snowballs at each other, and ride a sled down a hill, or ride standing on a board down a mountain side. She told me her favorite subject was English because one day she wants to come to the U.S. and only speak English. I said that was very good, and that her English was impeccable for being only 13. I also told her that even though it's good to learn English, she should embrace her culture, and continue to speak Ewe too, because there is so much history there.

Then she said something else: "I like your skin color; do you like my skin color? I wish my skin were like yours." I was surprised and told her that there are lots of different kinds of people with different skin colors, and it's good to be different. I told her she should be proud of who she is and what she looks like, because her skin was beautiful. She smiled and replied, "Your skin is beautiful too." Finally, they were satisfied and left. A moment later, they said "goodnight," once more at the window. I crawled into bed, listening to them giggle and run away.

JSS Questions for Christine & Denise

I mentioned we asked the students to answer some questions for us on a sheet of paper about school. The last section on their papers included free space for the children to write down any questions they had for us - about anything at all. Some are listed below, written verbatim.

- What is USA?
- What is it like in the US? How many schools do they have there?
- Can I visit you in the US?
- How do you like Ghana?
- Can you take me with you to the US? (this was written by Kosi)
- Please can you help me to pass through my education so that I can be like someone also better like the way you are?
- Mrs. Christine please I want to ask that will you come and teach us for two weeks.
- Please do you help me in future?
- What subject do you like?
- How do you feel about our village?
- What are you really doing in our village?
- I want to ask questions form bothe of you that teachers like punishment us, the beat hardly.
- Do you like our food?
- Please would you help me to enter university and becoming something tomorrow.
- Please do help me in my future.

- Please can you help me to pass my education so that I can becom good in future.

- What work do you do in the US?

- If I come to USA, which problem am I going to face?

- If I want to continue my education but don't have any support, why do I do it?

- If I come to America, how can I manage to find you?

- Please help me continue my education.

- Please I want two of you to care for me and I also want storys books thank you.

- I want to be a pilot in the future, what will I have to do to become a pilot?

- If I want to go to university to be a journalist, what subject will I have to study, what will I do?

- I want to be one of your learning partners—would you like it?

- Which time are you going to teach us the computer?

- Please would you like to take me to United State?

- Is there any idea about our school facilities?

- Do you like the water we drink, the food we eat, and the village which we live in?

- Because when you came to Ghana you did not do anything bad and you live happy in the village when you came to the village did you fill the village. *(I think this means, how do you feel about the village)*

- How did you fill when you visite Ghana, why?

- How would I do before going to USA?

- I want to go to United States—what can I do to reach that place?

- If I want to go to university, can I make it, and in what way can I make it?
- Can you bring us something that will make the school fun, things like library book, text books and to build up our schools?
- I want to go to America but what should I do before going?
- If I want to be a teacher, what should I do?
- If I want to go to school but my parent don't have money what would I do?
- Why did you come here?
- Why is it important to go to university? *(we did talk about this, but will have to go into more detail for the 2nd presentation I think)*
- I want to asked that when you come to our village did you like it or did you suffer for us? *(I think this means, are we coping or are we suffering living in their village)*
- Do you like our language?
- When I want to be journalist at university what is the core subject that I will do, and what can I manage to work on time?

October 10, 2008
Update on family compound details

We've received some clarification on Kosi, Grace, and Jessica's immediate family. Their mother is Cassandra, who is due to give birth in two months. This compound belongs to her aunt and uncle. Cassandra came here twelve years ago with Kosi and Grace, from Liberia, after she and her husband divorced. He is still in Liberia. She remarried to a man in Ghana several years later. They have a 6-year-old daughter, Essanam who lives with the father's mother in Ho, 3-year-old Jessica, and the soon-to-be-born December child. Sometime in the last 6 months, he left her with the children, and he now lives in another village nearby. He was apparently very close with Kosi and Grace. One week before we came to the village, Cassandra's father died. All of this could explain some of Grace's erratic behavior lately. We also found out that the guy who we thought was Jessica's father, here in the compound, is actually Cassandra's cousin. When we saw him hit Grace the other day, it was because Grace threw all of her dresses away in the garbage and had no dresses to wear, other than her school uniform. This is also why we've seen her draped in a large piece of fabric, like a robe, lately, and why her mother didn't let her follow us when we took Jessica for a walk with Divine the other day.

Primary Presentation #1

We began the day as usual with breakfast, though it was significantly later than usual. Denise and I joked that we had kept Sema up too late the night before. Sema walked in around 7 AM with the covered bowl. I called out to Denise to let her know the porridge had arrived. As Denise set out our bowls and spoons, I lifted the lid, and sadness crept over my face as I revealed the watery rice to Denise. I had two pieces of bread instead.

Today we talked to the six primary classes about education. We shortened our material by a good amount, but it still went over quite well. Going around the room in the upper primary class, kids said they wanted to be doctors or nurses or pilots. One child wanted to be the president. As we moved down to the lower primary classes, the answers shifted, to jobs they knew, which coincidentally required less education, like a seamstress, tailor, hairdresser, driver. Out of the three JSS classes, and the six primary classes, only one child said they wanted to be a farmer. Practically everyone raised their hands indicating they like school, and that they want to go to university. In almost every class, several students admitted they have a problem doing their homework because they go to the farm after school to work, and are too tired when they get home. In four of the primary classes today I recognized a child from our post-window discussion the night before. In ten days we will conduct our second presentation for the primary kids, which will focus on developing and maintaining habits for good hygiene.

After the Primary presentations, we went home to rest a while and test our new phone. Denise called her father to change her return flight to the same one I booked. She originally planned on traveling around Ghana on her own for a week following the conclusion of our assignment, but we still have a few weeks left of our assignment and we're both feeling like we'll be ready to go home.

Pretty soon, the children arrived, so we played with them for a while. Jessica attempted to brush my hair as I focused on my book, and after a while I noticed she was just shining the flashlight in my hair. Three kids from JSS came by to ask about computers. Denise opened the laptop and showed them MS Word. Amused but clearly wanting to explore another topic, they asked, "How do you play music?" Denise took the opportunity to show them iTunes, which occupied them for a while. At 3 PM, we told them we needed to work, to prepare for our 4 PM meeting with Anyo Group. They left and both of us fell asleep for a quick nap.

At 3:55 PM, we walked over to Sema's house. We wondered if it would be a short meeting since clouds were yet again moving in. When we came to the backside of the house, there were no chairs set up for the meeting. It was 4:01 PM, so we were early, but still chairs are usually set out for everyone ahead of time. Sema and Beatrice walked out of the house, surprised to see us, and exclaimed, "The meeting is postponed because of the rain." We walked by Richard's house (which is also the village bar with a sign above the entrance reading, *Kindness Can Kill*) and Walter's house to inform both of them of their next computer training time. Right as we turned out of Walter's yard, the rain came pouring down. We all ran back to our rooms, me, Denise, Sema, and Beatrice. Even though it was in the rain, it felt so good to finally run again and stretch my legs. If it's not raining, and still light out, it's almost too hot to run. We burst into our room, with the door curtain flying behind us.

As we waited out the storm, we showed Sema and Beatrice the fabric we bought in the market, and wrapped it around us to show our plans for skirts, and held up the other fabric we want to make into bags. Beatrice bounced around the room chattering to Sema in Ewe, smiling and saying, "Oooh, fine! Fine! Fine!" We brought out the beads to show them, and Beatrice got so excited that we had beads for our hips! She took mine and immediately started adjusting the length of the beads to fit around my hips. When it all tied together, she handed it to me to slip on over my head and down to my waist. Several children were in the room, and were immediately shooed out as soon as I stood there to put on the beads. I guess you're not supposed to put on those beads in front of other people, oops! One of the many cultural slip-ups on this trip. We showed Sema and Beatrice pictures of us snowboarding and pictures from the U.S., mainly of the Colorado mountains where Denise recently lived, which had them inspecting the images in awe.

We began reading over the JSS papers we collected as Tony walked in. He sat with us for a while and told us the children were really going to benefit from all we were doing. While presenting to the students, we were unsure about their responses, and Denise and I were both wondering if the kids were really absorbing what we were trying to tell them. From reading the papers though, and from Tony's expressed pleasure and gratitude, I really think the students were listening and took what we had to say to heart.

Around 6:30 PM, Divine walked in, a half hour early for his computer training. We hung out for a while, talking about the JSS papers, and took the opportunity to ask questions about the village. We still have no idea what an annual salary for a farmer would be, or how much it costs to live here. In talking with Divine, we learned a farmer can save at most 300 cedis per year. You can rent a room in the village for 3 cedis per month, or an entire house for maybe 6 or 7 cedis per month. A farmer will typically have a few crops to sell, but in just selling corn, you might be able to make 20-30 cedis per month. We set him up on the computer and let him practice on his own (he had some experience before but wanted to practice typing) while we ate dinner.

Dinner was incredible with white rice, pasta with tomatoes and onions (and oil of course) and small patties made of egg and canned corned beef, which tasted like breakfast sausage. As we were finishing an orange for dessert, Divine's cousin, Titus (22), walked in. Divine continued his typing practice while we chatted. Titus was tall and muscular, and spoke English with more skill and confidence than Divine who stuttered slightly. As much as I love the kids here, it was refreshing, and almost energizing, to hang out with people our own age, and who could speak English so well. Titus's father happens to be the counterpart of one of the other volunteers, similar to Tony's role for me and Denise. They live in Etodome (which means *between 2 rivers*) about six miles away. During our phone testing earlier, we ran out of phone credits, so we agreed to buy more the following day from Divine. In our conversations, we mentioned how it's so strange to us to wake up with the roosters.

Titus gave us a look and asked, "Why don't you just sleep through the roosters?"

Surprised, I asked, "You can *do* that?!"

"Of course!" he replied, "if I don't have anything to do that day, I can sleep late, until 6:30 AM!"

I couldn't help but laugh.

We said goodnight and got ready for bed. Denise noticed a lone chicken who wanders the compound at night. We saw it again, and Denise turned to me and said, "what about Clarissa?"

The look of confusion on my face prompted her to clarify: "For the chicken. Do you think Clarissa is a good name? Or Koko?"

About to roll my eyes, I stopped, and thought, *ok, Denise likes animals, and empathizes with them, I'll humor her.* "Koko, since *kokolo* is the Ewe word for *chicken*."

She agreed and we went to bed. Later, I listened as Denise agonized over killing a mosquito that found its way into her net. She didn't want to end a life of something that was so clearly struggling to survive. I stayed mostly silent during this. Denise then began talking about how the poor little lonely chicken must feel, and maybe an animal snatched up her eggs before they hatched and that's why she wandered, lost in the compound all night, or maybe she doesn't have any chicken friends. I sighed, and managed to fall asleep without making jokes, listening to Denise ponder the mental anxiety of a chicken.

October 11, 2008
Wedding Day

After getting up at 5:30 AM with the roosters, we took our bucket showers and got dressed. Breakfast was porridge and eggs loaded with peppers and onions, really tasty and my source of vegetables for the day! Sema walked in with one the seamstresses from the village, who was going to make long skirts for us with the fabric we bought on Thursday. With a baby strapped to her back, she took my measurements and my fabric, and then did the same for Denise. She was young, maybe mid-late 20s, and missing a couple teeth. One tooth in the upper front of her mouth was much longer than the others, and jutted out sideways through her lips, about ¾ of an inch. The wedding actually begins at 9 AM, but we're going to wait and go around noon. The drumming and dancing can last about 6 hours, so the fact that we're missing only the church ceremony part, which will be entirely in Ewe, is not so bad. The skirts should be ready between 11 AM and noon.

It rained off and on, all day long, more rain than the usual afternoon storms. I read my new book all morning (Water for Elephants), and Denise slept—she wasn't feeling well. Lunch was sliced boiled cassava, a tomato-onion mush, and more of the sausage-like patties of egg and canned corned beef. After lunch, Sema appeared with our skirts, which cost us

2 cedis each to make. It started to storm while Sema and Beatrice left to get dressed for the wedding. Someone in the compound had a radio that was turned up so we could hear it—soft jams from the 80s and 90s, including Boyz II Men, Westlife, Elton John, Bette Midler, Bryan Adams, and *A Whole New World* from Aladdin. It was nice to hear something familiar, and we sang along to every song.

After about a half hour, the rain had taken a break and we walked with Sema and Beatrice up the road to the next village, Deme. We saw Hans and he introduced us to his daughter, Forgive. Louis (the old man who gave us liquor distilled from palm wine the last time we came to Deme) appeared in a traditional African robe, as he was the father of the groom. He led us through the mass of people to our seats, and as we followed, a large woman dressed in a white robe and head wrap, printed with a black and gray pattern, smacked her lips in a dramatic air-smooch as I walked by—about 5 inches from my face. Another older woman stood facing us, walking backward as she watched us through the wrong end of a pair of binoculars.

Louis led us to our seats under a fabric tent, right next to the head table with the bride and groom! The scene resembled our welcome ceremony, but multiplied tenfold. There were more people than you could imagine, from all three villages of Saviefe: Gbogame, Deme, and Agorkpo. A group of young men were drumming and everyone was singing and dancing. A few notable women (one dressed head to toe in what looked like gold satin) were demonstrating their version of African booty-poppin'. Thirty people danced around the drums in a large uniform circle, twirling their handkerchiefs in the air. A woman came around and handed me a cold glass bottle of coke and a small slice of wedding cake, cut into four pieces. The cake was really good—reminiscent of rum cake and coffee cake at the same time. I was very careful to use only my right hand to eat and drink. A table was set up on the sidelines displaying rice and banku for people to partake in. With a crack of lightning, it started to pour heavily again. The rain was relentless, falling hard and plentiful over the celebration. It didn't stop anyone. Everyone continued to sing and dance to the drums in the pouring rain. We were soaked, but having a blast.

Later, everyone dispersed and we followed Louis back to his house. The bride and groom sat in chairs facing the entrance. We were seated next to them. Several people came in, greeted us, and congratulated the bride and groom, which is when we realized we were seated in the receiving line! This was a little strange, so when I asked Sema about it later, she explained that the bride and groom wanted to be our friends because they like our skin color. I guess that's nice enough, but I still felt like a monkey in a zoo. Everyone greeted us with "mia woezo," (you are welcome) and we replied, "yoo" (thank you).

One guy walked up, who was actually pretty hot but lost *major* points when he greeted us with "yavoo, yavoo."

I shook his hand, about to say "yoo," in response and stopped short looking at him with confusion, and asked, "What?"

He clarified, "Yavoo, yavoo. White, white."

I said, "Yea. I know that," and took my hand away.

Yavoo is not a greeting. What do I say to that? The next time an adult says *yavoo*, should I just reply with *ameyibo*, (the Ewe word for black)? The kids, now that we introduced ourselves in their classrooms, will call out our names instead of *yavoo*.

Louis gave us more palm wine liquor and we had our pictures taken with the entire wedding party. It seemed like we were the guests of honor, I had no idea we were so important. We met one woman from Accra who was related to the bride and groom somehow. We exchanged information so I'm hoping we can stay with her in Accra our last night before our early morning flight home.

We were just about to leave when the drunk, dirty, old Roka burst into the room, arms up to the sky, and exclaimed, "I FOUND YOU!" Sema and Beatrice quickly pulled us away and we headed down the muddy dirt road back home in the rain. On the way, a motorbike passed by, its driver donning a bright blue poncho that flew in the wind. He looked like a superhero.

Once home, I read more of my book and Denise took a nap. Dinner was plain noodles accompanied by a plate of cold baked beans, canned carrots and chopped tomatoes. I wasn't very hungry but the dinner wasn't very appetizing either. I picked at it and settled for two pieces of bread with jam, and tea. After dinner a boy from one of the JSS classes, Bright, came over to learn about the computer. He left at 7:30 and shortly after, we fell asleep.

October 12, 2008
The African West Virginia

I actually had to draw myself a little map to completely see the connections, which will be slightly harder to convey through words, but essentially, this entire village is related.

I'll start by saying that Cassandra (Jessica's mother) is cousins with Sema (28). Therefore, Sema is related to Kosi, Grace, and Jessica, who all refer to her at Auntie Sema. Sema is also cousins with Beatrice. Divine (22) is cousins with Titus (22), whose mother is cousins with Beatrice, therefore Divine is cousins with Sema also. Sema is cousins with Tony's wife, therefore also cousins through marriage with Tony (39). Tony's wife's brother is the chief, who is in turn related to Sema, Beatrice, Cassandra, Divine, and Titus, and the kids.

They don't introduce each other as family, but when we ask if they're related, they refer to each other as brother or sister, and anyone older than them are aunties or uncles, despite them actually all being cousins. This presented some confusion in the beginning but now we've got the connections straight.

Sunday

This very chilly morning began with rain clouds hovering overhead. This weather reminds me of being wrapped in a blanket on the couch back home, with a hot cup of chai tea, watching movies. Our breakfast was cocoa—a soup made of cocoa, corn powder, water, and anise. We dropped a sugar cube in each of our bowls and essentially had hot chocolate soup for breakfast. We decided to skip out on church today to do some work on this week's JSS presentation.

The sun finally came out so Denise and I went on a long walk down the road toward Bame. We noticed a large tree at the edge of the village bearing an incredibly odd fruit. The fruit resembled Granny Smith apples, but were the size of basketballs! The few people we passed were very friendly and stopped to shake our hands and exchange a greeting in Ewe. A motorbike slowed enough for both passengers to say "hello, how are you sistas?" and a truck stopped to wave and high-five me, and asked where we were going. I guess the sight of two white girls traipsing along the dirt road is cause for concern for some. When people recognize that clearly, we're not Ghanaian and we don't speak Ewe, they'll say "hi," "hello," or "how are you," sometimes addressing us as "sista," which is really nice and feels like a sense of inclusion, and especially being so far from home, I really appreciate it.

We returned home from our walk and worked more on the presentation for JSS. We were starving at this point and very curious as to when lunch might be. Divine appeared and asked when we might want to finally go to the waterfall that Denise had flagged from her guidebook. We decided on Wednesday, and asked if Titus might want to go also and just then, Beatrice appeared with our lunch! My stomach was literally growling, and Divine just sat there, and continued talking. Denise and I kept exchanging worried looks, as if to say, "Will he ever leave?" He wasn't about to. He continued to bring up an entirely new subject—one that would occupy the next twenty minutes. He asked if it was possible for him to go to school and be employed in the United States. This opened up a lengthy discussion of obtaining work visas and student visas, looking into a community college in the U.S., application processes, etc. After a while, he was very pleased and then asked to practice on the computer, which we immediately agreed to, set him up on the computer, and then devoured our food.

We spent the afternoon in our compound, resting and playing with Jessica. She had on a pink jumper and blue Velcro tennis shoes. Her hair was parted down the middle with two poufs of hair tied with bows sitting atop her head, giving her a Minnie Mouse-like appearance. If you've ever watched Disney's *Lilo & Stitch*, Jessica's demeanor would remind you of Lilo: adorably destructive. She hits crayons and sticks on stone until they break, and when they do, she lets out a little raspy giggle. We've unsuccessfully attempted to stop some of this behavior, like when she threw a large snail against a rock and broke its shell. She was in an extra destructive mood today so I was surprised when she reappeared from her part of the compound, holding a baby doll, ever so gently. She gingerly placed the doll in my lap and if the doll slipped or fell to the ground, Jessica immediately became concerned, brushed her off, and very carefully set the doll back on my lap. This doll played a song when you pressed her belly: "*I'm a Barbie girl, in a Barbie world…*" Definitely not something I expected to hear on this trip! Later, we saw Jessica walking around the village with the doll strapped to her back like all women in the village do with their babies. It was really cute.

I enjoyed my afternoon nap (which has become a daily habit) and we headed over to Walter's house for another session of computer training. On the way I realized that Denise was well on her way to naming half the farm animals in our compound, including the two spiders in the outhouse (Fred and Sheila). We passed a group of children, Grace, Selom, and Jessica included. We then became witness to a slight brawl between them. Jessica was pushed down over a wood and stone barrier, and some other girl starting hitting Selom with what looked like honest intent to kill. We broke up the fight, picked up Jessica, and tried to console the others. In the end, they gave us high-fives and were smiling again. We were a few minutes late to our computer training, but in Ghana, that never seems to be a big deal—my kind of people! To avoid another "aerial" incident, we decided to refer to the arrow on the screen as the "pointer." With chicks at our feet and goats all around, we conducted our lesson.

Afterward, we headed home to eat dinner with the numerous fruit flies and house flies that have set up camp in our room. Lying in bed, I was sweating and constantly adjusting my pillow. It's so hard that if I rest the side of my head on it too long, my ear starts to throb in pain so I think the weight of my head is causing the hard, flat pillow to bruise my ear. I couldn't sleep. Fully believing I'd suddenly switched back to U.S. Eastern Standard time, I was lying in bed wide awake, dreading the roosters I would hear in just a few hours.

Educational Finances

Primary school and JSS are now free for children to attend, however Senior Secondary School (SSS) still has tuition of 180 cedis per semester, per student. After SSS, students could attend one of ten Polytechnic Colleges (junior college) in Ghana—there is one in each region), which is a less expensive alternative to university if finances present an issue. Polytechnic costs about 300 cedis per semester. After two years, the student can transfer to university. Alternatively, a student could go straight to university from SSS. Another option is a training college for teachers, electricians, etc. You can only earn a bachelor's degree at a university, and there are 12 universities in Ghana, each with tuition of 500 cedis per semester.

There are no scholarships, only student loans, and only for university. You cannot be granted a loan for SSS, and you won't be granted a loan as a farmer because a farmer has no collateral to offer the bank. A JSS student, whose parents are farmers without enough savings to send them to SSS, is out of luck. They must work and try to save enough money to go to SSS later. To put things in perspective, Tony (a teacher) is paid 200 cedis per month. A farmer with 1 crop might make 40 cedis a month for that crop. When you look at the math, and the lack of support and opportunity for farmers and their children, it's no wonder the farming communities are plagued with poverty. Even the kids don't have a fair chance.

What's also interesting is the vast disparity between ages within the classrooms. JSS Form 1 could have a child as young as ten years old, or as old as eighteen. The cognitive and emotional stages are so drastically different between these age groups, it's hard to imagine the academic and social environment would be appropriate, or conducive to learning. Apparently, if a child moves to the village with their family, no matter their age, they will be placed in Primary 1. This seems illogical and hard to believe, but Tony explained that it happens often enough, which is why there are so many older students placed in lower forms with younger kids.

October 13, 2008
Grumpy

Time in Ghana is really just a concept on which to base vague intentions. For example, we were told that church lasts an hour and a half. This was a lie. It lasts three hours, at least. Tony said his meeting in Ho this morning with the election board would take thirty minutes… After an hour and a half, we called and he said he was almost done. We asked if he would be finished in thirty minutes more. He said again, "almost done." But what does that *mean*?! Thirty minutes later, he walked into White House.

I sat in the shaded patio area of White House, waiting for some vegetable pizza and French fries. I already had my coke, and took my malaria medication on an empty stomach which is causing some dizziness now. Denise and Tony walked up the hill to do some internet training while I wait here for our food. It's nice to have some time alone. After some time of waiting, I decided to try and call home with the cell phone we bought. The connection wouldn't go through to my mom and when I got my dad's voicemail at his office I was slightly discouraged. As I stared out at the paved road in front of me, the beaded curtain lining the patio swayed slightly in the small breeze. The air was thick today and something was in my eye irritating my contact. All I had to use as a mirror was the reflection in my American cell phone. Even if I saw the problem, my hands were filthy, I'd probably just make it worse. I was grumpy. I didn't sleep much the night before, and the roosters never did shut up.

Playing with our Ghanaian phone on the tabletop, I decide to try again. I dialed my father's cell phone and he answered. I said "hi," and waited for him to recognize my voice. He excitedly replied, "Christine!" I could hear the smile in his voice. He was tickled pink and speechless as he searched for words—picking the start of one sentence and then switching to another to ask me something else. His reaction was just what I needed. It made me really happy to talk to him and hear his voice, and of course I was smiling ear-to-ear, sitting in the otherwise empty patio. I got lost in the sound of a familiar voice and suddenly it cut out—the connection was lost, sending me back to the sights and sounds a world away. After a few more attempts, we were reconnected long enough to say a proper goodbye. The conversation made my day (and his too) but I could tell I was slowly getting grumpy again.

My stomach was growling at this point. Denise and Tony returned, just as the waiter placed Denise's food on the table. She ate it. I sat. I waited. After they took her empty plate away, I waited more. Then I went up to the bar area and asked the kid how long it would be. He replied, "Almost." Great. I waited more. Finally, my pizza appeared and lasted approximately 7 minutes on the table before it was gone.

Denise and I walked to the market with Tony. I need to mention here that shopping with a man is a bad idea, unless he's a friend. Tony led the way, stopping at several places he needed to go, including the pharmacy, and another place that looked like it sold fertilizer or something. This was annoying because it reminded me of being dragged to a hardware or carpet store, when I was too young to object.

We followed Tony as he did his errands and picked things up here and there. We told him we needed to get toilet paper, fabric, beads, and water. Describing cinnamon and peanut butter was a trying ordeal. I concluded there must not be any cinnamon in Ghana. Peanut butter though, we were not willing to give up on, especially since I had seen a jar last week in the market of something that looked similar. Tony had no idea what we were talking about, so we continued weaving through the market for other things on our list. Suddenly, we saw a jar of what looked like peanut butter. It's actually a jar of groundnut paste, which is essentially the same thing, only smoother and softer (like honey) and is made of ground-nuts. Not *nuts that are ground*, but the actual nut is called a *groundnut*.

Moving on, we managed to obtain both toilet paper and water. Tony had no idea where to go for the fabric or beads so we were on our own. Walking through the market, I started to recognize a few stands, and going on instinct, took a few specific turns through the pathways. I found the bead lady that Denise wanted, but we were unsuccessful in finding the bracelet lady. We had Tony call Sema to ask where the fabric was. He led us in the right direction, but his pace was very slow and leisurely, a stark contrast from trying to keep up with Sema's purposeful strides last week. It was also contradictory to his impatient manner. We arrived at the fabric stand only for him to pace around and try to force me into buying a particularly ugly piece of fabric. I became increasingly frustrated with both him and the saleswoman. I left the stand abruptly and resolved to try again with Sema after a week or so. Tony was eager to leave the fabric stand only to lead us to the tro-tro stop, so that we could stand, and wait for a tro-tro. This clearly was a brilliant idea to leave the market unsatisfied so we could stand somewhere and wait. Honestly, I'm tired of being polite. I wish Tony would stop being so impatient when all I want to do is buy some fabric to make gifts for a couple people back home. He wanted to rush us off just so he didn't have to stand by the fabric. He could have gone somewhere and waited on his own until we were finished.

The ride back to the village wasn't awful. I had a seat by the window and had enough room in front of me to set my backpack down under my legs. This tro-tro, like so many others, is devoid of any interior upholstery. Ceiling, walls, and floor of the vehicle are just metal. Sometimes painted, sometimes rusted, and with some effort, the windows usually open, sliding roughly along their rusted metal siding. I'm unaware of the anatomy of a tro-tro, but something—either the engine or exhaust or some unknown car part—was causing the floor beneath my feet to become extremely hot. The bottom of my backpack was hot to the touch, so I moved it to my lap, and set my feet back down. The heat radiated through my flip flops, causing them to actually stick a little to my feet. This wasn't from sweat—I do believe my flip flops were in the slow process of melting. Every now and then my foot would slip off the sandal and touch the burning metal. After a while, we were close to the village, and looking behind me, Tony, Denise, and I were the only ones left in the tro-tro: a rarity.

Our sack of water had burst on the floor, our individual water pouches scattered and hot to the touch. People were always standing at the roadside of the village (the prime gathering spot) so when we pulled up, Divine and another boy named Hope helped bring the water to our room. As always, I was more than pleased to be back in the village. It was dark by then and the four of us just sat on our stoop watching Kanye West videos on my iPod. Dinner was uneventful, a type of flake fish and yellow rice resembling rice-a-roni only by looks. I picked at it, and decided to make a PB&J sandwich with our newly acquired groundnut paste.

People were in our room for a while, alternating between young adult and child. Grace likes to hang out in our room, but lately has been pretty quiet. I try to engage her in conversation, but it's like pulling teeth to get her to respond. I know she's still learning English, but there are some things I know she knows, because she's spoken about these subjects before—like school. The problem is, she doesn't know how to handle not knowing the answer to a question. Instead of admitting she doesn't know, or asking for clarification, she'll either stare at the wall and ignore you, or she'll bashfully bury her face in her hands. Denise took some time to explain some things to her and was able to get some responses. Denise also tried to explain that it's ok if you don't know something, but I'm not sure that point was absorbed.

Bright (age 18, but in JSS, form 1 - similar to 6th grade in the U.S.) appeared for some computer training and I took the opportunity to ask him about other students and their motivation for Senior school. I also asked what the situation was as far as kids having sex, to which he had some interesting answers. In his opinion, girls don't really think they have a chance at university, so the girls believe their actions now don't matter. Also, parents don't have money to give the students for the school day, for instance the 5 or 10 pesewas lunch that is available on the school grounds, provided by some women from the village. Some boys will give money to girls, but Bright indicated that it's the girls who become sexually aggressive toward the boys.

During this conversation in our seating area, I became repeatedly distracted from noise coming from the bedroom. Denise had been working on the computer, and a small group of children had gathered at the window, trying to have a conversation with her but really, they were all just yelling random sentences in English. It was so noisy, I burst into the room, immediately seeing an adult figure (along with the children) standing at the window. It was dark so I couldn't see who it was. I yelled, "Are you an *adult* or a *child?*" After I slammed the door, I heard Sema's brother laugh, as he does with most things, and I felt a pang of guilt mixed with my frustration because I knew he was developmentally challenged in some way.

Outside the night sky became the playground for a lightning storm. The air was cool and refreshing so Bright and I stood outside for a while just watching the sky. The lightning would crack and glow between layers of clouds, illuminating the outer cloud's edges, and displaying rays of white, light blue, and purple from within. The rain came down fast, so we turned off the computer and sent Bright home with my red poncho, which he returned the next morning before school, dry and folded inside one of his text books. After the rain storm, a cool breeze came through our window, giving us a nice break from the humidity.

October 14, 2008
Village Life

I want to take a moment to thoroughly describe our living conditions and the daily village life. I'll begin by saying that even though everything is a process, I have actually become accustomed to most of it.

To summarize the transportation system, it sucks. Tro-tros are the main method of transport, affordable, and provide an equal amount of discomfort to all passengers. They are always over capacity with seated passengers packed tighter than stock animals. You can't move your arms or knees and you try to lose yourself staring out the window instead of being painfully aware of the other nineteen sweaty bodies pressed together in one van. Yesterday I saw a tro-tro packed full on the inside, and carrying a load on the roof matching the vehicle's height and width, with a goat strapped to the front of the roof-top heap.

There is constant noise everywhere, even when you try to sleep during the night. There are noises from roosters, goats, sheep, people, and the village band which in case you were wondering includes several drums and a trumpet. There are noises I didn't even know goats made, but they do, all day long. Children and adults alike run past our window, their footsteps noisily crunching the ground as they scream or yell to another person down the way. This begins at 4 AM, lasting well into the night. Sometimes you can hear someone's radio or TV, and every other day or so, a van or truck will pull into the village, blaring a loudspeaker to make announcements or encourage some type of action in Ewe. There is always someone outside our bedroom window trying to look in, or speak with us, or they're just standing out there relieving themselves against our wall.

I've never in my life been around so many farm animals. They've really just become part of the background here, contributing to the soundtrack of daily life, and wandering past my feet if I sit outside. The baby goats, if they're not sick, are actually pretty cute, about the size of a twelve-week-old puppy. Male goats, whether just a baby or a full adult, have testicles bigger than most human men, that swing as they trot through the village. Roosters are usually red or white, chickens are all colors. I especially like the look of black chickens, whose feathers are black like oil—they shine in the sunlight and reveal blues and purples and reds and greens. Goats and chickens will walk into any open door, so you need to shoo them out.

Gee, Christine, what animals did you see in Africa? Lions, elephants, giraffes?

Oh no, but I did see a lot of goats and chickens and sheep!

The air is hot and humid even at night, which makes the thought of a battery powered handheld fan just divine. The bank in Ho has air conditioning so it's always a treat to go exchange money there. My skin is always wet, whether from sweat or humidity. The dirt in the air then sticks to me especially after applying sunscreen which is essentially an adhesive for all things disgusting to attach themselves to my skin. I hardly get a moment where I feel clean except for the 30 seconds after I rinse myself during my bucket shower in the mornings, before I put dirty clothes back on to walk back to the room.

You need water from the well to bathe, and also to fill the "flush" barrel in the outhouse. I'll explain. You may assume getting water from a well is fairly simple, if you've never attempted it before, so I'll explain. The bucket is plastic, so it floats. If you just drop it in, it will float on the surface and you won't fill the bucket. You have a few options. You can drop the bucket from above, holding it upside-down so it lands open ended into the water. Then when you pull it up, you'll have water. Alternatively, you can drop the bucket and jerk the rope sharply from side to side, causing the bucket to swing as well, eventually grabbing enough water to sink the bucket. The most common method, however, is to swing the bucket down so the bottom of the bucket knocks against a metal hook about half way down the well. When the bottom of the bucket hits the hook, it flips upside-down into the water and sinks. You need to do this three times to fill the shower bucket. About eight shower buckets will fill the "flush" barrel in the outhouse. Have you ever tried to walk while carrying two buckets filled with water? They're quite heavy and inevitably will hit my legs as I walk, which causes some of the water to splash and spill. After about ten feet, I need to put them down for a second, then pick them up and try to go another ten feet. It's probably about thirty feet from the well to our room, and another thirty feet to the outhouse, and another twenty feet to the shower area.

We despise getting up in the middle of the night to pee. This, like all other things, is a process, and not a pleasant one. When we first go to bed, we brush our teeth and wash our faces, wash off our feet in a bucket, and then we apply insect repellent all over. We're sticky and sweaty as we sit on the edges of our beds brushing the dirt from the floor off our feet. I awkwardly do a backbend to shimmy underneath my mosquito net, which I then tuck in by the sides of the foam mattress.

A couple hours later, I wake up, realizing I need to pee, and I contemplate the odds of tricking my body into going back to sleep. With no luck, I sit up, un-tuck the mosquito net, awkwardly bend underneath it, and carefully place my feet directly into my dirty flip flops. I re-tuck the net so mosquitoes don't get in while I'm gone, fumble to find a flashlight, and tear off some toilet paper from our roll. I go outside, shutting the door behind me to discourage any farm animals or rats or bugs from entering.

I walk to the outhouse, slide the latch open, push open the door, and shine the flashlight at the light switch. I close the door, and twist a bent nail sideways to catch the door, essentially locking it from the inside. I go into a stall (there are two), check for spiders, and squat carefully, to avoid actually touching the seat. Outside the stall, but in the corner of the outhouse, I lift the lid of the large water barrel, scoop with the gray bucket that typically sits on top of the barrel, and pour the water directly into the toilet bowl, which is the *flush*. I untwist the nail to open the door, turn off the light, and exit, latching the door behind me. I wash my hands in a bucket in our room, un-tuck my net, brush off my feet, bend under the net, re-tuck the net, and lay, sweaty and gross, staring out the window listening to the goats until I fall back asleep. The other night, I had to get up 3 times. I was irritated with my body's inability to hold on to water.

Separately but related, we never see anyone else use the outhouse in the middle of the night. At first, we thought no one needed to go at night. But then we would see people relieve themselves against the wall of the compound, close to their bedroom doors, rather than walking to the outhouse. When we asked about this, we were told that "witches would come and knock you on the head if you went to the outhouse in the middle of the night to steal your blood." Obviously, we figured this was an urban legend. But then Tony and Sema actually corroborated with more detail: As recent as eight months ago, people were attacked (knocked out after a blow to the head) when they went to the outhouse in the middle of the night. The culprits had syringes that they used to draw blood from the unconscious person to sell on the black market (for what purpose, I'm not sure). I'm still not sure about the accuracy of what he told us, but… that's what he told us. Immediately thinking the syringes were likely not sterile, I asked if any of the victims had contracted infections from these attacks.

Tony assured me, "Oh no, no one has gotten any disease from this."

Surprised, I asked "Wow, so no one got hurt?"

Tony replied, "No, they didn't get hurt, they just died."

The bucket showers are exactly that—I get a bucket of water to bathe with. It's pretty simple and goes quickly. I stand in an open-air concrete cell with my bucket of water, and a small empty bucket you might use to make a sandcastle. I scoop with the little bucket, pouring water over my head to rinse. Then I lather up with shampoo, soap, and face wash. I rinse again with the little bucket to complete the process. My towel is draped over the cement wall and I set my clothes (that I've sweated through the night in) on top of my flip flops in the corner to avoid them getting wet, which does occasionally happen anyway. After I dry off, I put on my dirty clothes, brush off my feet, and step into my flip flops to return to the room.

I've become a village-body, similar to a homebody. I really don't like to leave the village now, for any reason. Even if I'm lured by something that might be fun, like a tourist attraction, or visiting Ho with the added bonus of using the internet café, I really dread the process of leaving our village. The people are nice here and transportation proves to be such a pain in the ass every single time, it makes me wonder if it's really worth all the trouble.

We take walks on most days that we're hanging around in the village. It breaks up the day and provides a small opportunity for exercise. Walking down the road, in the village people have yelled out, "Sista Christine!" or "Nava kaba," which means, *come back before it is late.* People from the village we meet along the way will stop and greet us, ask if we're ok and when are we coming back. The other day we were walking and saw our host family returning from the farm. We stopped and chatted for a moment before continuing. A man on a motorbike stopped to ask if we were volunteers and what we were doing in our village. His name is Mike and said he would visit us in the village and suggested his wife could make us fufu before we leave. The next day he saw us by the roadside in the village and stopped to say hello again, first yelling "Sista Christine!" in recognition, which was really nice. When we're walking along the empty road we usually start singing old Disney songs or sappy songs from the early 90s. As much as I love the people in the village, it's nice sometimes to separate ourselves from the politics of every greeting for every person we pass by.

When we're in the village all day, we usually take naps, and read, work on presentations or computer training for a couple hours, and then go back to reading or playing with the kids. It's a pretty decent way to spend the day.

October 15, 2008
Waterfall: Tourist or Ghanaian?

The night before our waterfall trek, the village band decided to practice outside our room until 10:30 or 11 PM. We were serenaded to sleep with loud drums, singing, and a particularly boisterous trumpet.

We woke up late, at 4:15 AM. Sema had already arrived and was preparing our porridge. We showered with our buckets in the dark under the stars. Divine came to the compound at 5:10 AM and waited for us to be ready so we could walk together to the roadside. We planned on catching a car to Bame by 6 AM, in order to get a tro-tro by 7 AM to drive us to Hohoe. At 5:30 AM, we sat at the roadside to wait for a car to drive by.

Hurry! Get up and get ready! We have to go wait!

Divine was feeling a bit antisocial this morning so didn't say much, and sat on the opposite side of the road. A tro-tro drove by and surprisingly was deemed *full* so it kept going. At 7:15 AM, we finally caught a tro-tro going to Kpeve, so we hopped on. Once we got to Kpeve, we took another tro-tro to Hohoe, and then a taxi to the waterfall. The journey was miserable and everyone lied to us about costs of travel, because they assumed we had money so they would constantly try to cheat us. Originally when Divine offered to accompany us as a guide, we thought it would be helpful to have a local with us to help in these scenarios. But apparently Divine had actually never left the area villages around Saviefe before. Thankfully, Denise's guidebook listed appropriate fares we could expect from one town to the next so we knew that a taxi should cost three cedi, not thirty.

Once we got to the waterfall area, some men sat carving wood and hosted a few stands with jewelry, bags, and fabric for sale. A guide was assigned to us at the entrance to the hike, and he walked incredibly fast, for any person—not just a Ghanaian. We essentially hiked through the African jungle, up a trail through lush green vegetation. Some sides of the mountains were clay cliffs, while the other sides were covered in trees. We saw several gigantic millipedes, and a few rivers of ants marching across the paths. The guide pointed out black berries that we could eat, and showed us mahogany leaves that we could chew to ease an upset stomach. We also saw a cocoa plant—a yellow fruit with giant white seeds within a white pulp that was really tasty. We walked over aged wooden bridges with the water rushing beneath us. Moss and other plants covered the rock walls at our sides and water dripped from all over.

After 45 minutes of hiking, we reached the base of the lower falls. You could feel the water in the air from a good distance away. We were wet standing 150 feet from the falls. It was loud and beautiful. Divine suddenly lit up and was yelling in excitement as he ran toward the base of the falls where we were standing. We found a vine looped from a tree that we decided to climb and hang from for some key photographic opportunities. It was high up so I needed Denise to lift me up to where I could grab a hold of the vine and pull myself up. She hoisted me up but then accidentally dropped me in the mud. Wet and muddy, and smiling from ear to ear, we headed back down the trail through the jungle.

On our way into the hike entrance earlier, we had seen a sign, *Waterfall Lodge: The German Couple Will Welcome You*. We walked 250 meters from the road down a path that felt truly African: huts with thatched roofs and fire-pits. At the end of the dirt path, we came to an opening overlooking the mountain with a view of the falls. There was an open-air pavilion with a young Ghanaian setting up chairs. At the end of the pavilion was a large enclosure—the habitat for Cocoa, the German couple's African Grey parrot. The pavilion had wooden lounge chairs lining the outskirts looking out toward the falls. The ground was soft and covered in lush grass. A volleyball net was positioned to the left, and wooden tables were scattered under the pavilion. Small round bungalows, painted a rust-red with thatched roofs, rested in the shaded area behind the couple's house, and a campground was situated back there as well.

The menu was like a dream. We had a salad (a real salad) with a vinaigrette, and we split two dishes: chicken with pineapple and rice (seasoned with curry powder), and beef sautéed with onions and tomatoes and a side of French fries. I had a coke, and for dessert we had fruit salad and crepes. We felt like we were on vacation. After a leisurely and very filling three course meal, we sat and took in the view for a while. I went to use their toilet, which was a clean, tiled bathroom with a flushing toilet, supplied toilet paper, a sink with running water, and a mirror! It was great.

Reluctantly we made our way back down the road away from the lodge and caught a taxi back to Hohoe. From there, after witnessing a small altercation between two tro-tro drivers over who had the right to take us as passengers, we boarded one and were taken to Kpeve. The tro-tro was actually pretty nice, we were only at 15 passengers, which left room for me to put my feet up on the ledge in front of me. This one had upholstery and a working radio, and the remnants of a cup-holder was visible on the back of the seat next to the driver.

Once we got to Kpeve, taxi drivers tried to convince us that there were no more tro-tros, and we could only get back to Saviefe via taxi (and a cost of 15 cedis). At this point, we only had 4 cedis left and I was sick of taxi drivers trying to cheat us and manipulate us. With plenty of attitude I yelled, "That is ridiculous! Of course there are more tro-tros, its only 3 o'clock!" I don't know why I thought that…Denise quietly corrected me, saying that it was 5:30 PM. Oh well. Either way, we managed to catch one tro-tro, but it would only take us as far as Bame.

When we arrived in Bame, it was dusk and there were no more cars, or tro-tros, or taxis. It's a nine-mile trek from Bame to Saviefe along a dirt road through the African farmland and brush. We started to walk. It got dark quickly but Divine had a small flashlight. We were equipped with 2 ponchos, 3 Clif bars, and my water bottle containing only eight ounces of water for all three of us. Denise started to sing Disney songs to keep our spirits up and I started to think about the farmland around us.

"Divine," I asked, "I know farmers carry machetes to cut crops, but why do the farmers also carry guns into the fields?"

"For the cats," he replied. "Big cats."

"I'm sorry, what?" I looked concerned, since again we were walking along tall brush reaching over seven feet, exactly where the farmers would encounter these "big cats."

Realizing his response caused concern, Divine assured me, "oh don't worry, the farmers never see the cats because they're nocturnal."

I stared past the rustling brush into the darkness, wondering if Divine understood what *nocturnal* meant. We couldn't see anything past the faint glow of the flashlight except when the night sky occasionally lit up from some lightening.

We found out later that the "big cats" Divine referred to were a type of large weasel.

Two and a half miles in, we came to the village of Etodome, where one of the volunteers lived with Divine's cousin, Titus. We figured if nothing else, it would be a nice break so we stopped to say hello. Titus emerged, shirtless, from a thatched covering, with his seven young brothers and sisters. He offered to accompany us for the rest of the six and a half miles to

Saviefe, which surprised us, but we were happy to add his company to our entourage. Titus put on a shirt, and his brothers and sisters (all under the age of fifteen) walked us to the edge of their village, holding our hands, and we departed with hugs all around. The next six and a half miles consisted of brief conversations between Titus and me, and then Titus and Divine would chatter away in Ewe while Denise and I walked in silence.

Mosquitoes were plentiful and annoying, biting at my neck and ankles and bare arms. My flip flops were worn and I felt every jagged stone I stepped on. Occasionally we would trip over rocks or ditches that we didn't see in the dark. A government vehicle drove by, but didn't stop. I guess they're not too concerned with distressed people. I was quiet and became increasingly aware of my right knee and left hip that were aching in pain.

Toward the end of the nine miles, the moon cast a dull light over the road, and after a while we began to recognize some landmarks from our usual walks. We heard drums in the distance, and felt some relief as Saviefe was only maybe another thirty minutes away. Denise started to sing again as we came upon the outskirts of our village.

We walked into the compound and hopefully called, "Family?" Sema and Beatrice emerged from the house, ran over and hugged us, squealing in excitement that we'd returned. Of course, none of us had thought to bring a cell phone so everyone was really worried about us. It was late, and we were dirty, but dinner was waiting for us on the table, which by that point was great because we were hungry again.

As we said goodnight to the guys, Titus looked up at Sheila, the giant spider Denise had named, who was just then crawling up the wall of our bedroom. He chatted casually and removed his shirt again, swinging it into a roll, and smacked it on Sheila, killing her instantly. Denise squealed and was visibly upset, but I was quietly grateful for Titus' company once again.

I dampened a white washcloth from our bucket to run along my arms and legs to clean up. The white cloth was dark brown when I was finished. I was sweaty and achy, and ready for bed. I downed another 16 oz. of water (the contents of one water pouch) and crawled under my net and fell asleep.

October 16, 2008

The next morning, we got up a little after 6 AM, and began our bucket shower routine, scrubbing extra hard with our soapy water. After breakfast, we decided to skip Ho and just do work in the village. At 8 AM we took a two-hour nap, and spent the rest of the day relaxing and reading, enjoying village life once more.

The Plan

Tomorrow is Market Day again, so after we give our 2nd JSS presentations, we will catch a ride to Ho, hopefully by 12:30 or 1 PM. We may stop in the internet café for a few minutes, but eventually we'll get a ride to Accra (a two-and-a-half-hour drive). We'll stay in Accra Friday night, and Saturday morning we'll get a ride to Cape Coast (another three-hour drive) for our vacation-weekend. We're planning to explore the Cape Coast Castle, Elmina, and Kakum National Park, where there is a *canopy walk* (350 meters long, 40 meters high) consisting of wooden and rope walkways suspended between seven trees.

October 17, 2008
JSS Presentation #2

The second presentation went very well. We stressed how important it was to not give up on goals of higher education. We outlined the steps needed to progress from JSS to Senior Secondary School, and then to University or a Training College. The biggest issue was obviously money. We encouraged the children to discuss their education plans for SSS with their parents sooner rather than later. It's not too late for the Form 3 kids, but definitely much easier to get this across to Form 1, since they have two more years to figure out a financial plan. If their parents did not have enough money we discussed opportunities for the kids to earn money for a year or two after JSS, to save for SSS. We also stressed that they should not lose sight of their goal, as many people do when taking a break from school to earn money. All in all, the children seemed very interested and hung on every word we had to say. I think most of them, if not all, desperately want to go to Senior School, and are really struggling with how to do so. I really hope they can push themselves to do this. I want them all to have more choices and more opportunities in life than their parents did.

Accra for the night

After the presentations, we were able to catch a tro-tro to Ho at 11:15 AM. Once we got to Ho, we saw a guy we recognized (Ernest) from our tro-tro that broke down three times that one night. He led us to where the busses meet before heading to Accra. We had a Clif bar for lunch, and at 3:30 PM we boarded a Metro Mass Bus heading for Accra. These busses are five seats across, separated by a narrow aisle. I sat by the window, leaving Denise to have a lengthy conversation with the man to her right. I wasn't feeling particularly social so I lost myself in the passing scenery.

It was a three-and-a-half-hour drive to Accra and after a short rainstorm when my window leaked all over me, I was glad to shut everything out for a bit while I read my book and listened to James Blunt, Norah Jones, Duffy, and Elvis. I could hear Denise and the guy but pretended to be absorbed in my music and book to avoid being pulled into the conversation. The most interesting thing during the bits and pieces of the conversation that I did pay attention to was apparently there is a place up north called Paga, where you can feed a live chicken to a crocodile and then pet the crocodile, sit on it, take pictures with it, etc. Denise was appalled at this idea but I was intrigued, half wishing we were headed to Paga instead of Accra. Apparently, if you don't feed a live chicken to the crocodile, he might bite your hand off. This is easier for me to comprehend because I don't humanize every single farm animal I come across with names. Obviously, I wouldn't feed Koko to the crocodile…

I should mention here that Denise had become increasingly ill over the last day and a half. Her slight cold from Jessica had turned into a full-blown sinus infection. I really sympathized for her because it really sucks to be *that* sick and so far away from anything familiar, especially modern medicine. We decided that while in Accra the following day, we would try to find her a doctor before heading to Cape Coast.

When we arrived in Accra, we asked the few people left on the bus where we could catch a taxi to our hotel. Two guys on the bus, in their mid 20s who go to college in Accra, offered to show us the way. They led us through some pretty seedy areas that I definitely would not walk through alone. It was dark by then, when good chop bars by day turn into prostitute hang-outs by night. In reflection, I'm surprised how trusting we were, of strangers who wanted to help lead us down dark streets at night.

Street vendors lined the sidewalks, their stands lit by kerosene lanterns and small canisters with flames otherwise designated for catering chafing dishes. The boys flagged a taxi, negotiated a fair price of 3 cedis, and accompanied us to our hotel. This was really kind because the taxi driver dropped us off in a fairly sketchy alley where some people were lurking in the corners by the road. The boys walked us to our hotel and once we checked in at reception, they wished us luck and went on their way.

Our hotel room ($9 USD per person) was probably the worst hotel room I'd ever stayed in, but definitely a treat in the scheme of things. The staff was really friendly, and our room had a *ceiling fan*! The room had two screened windows that opened, one to the hallway and the other to the stairwell, which proved quite noisy throughout the night and in the morning. There was a mirror and a chair and dark blue curtains with a white print pattern. The two twin beds each had a bottom sheet *and* a top sheet, and I had a nice squishy pillow. The shared bathroom down the hall was fairly clean, had a small sink with running water, the toilets actually flushed (if you weren't running water in the sink), and one stall even had its own free toilet paper! The showers consisted of two stalls, raised about a foot above the rest of the floor, which we didn't use, but all in all, I was quite pleased with our accommodations.

We walked to a Chinese restaurant (with arctic air conditioning) for dinner, and on the way a random guy asked where we were trying to go. We told him and he offered to walk us there. He waited until we were seated, found a piece of paper to give us his email or phone number or something (I can't remember because I didn't really look at it before I threw it away) and left. It's strange, you meet really friendly people who are more than willing to help you out or show you the way, but afterward they want to be best friends and exchange phone numbers, even if we're not ever going to be in Accra again. What am I going to say? How's your family that you've never told me about? Very odd.

In the morning we had breakfast at the hotel, and I had instant coffee! They had real cream that I could add which made it delicious. I had two cups of coffee with sugar and cream, which put me in such a good mood to start the day.

October 18, 2008
Visit to an Iranian Clinic

Shortly after 8 AM Saturday morning, a guy who worked at our hotel, Ernest (age 26), offered to walk us to the nearest clinic so Denise could see a doctor. Her sinus infection had gotten considerably worse overnight and she was absolutely miserable. He kindly walked us all over town before our third attempted clinic was finally open and accepting patients. Many clinics were closed because it was Saturday.

The clinic was Iranian, called Red Crescent. I figured this was similar to our Red Cross, operating in the same manner as far as helping people who have no other option. The waiting area was packed with at least two hundred people. This was discouraging because we had no idea how long we'd have to wait, or if we'd catch the STC bus to Cape Coast by the 12 PM departure time. By this time, it was already 9 AM.

Of course, two white girls walking into this clinic, especially with Denise looking as sick as she did, drew some attention. The clerk asked where we were from and whether or not we were volunteers. Denise filled out a short form, paid 2 cedis, and was told to wait her turn. Looking around for a few minutes, we wondered if maybe we should try another clinic. Ernest was still with us, and recommended trying another clinic since waiting could take all day.

Just then, the Iranian doctor appeared and called us forward. We (me, Denise, and Ernest) followed him up the stairs and into an office. A nurse led Denise away and took her vitals while Ernest and I discussed literature he'd studied in college. Before long, Denise was in talking with the doctor about the possibility that she's contracted malaria. Just in case, the doctor prescribed her a Malaria treatment kit, along with cough syrup and some other medication for her sinus infection. Because we were volunteers, the medication was free.

As we exited the waiting area full of the same sick people who hadn't moved from their seats, I felt ashamed that we had been rushed to the front of the line. Several people in the back of the room by the door watched us intently as we left. Even so, I was glad we got medicine for Denise and could be on our way. I was also grateful that Ernest walked us around. We wouldn't have known where to go otherwise, and he was really helpful.

Cape Coast

Once Denise was properly drugged up, we gathered our things from the hotel and took a taxi to the STC station. Usually when you wait for a tro-tro or any other bus, you are waiting for an undefined amount of time, gazing hopefully down the road anticipating its arrival. This is referred to as Africa Time. STC busses are the only busses in Ghana that actually start off on Real Time (i.e. with designated departure times) in the mornings, and eventually transition to Africa Time throughout the day. STC busses also happen to run fairly regularly between Accra and Cape Coast. Denise handed the woman at the ticket counter our money with her left hand. The woman called this out to our attention, explaining that we were in Ghana and in Ghana you use your right hand to give or receive anything. We stood corrected, and nodded in reassurance that we would remember. The bus ride was about three and a half hours long, but thankfully it was also air conditioned.

Once we arrived, we dropped off our things at the hotel and decided to walk around town. This led us toward the beach where a group of fishermen were tying lines and occupying themselves with the fishing boats beached on the sand. The beach is nice where the tide comes in, but as soon as you step above where the water would hit, you can't put your foot down without stepping on some piece of trash. Anything you could imagine to be thrown away was littered all over the beach.

We managed to find *Oasis*, a restaurant further into town that was owned by a German-Turkish lady. We sat outside and I actually began to feel like we were on vacation. An open-air arena was right next door and seemed to be set up for some type of performance. A tall guy with short braids came over to greet us, asking if we were American. He was really nice, and easy on the eyes as well. He introduced himself as a musician in the performance tonight and asked if we'd be around for it. We made small conversation and eventually he left us to our meal.

The salty air was relaxing and I watched the dusk sky turn palm trees into dark silhouettes, and watched the moonlight illuminate just the right sides of the leaves and trunks. You could see so many stars, it was so beautiful. Denise was feeling extremely tired from the day of travel and her medication so we grabbed a taxi back to the hotel, sharing it with two Belgian girls who were in Cape Coast for the week on vacation from their volunteer placement in Togo.

Our hotel in Cape Coast had then earned the title of the most disgusting hotel I've ever stayed in. The toilet was supposed to be able to flush but did not. The bathroom itself was filthy, with dirt and crud all over the floor. The bathroom light didn't work and the door didn't close. We did have a ceiling fan which seemed to blow hot air, so that was a bust. A grubby torn pillowcase did not cover the gray and lumpy "pillow" that was supplied, and the sheet was literally crawling with ants and beetles. You get the idea. At $6 per person, I guess you get what you pay for. I hoped I wouldn't catch the plague. I considered sleeping upright in the gross looking fabric chair in the corner but opted to lather on the insect repellent and sleep as covered as possible in whatever clothing I had with me. Needless to say, I didn't sleep well, not only because of the conditions, but poor Denise (who was still very sick) and I had to also share the double bed.

In general, the locals in Cape Coast were not very pleasant, calling out "obruni" and yelling at us. Sometimes children back in Ho or Saviefe would run up and grab our hands just out of curiosity. But here, even young adults easily twenty years old would grab our arms, and one girl even grabbed Denise's backside. That said, we are always impressed with and thankful for the kindness of a select few strangers. One young boy, probably ten years old, walked us through the city to show us where to catch a tro-tro to go to Kakum National Park the next day.

October 19, 2008
Kakum & Cape Coast Castle

Sunday was a very productive tourist day for us. Our first stop was Kakum National Park, an hour drive by tro-tro from Cape Coast. My flip flop decided this would be a perfect time to break, so Denise put on her tennis shoes she luckily brought with her and I wore her flip flops instead. We climbed 150 feet above sea level and then hiked along a rock pathway to the start of the canopy walk. The canopy walk is a wood and rope walkway, 350 meters long and 40m high, and is suspended between seven large trees. It was really fun and we hung toward the back of the group so we could take more pictures. In the early morning you can usually catch some of the monkeys in the park playing on the walkways. Forest elephants also live in the park, but are very hard to spot amid the jungle beneath the raised rope walkways. We opted out of the associated nature walk, which was an additional fee. We had our own nine-mile nature walk the other day, and decided to save our money. The souvenir shop at the park was pretty expensive and didn't have anything of interest to us so we walked back to the roadside to wait for a car or tro-tro heading back to Cape Coast.

Separately, we also came across a sign that said "USA Movies," and were hopeful that perhaps there was a movie theater we could visit that evening. We found out that it's an outdoor lot where they project one movie, usually Nigerian, each night.

After we were back in Cape Coast, we realized we had enough time to visit the Castle as well. For me, this was the most interesting and rewarding part of the weekend's excursion. Fishermen work just outside the castle grounds on the beach and locals were crowding the one safe area in the waves. The tide was too strong and dangerous much past the area where old ships came in. In an open area on the beach just between the rocks and the fishermen, a group of young men played soccer. When we first walked into the compound, it looked like any other fort you might see from that period that served as a trading post. Any other fort that is, until you actually tour the grounds and truly understand how grossly inhumane this structure had been.

There was a small museum with artifacts and descriptions about everything from the history of Cape Coast, the change in power from the Portuguese, then the Dutch, the Swedes for a few years, and eventually the British. Large drawings covered the walls depicting life in the 1600s. The women carried babies on their backs wrapped in cloth. It's interesting how some things stick throughout history. Plaques were mounted explaining how people lived before any foreign power, and other plaques briefly described trade in Ghana. It didn't go into depth about the gold trade though, which is strange since that's why Ghana didn't even join the slave trade until much later.

There was a diagram of a slave ship illustrating how people were stacked like books on a shelf for the journey. Other displays showed how slaves were shackled and marched through the African brush, how they were branded and sold, and another display acknowledged people involved in fighting for the abolition of slavery as well as some other key people in history. I remember learning about the slave trade in school, but only how it applied to the United States. One third of slaves exported from the African coast went to Brazil, and another third went to the Caribbean (which is apparently where most of the torturous treatment of slaves occurred). The last third was split between the rest of South America and North America.

We toured the castle, beginning with the dungeons where they used to keep 1500 slaves for three months before shipping them off overseas. They kept two hundred men in one small cell with only three small windows at the very top for light and ventilation. There was a small hole close to the ceiling which carried down British voices singing hymns in the church that sat atop the dungeon, calling to both Heaven and Hell it seemed.

Slaves defecated on the floor which ran down through the next room of 200 men. The women were held separately, but in similar conditions. The British would choose the most beautiful slave for the General. They would bathe her, clothe her, feed her, and take her to the General. If she refused to be raped, they would place her in the punishment cell, a small space of maybe 20 feet by 5 feet at its widest, for one week. Up to fifty women could be held in that space at a time. If a British soldier got a slave pregnant, she could live outside the dungeon, with the soldier until she gave birth. Once she gave birth, she would return to the slave dungeon, and the child would be sent to the first school that was built, the Cape Coast School. For three months, these people were simply held. If they became sick, they were condemned to a separate room, barricaded with three heavy locked doors with no light, no air, no food, and no water, to die. Domestic slaves who worked at the castle would come in to retrieve the bodies. Once it was time to be shipped off, the men and women were led, separately, through tunnels out to the sand, through the *Door of No Return*. About ten years ago, the bodies of two descendants of slaves who went through the *Door of No Return* were returned, through the same door, to purposely break the meaning. A plaque was placed on the outside of the door, titling it the *Door of Return.*

The tour was incredibly powerful. You can read about the slave trade and you can learn the stories and you can know of the horrible treatment that these people endured. But standing where they stood, in their dungeons, and looking at the same dark walls that haunted them during their three months in Cape Coast was utterly heart-wrenching. Livestock received better treatment than the torture forced upon them.

Inside the castle courtyard, several vendors had stands selling all sorts of drums and wood carvings. I picked up some gifts for my family and a small drum for myself. Afterward, we went to the Cape Coast Castle restaurant right next door for dinner. A guy sitting on the ledge outside looking toward the ocean sat with a drum, and he saw I had one as well. I sat down next to him and set the drum between my knees and looked at him for instruction. He smiled and slowly started a rhythm I could manage and sure enough we sat there for a short while as he tried to teach me how to drum.

Denise and I sat in the corner of the open-air restaurant and ordered food—I had vegetable coconut curry with jollof rice, and a pineapple pancake for dessert. While we were waiting for our food, Denise began to teach me how to play either gin or rummy. Neither of us are sure which game it was that she was teaching me, but it was one or the other.

After we ate, a young man who was deaf (age 22) named Kofi approached us. I'm not sure what prompted him to approach, but lucky for us (and him) Denise knew a little bit of sign language. She spelled words she didn't know how to sign, and we used a pen and paper for complicated sentences. He sat down and we taught him how to play gin or rummy. We played a few games, and then decided to head back to the hotel. We walked to save money, got a little bit lost on the way, but eventually found our street and our hotel.

A young guy who worked at the hotel was admiring my bracelet and asked if I wanted to trade for his Ghanaian style beaded necklace he was wearing. I agreed, knowing I have more bracelets at home, but was pleased to trade for something instead of just paying money. It felt more personal that way.

October 20, 2008
Monday – The Long Journey Home

I did not sleep Sunday night due to my anxieties of sleeping in a bed infested with biting insects, not to even touch on how diseased the foam mattress and pillows must be under the questionable cleanliness of the sheets. I had a headache at this point from dehydration, exhaustion, and stress, and decided we should try to get back to the village on Monday instead of spending more money for another hotel and more food. If we got back to the village, I could sleep in my own bed, under my own mosquito net, and could take a lovely calming bucket shower with my own pretty blue bucket in our clean cement enclosure, and eat good, free food. I made it my mission to get us back to the village. I had 25 cedis, which would cover my bus fares from Cape Coast to Accra, and then from Accra to Ho, and then we'd have to pay 15 cedis for a taxi, but it would be worth it to be back home in our clean safe village that night.

It was a long day to say the least. I had some delicious coffee with breakfast, minus the ants I picked out, and was ready to bid farewell to the coast. We walked to the Castle where we were told we could find the busses that go to Accra. On the way, a tall guy with short braids, a hat and an MP3 player stopped us. He explained that his friend was the musician we met at Oasis two nights before. They came back to Oasis after their performance to find us, apparently there was a party going on they wanted us to come to. After talking to the waiters, they found out we had left a short time before and ran after us trying to call us back! We were oblivious and obviously had gone back to our gross hotel room anyway, but it was flattering and I was a bit bummed we missed the party. I knew Denise wasn't feeling well, but I could have used a pick-me-up. At any rate, the guy was really nice and wished us luck with our travels and told us to hurry to catch the bus. *Wow, the first Ghanaian to initiate the end of a conversation!*

We boarded the Metro Mass Bus and then waited for about an hour before it departed Cape Coast. During this hour we read our books, listened to our iPods, and tried to methodically wipe the sweat dripping profusely from all over. The three-hour trip to Accra was thankfully uneventful. On the bus we heard a British accent from somewhere a few rows back. The Brit (Tolga, age 19) was actually headed to Ho just like us. When we arrived in Accra, I followed a woman in a pink shirt (who had a surprisingly fast pace) to a tro-tro lot, while Denise and Tolga tried to keep up. Once we were packed in our final tro-tro of the day, we waited for another half hour or so before departing the lot.

A tro-tro really is a unique extension of travel here that deserves a few more descriptive words to fully convey the atrocity of this particular compact budget mode of transport. As I mentioned before, a regular tro-tro is made to seat 11 people, but often manages to squeeze upwards of twenty adults into every possible open space, clearly challenging the laws of human physics. Every person may have ten or eleven inches to sit. Surpassing the bonds of physical closeness you ever imagined possible, you're pressed shoulder-to-shoulder literally like the infamous task of "how many marshmallows someone can possibly fit in their mouth." If you're leaning forward (usually over whatever cargo you are carrying on your lap) you may be lucky and able to move your arms at the elbows in a curling motion. Usually the only other things you can move are your toes. Denise had this glorious experience recently, though her trial was significantly more difficult as she was seated next to an incredibly well-fed woman. Everyone's bags are piled high with cargo and then occasionally topped with children. The ride is pretty noisy, not because of people, but because of the rattling metal pieces that are actually holding the vehicle together. The gauges don't work so you can't tell how fast you're going, or if you have enough gasoline to complete your trip. There are no seat belts, and only occasionally do they have rear-view or side mirrors. The only thing guaranteed to work on a tro-tro is the guy collecting your fare, and the sheer strength of the guys hanging on the back who inevitably help push the tro-tro up a hill.

I was sitting in the middle of the row just behind the driver, and Denise and Tolga sat in the back row. The driver's seat was separated from the rest of us by a metal wall with a wire mesh opening at the top. I think this tro-tro used to transport prisoners. A vendor was trying to sell children's books written in French, so would read aloud to us, "Good day, sir; Bon jour monsieur." Denise bought some plantain chips from a woman carrying them on her head. They were good but thinner than I'd imagined them to be. I sat and read my book as Denise and Tolga chatted about anything and everything for the entire three-and-a-half-hour ride back to Ho. I finished my book about halfway through the ride, and tried to sleep sitting up between the two men also occupying my row. I was unsuccessful.

We finally arrived in Ho and took a taxi back to our village. We surprised everyone with our arrival on Monday afternoon since we were planning on arriving on Tuesday. We arrived around 4:30 PM, and Kosi immediately ran up and offered to carry my tote bag, and Jessica carried my drum. With little Jessica leading us by the hand, we walked straight to Sema's house to say hello. There's just no way we could stay away. Sema and Beatrice were happy to see us, as was Jessica who seemed a little less sick, but still not 100% healthy. We had dinner of boiled cassava and palava sauce (the boiled cocoa-yam leaves) and crawled into our clean beds, under our clean mosquito nets, and fell asleep, so glad to be home.

October 21, 2008
Tuesday: Market Day!

The day began much like any other, though we were exhausted from our trip the day before. After our bucket showers, which I incredibly appreciated after the weekend's living conditions, we had breakfast and headed to the roadside to wait for a tro-tro. The men who seem to spend the entire day lazing on a small rock wall at the roadside saw us coming and they called to us to hurry up. One tro-tro had apparently already stopped and was on its way toward Deme but had stopped again to tighten the back-left wheel. We seized the opportunity, ran up and hopped in. Because the tro-tro was already full, we didn't have to stop at the usual other villages for more passengers. We made it to Ho in just an hour and went straight to the bank, where one of the tellers recognized me from our Monsoon day and called out, "Chris Brown!" when I walked in. We also stopped in the internet café to do some research for our upcoming sex education presentation, where someone else called out "Christine Brown!" but I honestly had no clue who they were. I turned and said hello but did not recognize them one bit!

Sema was planning on coming to the Market that day so we called her after we finished our research, asked where she was, and arranged to meet her a few minutes later at the entrance of the market. The entrance of the market was marked by a couple cinder blocks separating the dirt walkway between two street vendors. The cinder block entrance was wide enough for two people to fit through, and you'd step two feet down to the market area. The walkways in the market were dirt paths littered with trash and people sitting with baskets of goods for sale. You bump into a countless number of people as you meander your way through the vendors. Produce vendors monopolize the entrance of the market, casting out aromas of pineapple, herbs, spices, and fresh vegetables. This was also where you can buy cans of flake tuna in oil, one of the regular ingredients used in our meals. As you walk through the market, people carry all sorts of things on their heads, from baskets three feet high filled with anything from yams and cassava to clothing to bread to luggage bags. You might see a man push a wheelbarrow through, overflowing with toothpaste, aloe, and over-the-counter drugs. At the first major *intersection* you come to, men on both sides of the walkway pound metal pots with large metal spoons in a special rhythm. People hiss and click to get your attention, and soon you're ducking under vendor stands in another direction. I don't know how we would have managed to get everything we needed without Sema's guidance and blueprint knowledge of the Market layout.

After a very successful and cheerful shopping day at the market, we each got a small ice cream treat (I found a pineapple

Popsicle!) and waited by the tro-tros for the Saviefe-bound vehicles to appear. The tro-tros gather and pack themselves in a large dirt lot covered with trash and empty water pouches pressed beneath footprints. There is no concept of a trash receptacle anywhere in this city, or in the villages for that matter. I cannot express how much trash lay on the ground. People throw things out of windows or just drop whatever trash they have to the ground without a second thought. However, the trash isn't the worst part of the tro-tro lot. The stench of rotting garbage and old urine permeates the air, and no matter where you stand, or how hard you try to breathe from your mouth, you cannot escape the vomit-inducing smell of waste.

After waiting for a short while (maybe an hour), the first tro-tro going to Saviefe arrived. Looking up in hopeful relief that our ride had finally come, I was overcome with nervous disappointment as I realized this was the same tro-tro that had broken down three times just ten days before. This tro-tro is meant to seat twenty-seven people with five rows of five (including the fold out seats in the aisle) and room for the driver and one person in the passenger seat. We boarded the tro-tro with the same seats we had before, though Denise was the one hanging out of the window this time. When all was said and done, we had thirty-two adults, one ten-year-old child, three babies, one guy on the roof, and two guys hanging on the back. A relatively small family of monstrous sized reddish-orange ants crawled all over the ceiling right above our heads. After a couple freak outs, and a couple dead ants at the hands of Sema and me, we were on our way.

Denise acknowledged, "Wow, you really do fall out this window," and "ouch, it really does hurt when you hit your head against this thing." Yes. I wasn't exaggerating.

One of the guys hanging on the back of the tro-tro was Ernest, the same guy who led us to the Accra busses a few days before. Going up the infamous hill leaving Ho, the guys jumped off the back and the roof to walk up the hill. The police were apparently standing at the top of the hill to ensure no one was riding on top of vehicles. As soon as we rounded the bend, out of sight from the police officers, we stopped and waited. Soon enough, our guys came running around the side of the hill, took off their shirts in the process, and jumped on the back. I am happy to say that we made it to Saviefe Gbogame without any major break-downs or injuries. Denise and I were very pleased as this was the very first time we went to Ho without any major complications or disappointments, other than the monstrous ants. To top it off, we got to go shopping and we got a lot of really cool fabric. Of course, it takes coming to Africa to identify with my feminine side, but sure enough now all I want to do is make bags and quilts with all the fabric I've collected. Denise noted that with all this fabric we could easily clothe the von Trapp family two times over.

October 22, 2008
Sad News

Since our return home from Cape Coast on Monday evening, I couldn't help but notice that Cassandra (mother of Kosi, Grace, and Jessica) appeared to not be pregnant anymore. Wednesday morning I watched her as she washed clothes for the children and more and more, my suspicions seemed correct. Finally, after lunch, I asked Sema. She confirmed that indeed Cassandra gave birth to a baby girl on Saturday. Due in early December, the baby was over a month premature, and didn't survive. I wasn't sure of the details, whether the baby was stillborn or if there were other complications, or even if Cassandra had gone to a hospital. She may have just delivered here in the village, but at least she was alright. Too often, pregnant mothers don't survive the delivery if there is a complication here. If something had happened to Cassandra, it's unclear who would care for the children since Grace and Kosi's father was in Liberia. My guess was that Jessica would be sent to live with her paternal grandmother in Ho, along with her 6-year-old sister, Essenam. It didn't appear that anyone was planning a funeral, and I wasn't sure what they did with the baby if she delivered here in the village instead of a hospital or clinic.

A Teacher Falls Seriously Ill…

This morning we as we waited for the bus to Ho, there was a lot of commotion at the roadside. A taxi was flagged down by the villagers and Tony, along with the JSS headmaster spoke with the driver. One of the JSS teachers, Victor, had fallen seriously ill overnight. In his 30s, he seemed the picture of health yesterday as he taught the students as usual. This morning when he woke he wasn't able to speak. I saw him lifted into the taxi, sitting between the headmaster and another man. As they drove by me on the way to the hospital, I saw the headmaster was holding Victor's head to keep him steady. His head just bounced, limp from his neck. His skin was gray, his mouth was open and his eyes closed. No one knew what had happened or had a guess about what illness it might have been.

One Week Left

There was only one week left before I would be in a plane over the Atlantic, with an entire coach seat all to myself, a far cry from our tro-tro adventures. Our schedule for the last six days was filling up quickly.

The plan was to have our third and final presentation for the JSS classes on Friday morning, beginning at 8 AM. We'll separate the students into one classroom for the girls, and two classrooms for the boys. While we present to one class, the other two classes will write letters introducing themselves and describing why they are excited to have a library in the village. These letters will be used in our fundraiser back home in the U.S. As this would be the last presentation, we planned to focus on health and sex education, organizing the presentation into three categories: 1) puberty and hygiene; 2) sexual intercourse and transmitted infections, and HIV/AIDS; and 3) how teenage pregnancy would risk future opportunities.

Saturday will be the last big Market Day before our departure, so we'll take Sema and Beatrice out to Ho for a *girls' day*. We wanted to surprise them with a few thank you gifts for the excellent care they had provided for us over the past month. We thought we might find some fancy fabric they could use as a wrap or a shawl, and some beaded jewelry. We weren't sure what to get Tony, so hopefully Sema could help us with that. We had already planned on putting together a small package around the holidays for Cassandra, Kosi, Grace, and Jessica. Once I get back home, I will be on the lookout for a small backpack for Jessica, books for Grace and Kosi, and possibly a soccer ball. We will send photos from the trip with this package as well.

On Sunday, the village is holding a Farewell Ceremony for us, which will involve a lot of drumming and dancing, and members of Anyo Group told us we would be presented with small gifts in appreciation for our efforts. Monday is our last day in the village when I'm sure we will try our best to soak up life here in an attempt to hold on to the many friends and memories we've made. Tears will be shed, I'm sure, and it will be incredibly difficult to say our goodbyes, especially to the children, and also to Tony, Sema and Beatrice. I wish I could bring Jessica home with us.

Tuesday morning, we will take the bus to Ho for the last time, and board a tro-tro or another bus to Accra. We'll stay in Accra for the night, though it's unclear if we'll be in a hotel or stay with someone we've met. Early Wednesday morning we will head to the airport in Accra to begin our long journey back to the U.S.

October 23, 2008
Thursday

The day was fairly uneventful and began with the usual acoustics of animals and crickets outside our bedroom window, followed by children running and then we heard voices from our front room, indicating someone had come inside while we were still in bed. Beatrice and Sema switched our schedule a bit. We've been lazy since our return from Cape Coast - waking up close to 6:30 AM each day but this morning Beatrice announced our shower buckets were ready and waiting for us in the cement enclosure at 5:30 AM. I groggily crawled out of bed, having stayed up until well past midnight, writing.

Once we showered and ate breakfast, I gathered my things without realizing it was only 6:45 AM and we didn't need to be at the bus stop for another hour. I sat on our stoop and started reading a new book when Believe walked up with Sema. I gave her some fabric I hoped she would make into a skirt for my mother, and told her I'd have more fabric for her the next day as well.

We walked to Richard's house to chat through ideas for income generating projects for the community, and we came across a monstrous sized cricket and a dead rooster. Along the way, I watched a rooster strut with purpose in front of us. I had wondered since the first day about the logistics of chicken sex, and today was my lucky day. The rooster sped up his pace, wings slightly to the side and came upon an unsuspecting chicken in the path. The rooster took one wing and knocked her to the ground, hopped on top of her and performed for about four seconds, hopped off and ran away, leaving the chicken back to her business.

The afternoon passed with spending time with the children, conducting computer training for Bright and Kosi, and prepping for the JSS presentation for the next day.

October 24, 2008
JSS Presentation #3: Sex Ed

I was really nervous about giving the sex ed presentation. I didn't know how it would be received, I wasn't incredibly confident in my public speaking skills even though we'd presented before, and I wanted to make sure we were giving accurate information. We'd been researching specifics at the internet cafe around puberty, pregnancy, and symptoms and treatments of sexually transmitted infections, but I still felt nervous. The classrooms (one for the girls, and two for the boys) were absolutely packed with children sitting, sharing seats, standing at the back and leaning through the windows from outside. The teachers stood along the walls. We wrote *SEX* on the board, and began.

It was clear no one had spoken to these kids before about sex or healthy sexual practices. One 18-year-old girl (JSS Form 3, equivalent to 8th grade) asked, "if my friend has cramps, does that mean she has AIDS?" We were given guidance to *stress the importance of abstinence*, but I said several times throughout the presentations that if anyone had any other questions they could come ask us privately at our compound. And over the next day and a half, they did just that. I don't know how many children approached us at the compound, but it was a lot. Many had questions about the family planning method of preventing pregnancy, and others wanted to know more about condoms and periods and being pressured into sex. It was clear a lot more needed to be taught to these kids, but even this was a big step. Many adults in the community didn't want kids to hear about sex at all, for fear it would encourage the behavior. Long way to go, but today was a great start.

October 26, 2008
Farewell Ceremony

Sunday began with a quiet calm to the morning with Kosi and Jessica. Jessica sang quietly to herself on the stoop in her tattered clothes, the curtain swaying in the light breeze behind her. I sat, taking it all in. Jessica threw crayons on the ground, retrieved them, and threw them again while singing *Jesus is Knockin' at Your Door*.

The ceremony was lovely. Denise and I wore our new long skirts that Believe had made for us, and walked into the church with Sema and Beatrice. We sat at the front facing the congregation as we did last time, and everyone began to dance and sing. Sema and Beatrice approached us in the front and presented us each with a wrapped package. Removing the string and unfolding the paper, I could see a shimmery gold fabric with a wavy line pattern, sewn into a beautiful ceremonial dress, complete with headdress. Denise unwrapped her package to reveal the same shimmery type of fabric, but in light green. We were ushered to a back room within the church to change, and Sema and Beatrice helped us assemble our new outfits. We emerged to cheering from the congregation, and again were presented with gifts, this time beaded necklaces. Sema and Beatrice placed them around our heads, and the dancing and singing continued. We were led outside for a photo with the entire Anyo Group, and then wandered back through the village streets holding hands with as many children as could crowd us and reach for us.

After the ceremony, Jessica was clingy but distant at the same time. She pouted outside our room for a while, and then when I lay down to take a nap she decided to crawl under my net and join me. She woke me by climbing all over me repeating "airplane" over and over. Sema and Beatrice brought our dinner of Akple, a traditional Ghanaian meal of corn and cassava dough, with a side of gizzards. They listened to music on our iPods while we ate, and then we all sat on the stoop taking in the night air. Denise had a cup of Milo (which is a nutrient rich meal supplement that she treated as hot chocolate), and Jessica chewed sugar cane. Jessica would walk over to me and put her hands on my knees and look at me inquisitively. She touched her nose to my nose, pressed her cheek to my cheek, crawled onto my lap and hooked her head over my shoulder.

October 27, 2008
Last Full Day in the Village

We woke up late, at 6:30 AM and, after chasing some baby chicks out of the cement enclosure, had our last bucket shower. Sema brought us cocoa soup and eggs for breakfast, and a guest book to sign. Divine came over to listen to reggae on my iPod while Denise went for a run. I went to visit Richard, who had promised I could be his tailoring apprentice (since I had zero knowledge of sewing). He taught, I listened, and he refused to be paid.

I went back home for lunch, which was red-red (black eyed peas cooked in palm oil with plantains), one of my favorites. Sema opened a cocoa for me, and I sat on the stoop sucking the pulp off of the seeds and watching the baby goats and chickens wander through the compound. Jessica appeared, helped me finish the cocoa, and walked with me to Believe's house so I could see about the skirts she had been making.

After a quick nap, I woke to hear thunder in the distance and I felt someone grabbing my wrist. Jessica crawled in bed with me and slept for about an hour and a half. Selom woke us up and started to play with my hair, and Kosi appeared, wanting to play on the laptop for a bit. Jessica sat across the compound from me, looking sad so I tried to cheer her up by making silly faces.

We went to Richard's house for a final meeting with Anyo, giving our phone to Richard and a disposable camera to Tony. We chatted, and Richard and Tony thanked us for what we wrote in the guest book. Denise started to chase a rooster, I can't remember why. And we sat down to a group dinner with Anyo as it started to drizzle.

Tony and Hans walked us back to our compound and visited for a while. Tony was weeping at our farewell ceremony and expressed frustration with the chief and wondered aloud why more people didn't visit with us in the past month. Divine appeared with Kosi, Grace and Jessica. A sort of evening play time ensued, with Divine on the laptop, and the rest of us goofing around and dancing to music in our room. Believe, Beatrice and Sema came over as well. Imagine all of these people at once in our little 8x10 room! Jessica kept kissing my hand and seemed very pleased with the new toys we gave her - a flashlight, colored pencils, half a bottle of hand sanitizer, and a granola bar. I asked Kosi to explain in Ewe to Jessica that we were leaving the next day. Jessica said (in Ewe), very matter-of-factly, "I know, I'm going with them."

October 28, 2008
Back to Accra

Sema and Beatrice solemnly prepared our breakfast. As we packed up the rest of our things, Kosi, Grace, Bright, and Jessica hung around the room but didn't say much. Grace began to cry, hid her face, and left the room. Jessica was very tired and looked sad. We took pictures together and gave hugs. Tony arrived to say goodbye, and awkwardly hugged us as if he'd never hugged before. Richard came to say goodbye as well and actually walked us to the bus stop, which is a considerable effort on his part since his foot is handicapped from polio.

Grace, Kosi, Bright and another boy carried most of our bags before we could catch up. I grabbed my tote in one hand, and Jessica held tight to the other. She sat on my lap at the bus stop, looking quite pleased with herself as if she'd gotten away with some escape plan. Another 3-year-old walked by (unsupervised, as most toddlers are here), and Jessica yelled with all her might, "Kofi! Kofi! Kofi!" She ran to the road and continued, "Go home, I'm going to Ho!" She really thought she was coming with us. Sema asked her if she was going to school, and Jessica replied, "No, I'm going to U.S." I asked her if she'd said goodbye to her mother, and she looked at me and gave one very confident nod. This was going to be difficult…

This world is not my home played on a radio nearby. We said goodbye to the headmasters of the primary school and JSS, and the chief. When the bus came, I suddenly felt rushed and wasn't ready. As I hugged Jessica and said goodbye, at the last second Sema said to bring her with us (since the bus actually stops back through the village on the way to Ho). Knowing this was probably a bad idea, I held her close and climbed onto the bus. We waved to Richard through the window and headed to the other villages of Saviefe. Jessica couldn't get enough of it, and was a pretty great passenger. She sat on my lap and looked out the window with a smirk on her face. Her lips were closed tight but she was grinning ear to ear and her bright brown eyes were glowing with excitement. As we came back through Saviefe Gbogame, the bus slowed and I gave Jessica one last hug before passing her to Sema who took her off the bus and handed her into her mother's arms. Jessica looked confused and sad, and Cassandra whisked her daughter down the dirt path back to the compound.

The bus idled for a moment and we reached down through the large windows, grabbing hands with Emil and Richard, who had waited by the bus stop this whole time to say one last goodbye. As the bus pulled away, I started to cry and I could see Jessica standing in the pathway crying. Sema and Beatrice, who were accompanying us to Ho, became teary as well. I took a breath, and said goodbye to Saviefe as the bus continued down the road toward Ho.

Once we got off the bus in Ho, the four of us were loaded up with our bags: two large daypacks, two medium backpacks, one small bag, plus three tote bags. As we entered the tro-tro lot, easily a dozen men started yelling and grabbing and pulling us in different directions, asking where we were going.

I was way too emotional to be rushed through this process so I screamed, "STOP!" and held fast to Sema. I pushed away several men and yelled again, "HEY! I have to talk to my sister so BE QUIET and WAIT ONE MINUTE. BACK OFF!"

I guess not many people are used to a *yavoo* yelling orders so they stopped and stared. Some of them laughed but at least we got to calmly decide which tro-tro to take. We selected one, put our bags in, and said a very tearful goodbye to our beloved caretakers, Sema and Beatrice.

We climbed aboard for our last ride upon the infamous tro-tro. There was room enough for one leg on the floor and one leg on top of my bag beneath me, with my knee on the headrest in front of me. It was the standard bumpy, beyond cramped, ride and I listed to Coldplay on my iPod. We did have to get out when we were stopped at a police checkpoint, walked through a gate, and then we were allowed to climb back on. We got to Accra and took a taxi to a guest house just after 2 PM. We had lunch, and they gave us fresh pineapple which was really nice. We took a nap and a short walk before taking a shower (an actual shower!) and finding a place for dinner. I was mentally exhausted from the emotions of the day, so went to bed and read my book. I didn't sleep well, I kept waking up and was actually chilly for the first time in a month. We got up just after

4 AM, gathered our things, washed up, and headed downstairs for our 5 AM taxi to the airport.

The airport was confusing and the rules didn't make sense. Go to one table where they write the date in chalk on the bags you're checking. Another table (though the tables are not placed in order so you end up weaving back and forth) is where they check your passport and ticket and weigh your bags. Then you go to a counter where a person tags your bags, one at a time, and places it on a conveyor belt that doesn't actually move while you are "checked in." Then you carry your bags to another table where they take everything out of your bags to search. Then they keep your checked bags, and you walk to the immigration desk. They told me it was too early so we'd have to wait, but then Denise asked and they told her it was ok, and then started talking politics with Denise at some other security checkpoint.

We went to a duty-free shop with a snack bar, and picked up a cheese croissant and a pineapple juice. We had time to kill so I started watching a movie on the laptop but it was drowned out by some really obnoxiously loud Americans nearby, yelling at each other from across the room.

I still had 7 cedis so I decided to buy a muffin and a coke before heading to the first boarding gate (there are two). Once at the gate, my bags were searched completely, again, and they confiscated my unopened coke I had purchased two minutes prior. Then we waited for a few hours. The room was really hot and anytime we asked a question, we were just stared at.

When it was time to board the flight, we were ushered down some steps to a people mover, which only moved us 100 yards, but ok… We walked up two flights of steps to the entrance to the plane, and sat in the emergency exit row. I had an entire coach seat to myself, sitting on the aisle. As the plane took off, I watched the coastline get further away, and I whispered goodbye to Ghana.

Part 2

2010

May 2010
An Update

In April 2009 I held a fundraiser, *Guinness for Ghana*, to fund the completion of the village library, as well as to benefit the Saviefe Scholarship Fund. I created the fund to allow JSS students to compete academically for a year's tuition of Senior School. I worked with Anyo via email and snail mail. Richard made a few dozen handbags for me to sell at the fundraiser, and Tony said that my efforts had inspired the village to throw their own fundraiser, yielding 300 cedis! Together, we raised enough money to complete construction of the library, and we sent two students to their first year of Senior School.

In the fall of 2009, Tony emailed me to say that the seminars Denise and I conducted on education and health had been very effective. A year after we had visited Saviefe, there were no new reported pregnancies among the students! I was pleasantly surprised and so proud of the students we had befriended. Saviefe has had one other volunteer since then, and continues to make progress.

Research Intentions

I am now in my second semester enrolled in a Master's program at Clark University, studying International Development and Social Change. On May 16, 2010 I will arrive once again in Accra to work with Anyo and Bridge for another four weeks, this time with a friend, Samantha. I am hoping to assist Anyo in their projects as best I can, and I will also be conducting some primary research for my Master's thesis paper.

The plan is to conduct research by holding informal interviews and focus groups in Saviefe related to the social constraints that may limit the availability and accessibility to reproductive health care and sex education in rural areas. I wrote a paper on the reproductive health spectrum in Ghana already, noting the realities and repercussions for rural women, so I am hoping to leverage that as the initial backbone of this research.

May 14, 2010
Passport + USPS = Poor Choice

As an American, I am fully aware of the lack of confidence held by the general public regarding the accuracy and efficiency of the U.S. Postal System. I conveniently ignored this well-known fact when I decided to mail my passport to the Ghana Embassy for a visa. I was in school finishing up my spring semester in Massachusetts, far from the Washington D.C. embassy. I mailed my recently renewed passport via priority mail with a tracking number, and included another stamped, pre-addressed priority mail envelope (with yet another tracking number) inside for the Embassy to mail it back to my local address in Maryland since I would be back from school by then. In an alternate universe, I called the Ghana Embassy and asked them to hold my passport and visa until I could come pick it up in person. However, in this universe, I was royally screwed.

A change-of-address notice which had been placed for the Maryland address to forward my mail to my school address in Massachusetts was still in place, which directly countered the more recent change-of-address notice I had just obtained to send my Massachusetts mail back to Maryland... hence, the dilemma. My passport and newly granted visa, along with my certificate of vaccination against yellow fever, disappeared into the black hole of lost mail. Fun Fact: Did you know that once a package begins a forwarded journey, no one in the post office world tracks it anymore? Yep. Good to know.

The time frame I was working with was as follows: I find out the post office had no idea where my passport was—even what state it might be in—on Monday. I am scheduled to leave for Ghana on Saturday. Tuesday I frantically made phone calls, visited the Ghana Embassy to explain my situation, and picked up a replacement vaccination certificate ($5). Wednesday morning was the earliest possible appointment I could get for the Passport Agency. I waited in line starting at 9 AM, pled my case, and luckily was given permission to pick up my replacement passport ($160) at 2 PM. At 1:30 PM I arrived to wait for my passport, after which I ran it to the Ghana Embassy before they closed at 3 PM. I paid another $100 for an expedited visa, for which they said I could pick up at 2:30 PM on Thursday. Another fun fact: They close at 3 PM, and are not open on Fridays, and I had to leave on Saturday… no pressure…

Finally, Thursday afternoon, with my passport and visa in hand, and roughly $300 poorer, I breathed a sigh of relief and began to think about the other essentials I hadn't had time to think about due to the passport fiasco—packing, bringing what I needed for my research, resubmitting my IRB application to the university, paying bills, attempting to fix the forwarded mail situation, etc. Friday night was my last night in town and I spent the night with my friends, brother and boyfriend, Sean. It was a good night, and really good to see everyone I'd missed while I'd been away at school. After I borrowed money from a friend (since the passport thing set me back financially a bit), my brother walked me to my car and we said goodbye. I remembered my rent check was still in my purse so my brother offered to slip it in the mailbox when he got home.

At 2 AM, I got a text message from my brother explaining he'd put my rent check in the mailbox, and found a forwarded priority mail envelope: my long-lost passport. Of course. At least I have closure.

May 16, 2010
Goodbye USA, Hello Ghana!

The journey went fairly well. Advised by a friend as to where the secret non-crowded security checkpoint was, Samantha and I breezed through Dulles airport without any complications. The first flight with Lufthansa was ok. The seats were a bit small, but not terrible since there was a petite woman sitting on my left and Samantha on my right. We arrived for our connection in Frankfurt, Germany just before midnight. The second flight with Lufthansa was overall better than the first—our seats were the first right behind the first-class section, so we had plenty of leg room to stretch out. I tried to sleep most of the flight, unsuccessfully, but we were given plenty of snacks. Once we landed in Accra, as soon as we stepped off the plane onto the tarmac, the thick humidity of the Ghanaian air seeped into my lungs forcing a sigh of relief. Finally, I was back.

Everything looked the same, and details of my previous trip reentered my memory ranging from the familiar immigration line, to the currency exchange booth, and the two baggage claim belts. As we picked up our bags and headed to customs, I became increasingly aware of a pinched nerve in my shoulder causing excruciating pain. This was likely due to suddenly carrying 65 pounds on my back, especially considering my recent physical activity could be summed up by my haphazard attendance in a beginner Pilates class two months ago.

After going through customs, we hobbled with everything we brought in hand another quarter mile to see Joy standing at the exit to greet us. The air smelled the same: a mixture of sweet bread, exhaust and dirt baking in the heat and humidity. We took a short taxi ride to the tro-tro station, where there emerged the additional familiar scent of raw sewage. The tro-tro driver was quite bold with his driving on our way to Ho. One woman called from the back, "Driver! Take your time, please! It is already late." As he sped around potholes and people, and dodged goats and other cars, we made our way to Ho. On the way, we stopped along the side of the road with the windows and doors open for a sea of women to spill into the tro-tro with various things to sell—water, bread, kabobs, plantain chips, watches, and dried fish.

By the time we reached Ho it was 7:30 PM, too late to continue on to the village so Joy showed us to a modest hotel for the night. It was inside a church, just up the street from the BRIDGE office. Our room had a *ceiling fan*. We were pretty hungry at this point, so we dropped our bags and ventured off to have a night out in Ho with Joy. Wandering through Ho, we met several children who shouted, "yavoo" and tried to touch our arms. We stopped for a little while at Joy's house where we drank some water bags and listened to extremely loud music, I had no idea what Joy was saying most of the time. His two small speakers were about the size of a CD case and seemed to be fashioned out of wood and cardboard but I couldn't believe how loud it was! Joy handed me a brochure titled, *Meet Me There*, the name of a vacation spot where you can see giant turtles and crocodiles. He suggested we all go some weekend because he's friends with the owner, a 59-year-old Ukrainian man. It sounds like a lot of fun and really, you can't beat having an adventure with a local who's willing to show you around.

We walked through town and down back alleys with only Joy's cell phone as a light to guide our footsteps. Samantha and I ate fried rice and a small chicken leg across the street from the BRIDGE office (2 cedis each) while Joy watched, since he's a vegetarian. After dinner, we headed toward a local bar with a patio and strings of colored lights hanging all over the place. Inside, the bar was fairly dark with only the glow of a blue sign and a few strings of colored lights to contribute to the ambiance. The music again was excruciatingly loud, a trend that made conversation a difficult task, but three beers for three thirsty people helped the night flow. We had Star beer, made in Ghana, each bottle measuring 25 ounces for only 2 cedis and 50 pesewas each.

The conversation moved from topic to topic. Joy was surprised I returned to Ghana, and that I still remembered a few Ewe phrases. He said many people promise to return but never do. We talked about the World Cup, and how we want to get a Ghana jersey before it starts. Joy runs an electronic store on the side and offered to lend me an appropriate adapter/converter for my laptop. Though at first try, I got a painful glimpse into what electric shock therapy must feel like so decided to run on battery for a little while. We talked about flip cup and other drinking games. I tried my feet at hacky sack with a small ball Joy carries around and fidgets with as a nervous habit. We talked about friendship in the village, and how there has been one other volunteer since I was last in Saviefe. His name was Kevin. Joy told us of his plans to come the U.S. in August but he's not sure if he'll have to postpone his trip. In the back of the bar, a small TV was broadcasting a game show, "Who Wants to be Rich," a spin-off of "Who Wants to be a Millionaire." I glanced back at a few of the questions:

Question 1: Which person directs a choir?
A) Driver B) Conductor C) Teacher D) Coach

Question 2: Which one of these is a plant?
A) Glee B) Free C) Tree D) Flee

Samantha and I continued to laugh with Joy and make plans for travel and hanging out together over the next month. At the end of the night, my body ached all over from sitting for so long, carrying all my bags, and using muscles I haven't used in quite a while. I peeled off my dirty and sweat soaked clothes and savored the all mighty power of the ceiling fan as I drifted off to sleep.

May 17, 2010
Rainy Morning & BRIDGE

After a good night's sleep under the ceiling fan, I woke up at 8:15 AM to get ready for the day. I changed into a clean shirt, packed my things and waited for Joy to arrive to take us to the BRIDGE office. Having run out of water the night before, I was very thirsty. I also did not have any water to brush my teeth. I felt sticky with dirt and sweat, and I craved the bucket shower that I would get the following morning in our familiar compound.

I watched the sky through our window turn grey and the trees began to sway. A storm was coming. Soon the rain poured out of the sky in buckets causing the air to cool and sweep through the room. The fan was still going at full speed, and knowing that rain tended to paralyze time even more so in Ghana, I assumed Joy would be running late. I stretched out on the bed and began to doze off while the rain fell rhythmically on the tin roof and the breeze brushed my face, arms, and legs.

At 10:30 AM, a faint knock on the door woke me. It was Joy, and it had stopped raining. After carrying our things to a taxi, and then again up to the third floor of the KK House building, a familiar face walked out of the office to greet us. It was Emil, the chancellor of the church in Saviefe, and a member of Anyo. Tony, the previous counterpart, had been transferred to another village and was no longer living in Saviefe, so Emil had taken his place as our new counterpart. Emil and I hugged and greeted each other, and then listened as Bismark (BRIDGE Director) briefed us on our upcoming month together.

The BRIDGE office now has internet so rather than pay to use the internet café on the floor below, Samantha and I attempted to check our emails, and update Facebook, you know, the important things. After an hour of trying to open the internet, I almost gave up. I was finally able to access email, so I sent two quick notes to let family and friends back home know that we arrived safely. Immediately after I clicked *send*, the internet encountered an error and shut down. With a sigh I remembered that this is how the internet works in Ghana and I should be thankful that I at least was able to send those two notes. I was so thirsty; my mouth was dry and I was getting tired and feeling nauseous. I walked outside to take in some fresh air, and talk with Emil as we looked out onto the skyline of Ho.

Disappointment

I asked Emil how the library was, and asked what time school let out in the afternoon. I explained I wanted to see Kosi, and ask him how he likes Senior School. Kosi was one of the two children that were given a scholarship to Senior School because of the Guinness for Ghana fundraiser. Emil said the library is fine and couldn't wait to show me the improvements they were able to make.

What he said next made my heart sink. He explained the two children did not go to Senior School because other parents in the village were envious, and didn't understand why their children weren't chosen to go to Senior School. To not disappoint anyone, Anyo decided not to send either child to Senior School and instead put the money into the improvements on the library. I was utterly disappointed and angry and saddened by this news. I kept thinking about it the whole ride to the village.

The taxi swerved around potholes and we found ourselves on the familiar dirt road that led toward Saviefe. I didn't feel excited anymore. I couldn't stop thinking about Kosi and how much he wanted to go to school. I couldn't stop thinking about how inappropriate Anyo's decision was. If you receive financial support from any outside organization for a given purpose, you are supposed to follow through on the promise of what the money would be used for. The last I heard, Tony said he would send me updates of the kids' grades and how they were doing in school. I felt like they should have told me. They should have let me know what was going on. I was so angry, and I felt helpless. I really thought I had made just a small difference, and it turns out it was all for nothing... just a library. A library is great, but it won't help anyone climb out of poverty if they can't afford to go to school. I wanted to cry I was so upset.

Village Life, Once Again

The taxi arrived in Saviefe and pulled up next to the family compound where I stayed before. I stepped out of the car and stretched a little. No one around paid any mind that we had arrived. Around the corner, Sema came running with her arms outstretched, calling out, "Sista Christine!" I smiled and we embraced. We were happy to see each other, and I was also happy that *someone* was happy to see me.

Beatrice had recently moved to Accra in search of work so Sema had enlisted the help of Mama, who I think might be Cassandra's sister. Accompanied by Mama, Sema, Emil, and Hans who joined us from the roadside, we carried our things into my old room. Nothing had changed, it looked just as we left it two Octobers ago. The same mosquito nets hung from the ceiling. The same Spiderman sticker clung to the wall. We walked into another room in the compound to greet our landlord, Mr. Koju Asafu (the grandfather of Jessica, Grace, and Kosi). We then took part in the ritual of washing the feet of guests (i.e. having a couple shots of palm wine). By now it was 2pm and neither Samantha nor I have had anything to eat or drink since the night before. Afterward, we were served lunch and finally drank some water. Lunch was white rice with a red sauce. The sauce had onion and peppers with canned flake tuna in oil, Sema style. We ate quickly and washed it down with water bags, sighing with satisfaction. I asked Sema where the children were, referring to Kosi, Grace, and Jessica. She said that a year ago Cassandra married a new husband so they all live elsewhere in the village, no longer in the familiar family compound. I asked if her husband was nice, but Sema shook her head and said no. It was sadly quiet without the children.

After lunch we walked over to meet with Richard. He sat on a bench with his crutch leaning against the wall (Richard was handicapped from having Polio as a child). He didn't get up to greet us as he used to. He also looked like he'd lost some weight. However, he did inform me that I had gained weight. Thanks Richard. We then walked over to the JSS and visited with the headmaster. On the way I passed Selom, who revealed his shy smile, and Grace, who maybe didn't remember me. She didn't seem happy to see me. We walked around the group of children who stood outside, each of them in line to be caned for misbehavior. The line was moving slowly. Usually two or three hits with the cane, and then that child would go to the back of the line. We saw the outside of the library, covered in fresh paint, topped with a shiny new tin roof. The inside was locked because it's only open during school hours, and the teachers keep the key. This seems counterproductive since the library was supposed to be accessible to complete homework after school, or have leisure reading time over the weekend. If the kids are in the classrooms when the library is open, they're not in the library, and when they leave the classrooms, the library is closed.

We walked back to the compound and sat with Sema for a little bit on the front steps. She told me of the volunteer, Kevin, who had been here after my last stay. Kevin wired electricity to a new street light that now stood directly behind the compound. He also put lights in the school, which was good.

Kosi came by to say hello. He was in tattered clothes and rode a bicycle. I asked him how he was and what he did that day, and surprisingly he said he went to school, and that he was in his first year of Senior School. Sema told me later that his grandfather, our landlord, was helping to pay for the tuition. At least he was in school. But it didn't take away my disapproval with how the situation was handled. After I showed Samantha the ropes regarding toilet and shower procedures, we began to unpack against the backdrop of bleating goats, screaming chickens, and drums.

The rest of the afternoon was uneventful, and absent of any children. We had a small omelet for dinner with a piece of bread and a couple crackers. After dinner I sat on the front steps to look at the abundance of stars that illuminated the dark night. But when I looked at the sky, I was looking directly at Kevin's street lamp, which not only impedes the view of the stars in the night sky but also attracts a vigorous swarm of insects. Ugh, *development*. It was better before when you could see the sky, and when there were less bugs flying about your head. That money could have been put to better use that could actually improve the daily life in the village, like fixing leaky roofs, repairing broken down shacks that people live in, or building a fenced area for the animals. Instead, there were bugs flying into the room, all over our faces.

As a child, I loved summer camp, but when I went back in the fall to visit the camp, everything had changed. The tents were gone, the grounds were quiet, and the feeling was gone. I kept thinking of that feeling all night. How I wished Tony and Beatrice were still living in the village. How I wished Cassandra and the kids were still in the compound and didn't have to deal with a stepfather who "wasn't very nice," whatever that meant. I wished the scholarship had worked. I wished the library was more accessible. I wished I could only savor and remember the first time I was here, when everything seemed so much better. But this, this was reality.

May 18, 2010
Realizations

I tried to ignore the bleating goats and obnoxious chickens until it was light out. I got up at 6:30 AM and sat on our front steps. Soon Sema greeted us with porridge for breakfast, and Samantha and I headed toward the bath area for a bucket shower. Samantha quickly got over her stage fright of showering together, and we both gasped in shock as we poured the cold water over our heads. Now we were awake! It didn't take long for me to remember the efficient routine of showering with a bucket that took me days to perfect the first time I was here. It felt so good to wash off the dirt and sweat from the sweaty night, the day of travel, the night in Ho, the tro-tros, and the airplanes. Clean never felt so good. We took the morning to relax, and had a short visit from Emil who peppered us with questions about life in the United States—farming, poverty, jobs, money, government, crime, prisons, divorce. Then after lunch (fried plantains with beans), I took a nap.

I spent some of the afternoon sitting on the front steps watching some kids play. The boys were between 4 and 6 years old, Kofi, Michael, and another, plus Fafali (the 18-month-old who lives in our compound, sister to Kofi). They positioned a stick with one end on the wall ledge, and the other resting atop a tin can, creating an appropriate obstacle for them to jump over. Fafali often walked into the stick, wanting to join in on the fun, knocking it over and clapping with gleeful satisfaction. Soon they figured out how to raise the stick higher and higher, almost to their height, and took turns jumping off of the 5th step across the compound.

Grace visited briefly, long enough for me to give her the gift I had picked out for her- a brightly colored bag, flip flops, and a red cotton dress. Kosi came by as well, and spent most of the afternoon in our front room reading the books we had brought, one after the other. Emil and Hans came to walk us around the community. Hans was fairly quiet with only his wide grin and smiling eyes to express himself since his English is quite limited. A local man who was described to us as *mentally ill* approached us, grabbed a hold of both Samantha's and my arm and refused to let go. Once he started walking and dragging us along, Hans stepped in and pulled us apart, and walked deliberately between the man and us until the man gave up. Emil asked more questions: what did Americans do with the mentally ill; do we have villages like Saviefe in the U.S.; do we have goats running around, etc. The four of us walked to the library, which I was anxious to see.

The library, only open during school hours, has obvious limitations as far as the hours of operation. We discussed this, but Emil explained that no one is willing to volunteer their time without pay to oversee the use of the library. This was extremely frustrating. If the community wants to use the library, they should be willing to take ownership of its operation and maintenance, and volunteer one afternoon per month. Obviously during school hours, the children are occupied in their classrooms, and adults are working on the farm. No one was using this library. We peaked through the open window slats to see a long table in the center of the room. One desk with an ancient desktop computer was on one side of the room, with two desktop computers on the opposite. I wondered where the 5 donated laptops were. The two desktop computers, which looked old enough to still be running MS DOS, were crowded together on one small desk. There were no benches or chairs in the library at all. The right side had a long bookshelf spanning the entire wall, as did the left. It looked like mostly groupings of textbooks. It was clear the teachers were not making use of the text books or teachers' guides that accompany them. We couldn't tell much else because the books on the shelves were turned with the binding side facing in, so all you see are pages. You can't tell what books they are unless you take them off of the bookshelf. I stared through the window and rested my head against my arm on the wall. I just don't know.

We continued to walk through the village, visiting the chief and elders first. The chief was cheerful, and seemed more welcoming than the first time I came. We got into an argument over whether there were fifty or fifty-one states in the U.S. He swore that Hawaii was the 51st state. I dropped it. He then gave Samantha and I two bottles of Star beer. We continued on our way, and visited Peace at the roadside store. We saw Walter very briefly and then visited with Richard at his house. Richard, Hans, and Emil spoke with us about our plan for the next few weeks. They then recounted their experiences with Kevin, the previous volunteer. I already had my biased views of the kid based on the street lamp outside our compound, but I was ready to hear what they had to say. Despite the fact that Kevin refused to learn any Ewe phrases, and that he bullied everyone in the village to do what he wanted, Richard and Emil still held Kevin in high regard and said they liked him. I wasn't sure if it was because he contributed a flashy and tangible donation to the village, or if it was because he was a man instead of a woman. I rolled my eyes and exhaled slowly in suppressed frustration.

It became dark so we walked home. I met Mama at the entrance of the compound who told me that because we had plantains and beans for lunch, we would only have bread and tea for dinner. I ran a wet washcloth, previously white but now brown from the night before, across my face and down my arms and legs and got into bed.

May 19, 2010
The Mass of Children & Reunions

We woke up late, at 6:30 AM, and waited for Sema to appear with porridge. Fafali, the little one, is such a cry baby. All the time, crying. After breakfast and our bucket showers, I read for a little bit and then Samantha and I decided to take a walk. Fully armed with sunscreen, and Samantha with her giant beach hat, we set off away from the compound. On our way along the path that leads from the compound to the main road, I looked up in disgust to see a new sign: *Kevin Street*. Seriously? Ugh! The walk helped both of us calm down. We were getting restless in the compound. We walked my old route past the pile of sticks (which had moved to the opposite side of the road and were now resting in the brush) to the two big trees. We walked slowly, and took in the sun and light breeze as much as we could. I took a nap before lunch (boiled cassava and macaroni with flake tuna in a red sauce) and awoke to a familiar raspy little laugh…

I walked outside to watch Jessica and Kofi play, jumping over the stick from the day before. Jessica was a head taller, and her alfalfa sprout had been cut from atop her head, but she had the same sassy little smile. She was very bossy, telling Kofi when to jump, and hassled him when he was tired. Sema said something in Ewe to Jessica, who responded with "Christine," and looked at me. She remembered me. She didn't come close, but she watched me to make sure I was in view of her showing off her jumping skills. They disappeared after a short while, and Samantha and I decided to take a more in-depth tour of the library, knowing it would be unlocked during school hours.

The library was exactly as it appeared through the window. There were labels on the shelves indicating subject, though the books did not match the labels. After facing the binding outward on all the books, which took a fair bit of time, I rolled my eyes at some of the donations. Books on college algebra, mechanical engineering, organic chemistry, C++, Photoshop, feminism, and child development lined many of the shelves, all of which were appropriate for a college-reading level, or a specified program. Obviously, the ancient desktop computers were not equipped with fancy programs for which those books would be helpful… It occurred to me, after contemplating my frustration on the lack of organization in the library, the people in the village may have never been to a library before. Unable to picture how a library should look, how it should be organized, how it should run, or how to use a library, the people in Saviefe were at a disadvantage. It's like the saying: *give a man a fish, he will eat for a day; teach him to fish, he will eat forever*… If you only give him a rod and reel, and neglect to mention bait, or time of day to fish, or show him the motions of casting, he really does not have his best chance at catching a fish.

We returned to the compound, sweaty, and pensive about the library. Jessica and Kofi soon appeared and we invited them to color with us. After breaking out the crayons, it started to rain so we moved ourselves inside the front room to continue the impromptu art session. Jessica impressed me with her English. She knew her alphabet, her numbers up to 24, and her colors. Though when I asked her age, she recited the same familiar response from two Octobers ago, "I am three years gold," and yes, she said *gold* instead of *old*. Only later did she put up 4 fingers indicating her correct age. She'll be five on July 4th. I watched them color and noticed that Jessica's legs were scarred from random scrapes and burns, and her feet were calloused with skin that looked like an older woman's.

Soon there were nine children crammed into our front room, all crouched on the floor coloring away: Sarah (13), Auntie (10), Juliet (10), Selom (9), Minia (8), Worlanyo (7), Michael (6), Kofi (4), and Jessica (4). After each child drew something new, they would shove the paper in front of you for approval and praise. If I started to draw an animal on my paper, slowly all 9 children would surround me, watching carefully. Throughout the afternoon, Jessica would look up at me and smile. After a couple hours, we sent the kids home and got ready for a meeting with Anyo.

The meeting lasted a while. I explained, for the fourth time, my proposed research and our plan to tutor children in the library after school. We also mentioned that the library needed to be organized better, and the books rearranged. We will speak with the headmaster about it Friday morning, and we hoped to spend most of Friday doing the work ourselves. Perhaps I could scrounge up some benches to place inside. After the meeting, Mama brought us dinner, a small omelet to share. We ate, and had a piece of bread and tea. Mama returned to ask how her son, Michael, did with coloring that afternoon. She explained that he's not learning what he should because he plays too much, but she encouraged us to work with him and to encourage his learning of numbers and letters. Kofi hung around our door for a while. Mama asked him if he was sleepy, but he said he wasn't, though he tried to keep his heavy eyes open, locked on us, afraid he might miss something the yavoos did if he actually closed his eyes. Mama said she wanted to help us organize the library on Friday, and also invited us to spend the afternoon at her house tomorrow after we get back from Ho for Market Day. She was excited to have us in her home, and claimed the breeze could be felt perfectly in her room. Kofi finally sat on the ledge, with his back against the wall, and his head hanging straight down in slumber.

Bright, who must be about 15 or 16 now, came to visit. It was good to see him. Quickly thereafter, we had two more visitors when Cassandra and Kosi appeared at the door! Cassandra flew in and hugged me, and told me she missed me. It was so good to see her. She looked happy. She also had a new little bundle on her back, 7-month-old Christopher, sound asleep and beautiful. Cassandra will be going to Ho in the morning as well, so we exchanged goodbyes for the night and planned to see each other in the morning.

It was very hot and muggy, and I was sticky with sweat and dirt from the day… just like all other days. I'm not going to lie, I smell. Bugs were flying into our faces constantly. I wished I could take a cold bucket shower in the cool night air, but that probably wasn't going to happen. So, I just drank some water, ran the washcloth over my body, and sprawled out under my mosquito net to try and fall asleep, breathing the thick humid air as deeply as I could, and dreaming of Market Day.

May 20, 2010
Market Day

We woke up at 6 AM and had cocoa soup for breakfast: a semi-thick, light brown soup with a hint of cocoa and a hint of pepper. It's slightly textured but after adding a couple sugar cubes, it's like melted African cocoa puffs. I was starting to worry about Samantha—she wasn't sleeping at night because it was too hot, and she had lost her appetite. She had a bewildered look on her face and had lost her bubbly spirit.

We got ready to go to Ho. Sema couldn't come because she had to harvest crops on the farm, so Emil insisted he accompany us to Ho. I tried to tell him we would be ok on our own, since I knew he would probably be bored since we wanted to look at fabric and beads, and have lunch at White House, but he persisted. The three of us embarked on a very bumpy and overcrowded bus ride to Ho. We had a long walk to the BRIDGE Office, where we briefly greeted Bismark and then tried to use the internet on the few computers in the room. Emil sat patiently, walked around outside, came back again, and waited while we fought with the internet. At first, the speed was decent; I was able to check both my email accounts, and send a couple emails. However, quickly I started to have problems. The internet slowed to an incredible crawl, and the only computer that recognized my USB drive was broken and would not start. I used Bismark's laptop to email the file to myself, but then could not get the internet to work any further. At this point, we had been at BRIDGE for almost two hours dealing with computer antics. Finally, I gave up and walked downstairs to the internet café I used to use last time I was here. I found new computers and fast internet—seven minutes and 20 pesewas later, I had uploaded everything I needed to. From then on, I wouldn't bother with the free internet at BRIDGE, it just wasn't worth the trouble! As we were leaving, Joy caught us by the side of the road and we made tentative plans to go to that *Meet Me There* place next weekend. Seeing him just for a minute was refreshing—he seems to be the only person who understands where Americans are coming from, especially those of us in our 20s.

From there we walked to the nearby bank to exchange some money. Walking in was like walking back into the real world—air conditioning, people dressed in suits, and BBC News was on the television. Despite my earlier invitation for Emil to join us for lunch, he had eaten while we were at BRIDGE, so he headed off to a bar while Samantha and I ate lunch in the shade at White House. Emil didn't seem bothered that we took forever with everything, and said he was just fine waiting at the bar. He was cheerier after he met us again, too.

At White House, Samantha and I each had a small vegetable pizza (they improved their recipe by adding cheese, and omitting canned carrots), one small order of potato chips (French fries), one cold coke, and one cold orange Fanta. Samantha seemed much better too, more talkative, and she ate everything! It was a very good sign. Samantha said she started feeling better just being out of the village, and walking around. Emil walks much faster than the average Ghanaian and by the end of the day we must have easily speed-walked three miles. He also is partial to shortcuts through Ho, during which he would proudly exclaim that "Kevin can walk from Ho to Saviefe." He took us, quickly, through the back alleys behind homes, through the littered streets, and stepping over obstacles of rocks and stones through a teal-green stream of trash and sewage. I tried not to breathe, because even if I breathed through my mouth I thought I might vomit. Garbage littered the ground everywhere in Ho, but I was sure we were trudging through the worst of it, in flip flops no less. Gross.

Finally, we made it to the marketplace. We bought a table fan (for 32 cedis—expensive!) to help break up the stiff heat so Samantha might sleep at night. We went into the market and picked up a handkerchief for Samantha as well (it's for dancing and waving it around and also doubles as a sweat rag). We also bought toilet paper—an essential, obviously. We attempted to look at fabric and beads but though he tried, Emil is no Sema. We'll get fabric and beads next week with Sema. We headed back to the tro-tros and I picked up two pouches of cold pure water on the way. Suddenly I felt someone grab my arm quite hard, almost hitting me, and demanded, "yavoo, give me one!" I had briefly forgotten the torment of being a *yavoo*.

We climbed inside the tro-tro and the taunting didn't stop. A young woman sitting behind me, probably about my age, kept trying to talk to me. The thing is, she was eating a piece of corn on the cob (which is very mealy) and spitting at me while she spoke. Several of her chewed pieces ended up on my arm and shoulder. She didn't know enough English to ask what she wanted, so she resorted to talking *about* me very loudly for a while. I kept hearing "obruni" and "yavoo," both interchangeable phrases for "white." When I turned to give her any response, she would just laugh at me—and not in a "laughing *with* you" kind of way. Of course, it stopped after a while, and if Emil asked me a question about the U.S., I could feel her move inappropriately closer to my face to hear what I was saying. Sure, now you're interested in me as a person... ugh. I was sweaty and exhausted by the time we reached Saviefe. Samantha and I took a very quick nap with the help of our new fan.

Mama brought by plain spaghetti for dinner (very early, at 4:30 PM) with the tuna red sauce that we've had several times. I think the tuna is what's making Samantha's stomach upset. It was a clue when walking through the market we both fought back gag reflexes at the sight and smell of barrels of dried fish. I really can't explain that stench, so I'll just leave it at "assaulting." Just imagine, Ho is a good three hours from the coast, wherever fish might be caught. They are then dried in coils around wooden pegs and then carried on pegged platters in the sun all day long before someone might buy one.

We ate the plain spaghetti, and then ventured over to Mama's house to sit in her compound while she made supper for her children. There was a pleasant breeze accessible by her home, but the breeze is clearly blocked somehow in our compound. Mama's aunt sat nearby, who had suffered a stroke some twenty years ago. Her brother is deaf and also came by to greet us. It was interesting watching him interact with everyone. He used subtle movements to express himself, and there was an understanding between him and Mama and her children to understand his movements, though it was obviously not the official ASL (American Sign Language) that most of us have seen.

There was an abundance of goats and chickens and baby chicks running around, and Mama's children seemed to enjoy our presence. Michael (5) would hide and pop out with a shy smile, and then would make faces waiting for me to imitate him, which I did. Mawufemor (pronounced *Mow-Fway-Mo*) (4) is his younger sister who would sneak up quietly to my side and just slip her tiny hands within mine and smile the biggest smile I've seen a child display here—I could see almost all of her little teeth. I watched Mama's brother (she didn't tell us his name) bathe Mawufemor at the edge of the compound, which was much more efficient than Mawufemor trying to do it herself.

We left Mama to head back home and sat for a short while with the mother in our compound, also named Mawufemor who looks no older than 23 but I think she must be in her late 20s since her daughter Sarah is 13. Sarah, Kofi, and Fafali were eating akple with their mother. Akple is very similar to banku and fufu, but the dough just sits like mashed potatoes in a dish rather than being rounded into a round dough-mound. We sat on our steps for a while that night, taking in the cool air. There were several nice breezes, and some heat lightning, but it was overcast so we only saw a quick flash of glow in the sky.

Tonight, we will sleep with our new fan oscillating its fine self all over our room.

May 21, 2010
Operation: Library

We weren't given breakfast this morning; I guess they forgot about us. So I had a Luna Bar to get me through the morning. As I tried to carry my bucket to the shower spot, I realized I'm horrible at basic survival skills. The bucket kept knocking against my knees, splashing absolutely everywhere. Mama says it's because I'm short and not as strong as Samantha. The strength thing I get, but honestly, people in this region of Ghana at least are quite small- men are my size or a bit taller, and women are usually smaller than me. At any rate, the bucket shower was cold, but refreshing.

The early part of the morning brought along little visitors- Kofi, Michael, and Mawufemor. Flies accompanied the children, swirling around their eyes, hair, feet, and open cuts and burns. Kofi and Michael attend a private school in the next village over, but the teacher had a stroke and because there is no replacement, they haven't been attending school all week. We practiced numbers with the kids—Kofi did fairly well, despite his troublemaker character and lack of attention, and Mawufemor was catching on too, but Michael was clearly behind. Parents are so busy working all the time, they barely have any free time to spend with their children to teach, let alone play. Cognitive development isn't helped by anything here.

We went to Mama's house to wait for her to be ready, and then the three of us traipsed off to the library to begin the reorganization project. It was quite a task that engulfed most of the day. There were two long bookshelves that face each other from opposite ends of the rectangular room. Books were somewhat grouped together, but both sides of the room had English and math and science books. We removed everything from the shelves and piled the books in the center of the room on a long table, sorted them, and decided where they would go.

We placed them back on the shelves, binding facing out, and proceeded to make new labels by subject. Some books were too challenging, almost inappropriate donations, which we placed on high shelves, probably never to be opened: college algebra, C++ programming, Photoshop, algorithms, mechanical engineering, principles of thermal mechanics, and parasitology. The more appropriate level texts were placed at eye level, with story books on the bottom shelf. We took a short break for lunch and accidentally fell asleep, but woke at 2 PM to have red-red (beans and plantains) and hurried back to the library to finish.

The headmaster looked in on us at 2:45 PM to check our progress and seemed relatively disinterested. It was clear that neither he nor any of the teachers had looked through the text books in the library to see what could be incorporated into the curriculum. He came to ask us a favor. He wanted us to order two books, one for him and one for the school, which he did not describe. Apparently, it needs to be ordered and he asked if we would use a credit card and he would pay us the cedi equivalent. Uncomfortable being asked for money, I quickly declined, fully knowing that there were plenty of resources in this library, and anything he absolutely needed, he could get himself. Sam told him she'd think about it. He left us the key to the library and we finished up while accumulating a few onlookers as I put up the last shelf labels. It started to rain so we decided to lock up and head back. Before I shut the door, I looked around at the bare floor (the only seating area) and wondered if it would actually be used any more than it is now, or not.

On the way back, we decided to pay Richard a visit. Richard, the village tailor, also runs a small bar out of the same room. I was hoping he would be warmer and slightly more upbeat than in our recent exchanges, but had little hope. I quickly found out why. As we walked the worn pathway to his bar/tailor area, I could see his head was resting on the bar counter. I softly said his name, not to startle him, and he looked up at me, his right eye swollen and wet with discharge. I had noticed when we arrived that his eyelid was swollen, almost so that the eye was shut, but he hadn't mentioned anything. This time, it was swollen shut.

I glanced at the counter and took in the 5 mismatched small glasses that appeared cloudy, the measurement spoon used to serve a shot, and the shallow bowl of dirty water used to rinse glasses after use, flies everywhere. As Richard rubbed his eye with a dirty bar rag, he explained that 3 weeks ago he woke with a severe pain in his eye and went to the hospital. There he was told that he has cancer of the cornea and must have the eye removed before it spreads to the other eye, rendering him blind and unable to work. At this point his eye was leaking and I wasn't sure if it was discharge or tears from the pain. The discomfort and pain were written all over his face. He lifted the lid to show me his eye, which was red and also swollen, the color of his eye indiscernible through the cloudy and almost bloated image of what used to be his pupil. For the pain he was given the equivalent of basic Ibuprofen. He hasn't returned to have the procedure because it will cost 250 cedis- almost 10 months' salary. I started counting in my head the amount of money I had with me. I did have some extra Ibuprofen I had brought, so I promised to drop it by later, wondering what would happen with Richard.

When we got home, we were joined by several kids who came by to color for a while. Mama brought us dinner (a small omelet to share) and told us to tell the children to go home if they are smelly and not to come back until they have bathed. Good information to have! Sema, Hans, and Emil joined us after dinner where we discussed Richard's condition. Mama's deaf brother, Kujo, has the same problem but it's not as bad. He has been to an eye treatment center closer to Ho, and they claim the eye removal procedure would only cost 65 cedis—much more manageable. We decided to encourage Richard to go there while Emil joked that if Richard dies, who will care for his baby, and suggested that I take the baby home with me to America. I was caught off guard and said, "I'm sorry, what? Richard has a baby He's almost an elder!"

As I declined taking the baby with me, Emil noticed the 2 bottles of unopened Star beer from the other day. He asked in surprise why we had not drunk it, and I explained because we were full and tired when we were given the beer, and now it's hot. I told him he was welcome to take it if he wanted. His response was, "Kevin could drink three beers at once." Automatically I replied, a bit more harshly than I intended, "Kevin, Kevin, Kevin! I'm not Kevin!" I couldn't tell if Emil understood me or not.

We have to go to bed early since we're trying to go to Wli Falls tomorrow. We have to get up at 4:45 AM so we can wait by the roadside by 5:30 AM for a tro-tro. Rush, rush, rush to get ready to wait… such is the life in Ghana. But hopefully we will get there early so we can come back early so we won't have to walk home like Denise and I did the last time!

May 22, 2010
National Geographic Attack

Well we were up on time, I would say *bright and early*, but not so much bright at 4:45 AM. We took our bucket showers under the night sky, the water feeling warm against the night air. I gathered our things as quickly as I could, still not having time to eat the porridge that sat on our table. I grabbed enough supplies for any type of "just in case" emergency moment: 6 granola bars, flashlight, toilet paper, hand sanitizer, camera, poncho, a full 32 oz. of water, extra tote bag to carry back goodies, sunscreen, and Deet. We got to the roadside at 5:40 AM, where Mama told us we were late, and Sema waited in her matching silk PJs, robe, and head-wrap, slightly out of place here. As we waited by the roadside, I applied sunscreen and Deet, pulled back my wet hair, and sipped my water, fizzing with the rehydration tablet I popped in the bottle. After 40 minutes of waiting, finally a tro-tro came by and we hopped in to head to Kpeve (pronounced *pway-vay*).

On the ride I ate a granola bar for sustenance. At Kpeve we caught another tro-tro to HoHoe (*hoe-huoy*). This tro-tro was one of two heading to HoHoe, and both were competing for passengers which fueled a full-on race between the two, the entire ride to HoHoe. We then caught a taxi from HoHoe to Wli Falls, and we were doing really well on time. Then the taxi stopped to let a woman, her two daughters, and their basket of dried smelly fish into the car. For a while I was really fighting with my gag reflexes, and if I breathed through my mouth I could taste the fish. I pressed my hand to my nose and decided to breathe, smelling only my hand—which smelled of dirt and sweat, but that was *way* better than the vomit-inducing stench of dried fish. Finally, at 9:20 AM, we arrived at the Falls.

The thirty-five-minute brisk hike to the Falls is probably about a mile and a half or two miles one way. The guide wasn't slowing down or stopping at all so Sam and I would pause to snap a few photos and then run to catch up. At one point we stopped at a picturesque worn bridge over a babbling brook. We paused, posed and before I could snap the picture, our flip flops and feet were burning, crawling with a swarm of *giant* National Geographic sized ants that didn't just bite, but actually began to sink their teeth into our feet and burrow themselves in our skin. To say that it was painful would be an understatement. I really can't describe the chilling feeling that runs through you if and when this should ever happen, but I can say that in addition to the searing pain, panic washed over me and clouded my immediate judgment as I screamed, threw off my flip flops and tried to pluck the ants out of my skin… while still standing in the middle of the ant pile… genius. At any rate, the guide came in useful, moving us from the ant horde, making sure our flip flops and feet were picked clean, and we continued on our way. I checked every now and then to make sure I was still breathing, which I was… intermittently.

I no longer looked at the surrounding jungle, but rather I stared at the ground, trying ever so carefully to step exactly where the guide had stepped. There were ant parades or marches or whatever they do when they travel in vast millions, but usually they're easy to spot: a moving trail of darkness running across the path, dense and about an inch wide. However, another ant parade was not following the rules and had created a chaotic sea of ants spread over 3 ½ feet of the trail. I was too close by the time the guide pointed it out, as he was already past the sea, and I held my breath and prayed the biting wouldn't happen again as I took three long leaps from a running start. To no avail, I landed at the edge of the ant sea and the biting ensued once more, though this time I was slightly calmer. There was less screaming, and it was over much quicker.

Finally turning around the corner, we stood in a small clearing of jungle, staring at the falls. I kept thinking those falls were so not worth the ants, and I couldn't shake the idea that we have to go through those same ants again on our way back. We snapped a few pictures, and I rinsed my hands in the water like a raccoon. Samantha and I exchanged looks when an American family nearby asked us if we were going swimming as well, and if we had seen the mass of bats on the rocks flanking the falls. I recognized the vine I had climbed two years before, but it was overgrown and inaccessible. We turned, ready to brave the ants once more on our way back to the start of the trail. We were attacked again on the way back, every single time we had to cross the rivers of ants.

In order to make it back in a vehicle rather than walking, we opted to skip lunch as well and again turned to granola bars. We waited by the road for a tro-tro, climbed aboard, and waited, parked, baking in the hot oven of scrap metal that was our mode of transportation, for forty minutes. Finally, we were moving again and reached HoHoe. From there we took a tro-tro back to Kpeve, where I fell asleep and likely resembled a bobblehead as we moved along. In Kpeve we had to wait, sitting in yet another baking tro-tro for a little over an hour before heading to Saviefe. I had a lot of time to memorize the interior, or lack thereof. There was no interior on the doors or insides of the tro-tro, exposing rusted metal. The windshield was smashed in a thousand places, its cracks growing with every bump we went over. The driver's side door was held in place by a thin blue string, which was removed completely to let the driver in, after which he would pull across a horseshoe looking thing to latch over the window. At one point, it came loose as we drove and the door flung open. My head banged on the side of the rusted metal often, which didn't help my hunger headache that was forming.

When we got back home I had a granola bar, and started to feel better. We took posing pictures with our two cocoa fruits we picked up, and headed to Mama's. She told us they weren't ripe, but said in three days they should be fine. She then gave us mango that would be ripe in two days, and a group of bananas that would be ripe tomorrow. Anticipation really is driving me crazy, I just want some fruit that I can eat *today*!

We ate dinner, and entertained some kids in the evening. To my surprise, my old friend Divine came to pay a visit, so that was nice to catch up briefly. He agreed to be interviewed tomorrow too, which is awesome. As we chatted, Samantha started moving strangely in her seat with a worried look on her face. Turns out, she's got fleas! They came from the kids we think, so they're not allowed in the house anymore, just outside. Gross. We threw her clothes outside and killed about 20 that we found on her and in the room. I think we have had enough of nature for one day. After Divine left, we visited outside in the night breeze with Mama and Sema and decided we were too exhausted for further social interaction.

May 23, 2010
Research Begins

Sema had told us that because we were so tired yesterday that we were allowed to sleep in until 6:30 AM! What a luxury! (I'm not being sarcastic.) However, promptly at 6:20 AM, Emil was knocking at our door, asking if we were ready for the community announcement, which we had done so well to completely forget. The announcement was to focus on my research and my invitation for interview and focus group participation, as well as our plan to hold study sessions after school to encourage reading and language skills.

Sweaty and disheveled from the hot night's torment, we quickly dressed. I was really grumpy and fought the urge to ask if we could skip making appearances at the announcement, and rounded the corner of our compound toward the *Meeting Tree*. The Meeting Tree is a tree in the center of the side path between homes, whose shade provides an opportune spot for the elders to gather and hold meetings. I had seen such a gathering just days before, where maybe thirty or forty people crowded around the tree and faced the elders at the center. The scene before me now caught my breath.

The entire village sat, organized and still, flanking the path. Women on the left, men on the right, the elders and chief were situated at the center under the tree, adorned in their formal robes. I gasped with the sudden shift of attention on us as we walked through toward two empty chairs beside the Anyo Group and the chief's wife. I noted that Sema and Mama, our permission for sleeping in, were both absent. The entire meeting and announcements were conducted in Ewe, which made me anxious. Walter began to walk around the women, grouping them by six, and wrote down their names. He presented the list to me, explaining those were the focus groups. I wondered how much these women understood that participation was voluntary. I decided I would cross that bridge when it actually came time to conduct the focus groups. I did tell Walter I needed a few more groups though, one of men, one of elders, one of teachers, and one mixed with everyone. I tried to explain that I probably wouldn't be able to conduct *all* of the focus groups Walter had just organized, but that I would try. He asked about the people who wanted to be interviewed but wouldn't get the chance. I explained that I would try to complete as many as possible, but that I would need more time and more manpower to conduct interviews for everyone, and it just wasn't possible. He seemed relatively satisfied with my response, and moved on.

A man behind me spoke up, in Ewe, and started arguing it seemed. I didn't know what he was angry about, but I was again getting nervous, jumping to the conclusion that he must not agree with my research or something. The chief spoke, and the man retorted with something that caused an uproar of laughter and hushed conversations among the community. I was dreading knowing where the conversation had turned. I reluctantly asked Emil what was going on. Thankfully he explained that the man noted that some people were not at the meeting because they chose to stay at home, and the man wished those people to be punished for not attending. Apparently after that, they began to discuss the problem of stray goats.

Because of the early morning assembly, we decided to skip church. Instead, we took a late bucket shower and porridge for breakfast, followed by rest. As we lounged on our beds, we reminisced about Magic Hat Summer Ale, smores, coke, and pizza. We had a single electrical outlet in the room, and since my laptop had enough battery, we plugged in the fan, situated the laptop between us, and proceeded to watch the Lion King. It was really nice to watch a familiar lighthearted story. After we finished, we took a short nap before the children came by. Jessica and Mawufemor were decked out in their church dresses, looking ever so cute. Kofi on the other hand was a mess like always, constantly resembling PigPen from the Peanuts. His clothes were filthy and he attracted a gang of flies around him everywhere he went.

My first interview went pretty well. We were interrupted a couple times, but nothing too severe. Divine's familiar ways of communicating were still present, while stuttering, Divine would chat about topics that go in circles but don't ever seem to get anywhere. Afterward, the grandmother of the compound, whose name I forget, stopped by to borrow another book. I'm glad people are excited about reading. Everyone seems intrigued by the books we brought. Samantha and I decided to visit Mama for a little while, and then Mama took us to meet the village midwife. She seems like a sweet woman. She is trained as a midwife though she is illiterate and doesn't speak or understand any English. She did agree to be interviewed though, which made me beam with excitement—who better to talk to about reproductive health in the rural areas than the village midwife?

We followed Mama back to her house and on the way, she explained that she delivered Michael and Mawufemor with a midwife, but her most recent child, 2-year-old Cicho she delivered by herself. When we arrived back at Mama's compound, Samantha and I ate our cocoa plant we picked up at National Geographic Central the other day. It was quite tasty. As we sat, I observed everything in the compound for its purpose rather than signs of impoverished living. There were basins set aside for washing, another for rinsing, tools for cooking, barrels and bins for storage. The goats among us were making antagonistic advances on each other, warning other goats by somehow using their lips to make a distinctly accurate farting sound. Mama gave us two small baggies of groundnuts (like very tiny peanuts) to take back to our compound. Once we were there, we each enjoyed a bag-full very happily. Dinner was two small biscuits to share that Mrs. Agnes Asafu (the landlord's wife) had made. Delicious as they were, they were not plenty, and my stomach growled for more food. No wonder I lose weight here!

After "dinner," Mama came to participate in an interview. Sema didn't show up, probably because her aunt is 85 years old and not doing very well. The interview with Mama went swimmingly, and she promised to accompany me to interpret for my interview with the midwife later this week.

May 24, 2010
Market Day with Sema

We woke up early, had cocoa soup for breakfast after our invigorating bucket showers, and headed to the roadside to wait for a ride to Ho. The bus and market were relatively less crowded than before, putting me slightly at ease. With less people to weave around and deal with, it was easier to follow Sema through the market too. She knew exactly where to go within the maze, and was happy to indulge our wishes for jewelry and fabric. The market stands had an array of batik dyed fabric hanging from the walls and folded in front of you. Bright orange with white, purple with orange and green, sweeps of blues with teal and brown, green with white hearts, and magenta with lavender swirls. Things were a little quieter than usual, and there was less garbage on the path and in the street. At the internet café, I had two relevant emails: one from my mom saying she loves reading my updates, and one from my dad asking about bills in the mail that had been forwarded from my apartment. I guess the post office is back on track somewhat.

Samantha and I treated Sema to lunch at White House, where we shared jollof rice, French fries, and a small vegetable pizza. I had my weekly caffeine intake with a bottle of coke, and savored every drop. The tro-tro ride back was also much better than the ride last time. Samuel, the tro-tro helper, smiled at us and was friendlier than before. He had also run into us earlier that day in the market and said hello. We sat in the back, where curious eyes couldn't linger too much on our skin, and the gaping window at my side forced the fresh air into my lungs much faster. The window is one that I remember from last time as well. If I slouch, the top of the window comes to my temple, and the base of the window hits one inch above the seat. It feels like you might fall out, but I knew from my previous experience that I wouldn't. I did however hit my leg pretty hard as I exited the tro-tro, which left a giant deep purple bruise.

I was pleased with the shopping from the day. I got a couple really cool necklaces, and a few bracelets for friends. I'd spent way too much on fabric, considering I still had a pile of fabric from last time sitting in my apartment, waiting for me to have the time and expertise to weave them into a Ghanaian quilt. But the most expensive piece (4 yards of it) has three large designs in the middle, and would look nice hanging over my bed. The other three pieces were 2 yards each and I'm hoping Believe back in the village can make a couple of skirts and a dress for me.

Over our heads…

After getting our things back to the room, we had just enough time to savor the fan for a little while, and change into non-sweaty shirts before going to the schoolyard to begin the first study session for primary students, grades 1-3. As we rounded the corner of the library to the primary school compound, my anxiety caught my breath. What looked to be a mass of 70-80 children waited for us, full of excited energy. I like kids, don't get me wrong, but here we were, in a compound, just the two of us with no other adult who could help translate or keep order. I even have trouble controlling the dozen children that frequent our compound every day seeking attention… we were in way over our heads.

We called their attention and gathered them together around us. Sam brought stickers to pass out which originally seemed like a fun idea, though quickly we were literally buried under anxious hands and faces. Stickers to these children had the same effect as if we'd held a weak baby antelope over a pride of hungry lions. We stopped short of handing stickers to everyone as chaos took over and began to eat us alive. I got them to be relatively quiet and attentive enough to have them sit in front of us under a tree while Sam read a story. Within the first two pages, the children inched and pushed closer and closer until I barely had room to breathe. Children were pressed up against us in the front and from behind we could feel children breathing on our necks they were so close. I was getting claustrophobic very quickly. Hop on Pop did the trick—Sam would say a line or two and most of the crowd of children would repeat it, looking at the words and pictures on the page.

The sanity didn't last long; children were pushing each other to get a better look, fighting and yelling at each other. An adult thankfully walked by and told the kids to back off so we could breathe; he then suggested we move them into a classroom, which is great in theory but in practice we were doomed. First of all, rather than only dealing with Primary classes 1, 2, and 3, all of Primary 1-6 had shown up… a miscommunication to say the least. Second, when we got into the classroom, I sent the older kids home but a few stayed behind to keep order by arming themselves with giant sticks, smacking the desks and threatening the younger ones. I thought for sure a war would break out. The classroom was loud and echoed and it became impossible to do anything. We tried, but reluctantly (and with a simultaneous sigh of relief) sent them home.

The children didn't go home. That would have been too easy. Some had, but easily sixty children or so began to follow us back through the village. Looking behind me in slight panic, I planned our escape. We couldn't walk home because then all sixty of them would know where we lived and any chance of future privacy would be lost forever. As we neared Mama's house, we decided to bid the children goodbye, for the eighth time, and take refuge in Mama's compound. It didn't work. They ALL followed us into her compound. In shock, Mama looked between us and the swarm of children that poured into her home, fully comprehending the look of apologetic panic written across my face. It took a few minutes but she sent most of them out of the compound. Samantha and I waited patiently for a while… knowing well enough that at least twenty or thirty still lingered behind the compound walls, ready to attack the minute we let our guard down.

After about fifteen minutes I snuck to the side wall to check, and sure enough, they were waiting to pounce. I was running through the options in my head: a) we could make a run for it, but they would probably chase us thinking it's a game; b) we could try to reason with them, but we already had and they were clearly too persistent; or c) we could climb out a window in Mama's back room, sneak around behind the schoolyards, take a different path behind the chief's house, go through the alleyway next to his house, cross the road by the bus stop, and run down the side alley back to our house. Yep, option C seemed the most appropriate.

Luckily, we didn't have to stoop to such measures. Just then, Mrs. Agnes Asafu (our landlord's wife who strangely doesn't live with him, rather she lives across the road next to Mama) greeted us and asked about being interviewed. She wanted to show us her house so we followed her out of the compound, and suddenly were free! Afterward, Sam and I took the chance to head home, and I took refuge in my book on the front stoop. Soon, Kosi showed up wanting to read more of our books so while I sat on the steps outside, Kosi sat quietly behind me and read, shielded by the curtain.

Shortly thereafter, the strange man who grilled us about Ewe yesterday showed up and began asking me questions again, this time talking faster and using expressions I didn't remember. Luckily, Kosi whispered the answers from behind the curtain, completely hidden from the man—I really love that kid. Kosi left, and Hans and Emil joined us for some evening conversation that was mainly more questions from Emil. He asked about Ho, about food in the U.S., crocodiles, and zombies. Over our dinner of plain rice, Sam and I talked about pets, then talked briefly with Mama, and got ready for bed.

Getting ready for bed tonight was a bit more involved than usual; I wiped myself down with a washcloth, then used my fancy bathing wipes I had picked up at REI, changed, and then lay down in front of the fan. My stomach was uneasy, and cramping which is never a good sign, especially when the outhouse is dark, crawling with lizards, and has a padlock on the door that I forget the key for half the time… I just hoped that I could sleep through the night.

May 25, 2010
Empty

We had the cocoa puff soup again for breakfast, which was tasty. I also found out that it's not actually cocoa, but rather it's a hot soup made from ground corn, soy beans, groundnut, and spices. But it still tastes like hot cocoa soup with a smidge of peanut butter and a smidge of cayenne pepper. Mr. Koju Asafu caught us outside and explained that today was a holiday and there will be no school, thereby cancelling our plans to have a study session with the older primary school kids this afternoon. I was pleased for the unexpected break.

The plan was for Mama to come over sometime around 9 AM to accompany us to the midwife's home to conduct an interview, so from 7:30 AM when we finished breakfast, until Mama arrived around 10:15 AM, I read my book on the front step quite happily. It was around 10:40 AM by the time we were settled in the midwife's compound. The interview went well enough, I had more specific questions for her regarding pregnancy and delivery in the village so it lasted an hour and a half or so. Two men sat nearby and constantly interrupted to give their two cents on every other question, which was distracting and not helpful. I was getting super annoyed but thought it best just to endure and learn from my mistake of having the interview so *out in the open*. Though to be honest, everything is *out in the open* here.

Afterward it was noon and Mama had to tend to her children, and Agnes Asafu was ready for her interview. We conducted Agnes' interview in Mama's house in one of the rooms away from the children and other distractions. It was quick, only forty minutes and went very well. At 2:45 PM Mama brought us rice and palava sauce, which is a green sauce made with spinach, onion, egg, and some palm oil. From 3-6 PM I continued to read my book, without really wanting to conduct any more interviews for the day, and pleased we got out of the originally scheduled study session with the Primary 4-6 classes.

I don't really know how to explain how I'm feeling today. I guess discouraged, or an *indifferent existence* would be an appropriate term. I expected some contact from home when I checked my email in Ho yesterday, but not seeing what I expected made me feel insignificant. Things at home are going on as usual, probably without anyone caring all that much that I'm not there. Things stay the same, no matter if I exist or not. Similarly, things stay the same here in the village, whether I try or not. I really wanted to prove all those skeptics wrong. I wanted to show that small projects do work well, and all you need is a little faith, and a push in the right direction.

I am feeling deflated, defeated, and helpless. Maybe those people are right. What am I doing here anyway? The library is built, but it's not being used, and no one seems to care enough to even say, "this isn't right, we should be using the library, let's think of a way to fix this." There's just nothing. You can afford to send two children to Senior School, but because you can't send everyone, you decide to send no one. Sensibility is absent, along with hope. Today at least, I feel numb. I'm not even upset that I hadn't gotten many responses from home… I did get a quick note from my mom and my dad, a couple comments from my brother, and my friend Mike. I guess I just expected something more from a few other people. But when there was nothing, I wasn't upset, just numb. Even when I think about going home in a few weeks, I don't even want to go out and see people. Why does it matter if clearly keeping in touch with me isn't that important to them, and clearly isn't on their mind?

I'm here, with Samantha, and really our company is Mama and Kosi. Kosi visits every night to read quietly with us. Mama is like our best friend—the only one who cares to spend time with us, just to hang out and joke with each other. I know more about her than anyone else, and truly feel a companionship with her. I don't know what's going on at home, but life goes on without me just fine I've realized. And here… well, things here continue as they are, without real improvement, which is tearing at my heart, especially when the community does nothing to help themselves. What am I doing? Why are things happening this way?

We ate leftover rice and palava sauce for dinner, though it had still been sitting out all afternoon and was now cool in temperature. It wasn't bad, and I ate a small bit, but I'm still a little hungry. My stomach technically is not uneasy tonight, however there is a strong stench of trash and sewage somehow seeping through our window, next to my bed. I hadn't smelled it before, so I'm wondering why it has surfaced now, but I really hope I can ignore it when I sleep, otherwise I may vomit. I'm exhausted.

May 26, 2010
Rainy Day

We had porridge for breakfast, and started with a cold bucket shower when Mama interrupted with an extra bucket of boiled hot water. We added it to our cold water in our buckets. It was almost too hot, but it did feel good. As soon as we dressed and ate, I realized it was only 7 AM, and we really had nothing on the agenda except for a few interviews and conducting another study session with the Primary 4-6 kids this afternoon. We both laid back in our beds and rested while the fan blew. I dozed for 10 or 15 minutes, and then stared out the window. The curtain blew in and out, and the sky behind it turned from the light grey of an overcast morning to a dark grey of a coming storm.

I looked out the front room and saw Kofi situating a large metal basin on some steps to catch the rain water. The wind whipped around in several directions, and the sky became very dark. By 7:30 AM, the rain poured from the sky, pounding down on the tin roof. I tried to close the window slats as much as possible, but some rain was still pouring down the sides onto my bed, so I stuffed some hand towels into the slats to catch the water. The rain came down heavily for thirty minutes, and then subsided to a steady pace for another hour or two. By 10 AM, the rain had mostly stopped, and left behind a new cool air, free of humidity. The sun stayed behind the clouds, leaving the grey haze to engulf the day into a lazy respite from everyday work.

For most of the morning I sat just inside the front door, with the breeze flowing in with the curtain, and read my book. The kids (Kofi, Michael, and my favorite—Mawufemor) arrived to color. Mama and other children sometimes call Mawufemor by her nickname, *Akiti*, which in Ewe means "little," because she is so petite for her age (4). Around 11 AM, Emil came by to be interviewed. It went very well, to my slight surprise, and he volunteered more information than I'd asked for, and spoke about 50% more than the other interviewees. I also mentioned to him topics I wanted to discuss at tonight's Anyo Meeting, mainly the library issue and the lack of interest or care on the part of the teachers. I also wanted to ask at the meeting about the money Anyo received from BRIDGE for our volunteering with them, but decided I would wait to just bring it up tonight.

Bismark told me Anyo received 200 cedis, and that it was their decision alone what do with it. I wondered what constraints there might be. I wondered if it had to be involved with community decision making, or just Anyo. I wondered if they were restricted in any way from using the money on themselves. If so, I had a plan.

After the interview, I was getting really hungry. I did have a small granola bar to tide me over midmorning, but it was wearing off and my stomach was growling constantly. Mama brought us lunch, a plate with another covering the top—usually this signified a small omelet between the two plates, but something seemed different. As I looked at the plates, the one on top that covered the food seemed… higher than usual. She also brought a small container of freshly cut pineapple—the same pineapple we picked up in Ho on Monday. I lifted the covering plate to reveal our lunch. Samantha and I gasped and stood for a moment in shock with our mouths gaping open. We exchanged glances, a few times, and then sat down quietly and both seemed to whisper, "oooooh." Mama had brought us French fries! Pineapple and French fries, we must have been really good to deserve this. Or Mama just likes us a lot. We ate everything. The fries were really good, we didn't have ketchup but salt was enough. The pineapple tasted ever so fresh, sweet and juicy with almost a coconut essence. Samantha and I decided that this was for two reasons. First, Mama had been worried we hadn't been eating enough because our stomachs (and secretly some of our taste-buds) couldn't handle it. Second, Sema was with us in Ho on Monday and witnessed us devour a plate of French fries with a side of jollof rice and a vegetable pizza. She must have told Mama what we ate and how much we looked forward to it every time we went to Ho. I felt guilty that Mama thought we didn't like her food. We do! It's just hard on our stomachs, and it's hard to eat the same thing every day, and when almost everything is made with palm oil that seemed to lubricate the digestive tract more than necessary, it's hard to indulge the gesture. My guilt slowly faded with the intake of French fries and pineapple.

The rest of the day was pretty quiet. No more interviews, and the kids didn't bother us too much. Samantha and I had originally wanted more human contact here, but with the vast numbers of ankle biters constantly in our room and in our faces, we were starting to think differently about our previous wish. By 3 PM I had read almost the entire second half of my book.

At 4 PM we walked to the schoolyard, and my anxiety was already giving me heart palpitations. I don't know why children make me nervous, but they do, especially in large numbers, especially when there are no other authority figures around, especially when English is lost in most of their ears. I was picturing the madhouse from Monday, being suffocated by seventy-five excited children. I was silently panicking, again, as we walked toward the schoolyard. We were fifteen minutes early to survey our impending doom, and surprisingly I didn't see the same mass of children. We walked to the library and waited a few minutes. Soon, I saw two young girls come down the path toward us. Several others joined, and when we settled on the steps of the Primary School, perhaps only a dozen children surrounded us with eager eyes. This was *much* more manageable.

Samantha read a couple stories and asked the children who the characters were. This was a challenge. Earlier this morning Sam had told me her plan, and I mentioned that I thought it might be too advanced. She scoffed and exclaimed that of course it's at their level, and that she wasn't asking them about Shakespeare. Mainly as a direct result of my anxiety I have with children in large numbers, I shrugged and let it pass. After the study session, Samantha walked warily beside me, almost defeated, and with an expression of exhaustion and pity and helplessness, she said she was really disappointed at the level the children seem to be at in school. Throughout primary school, they do not read stories, they do not read poems, they do not write. Teachers speak at the children in English; the children don't comprehend, but simply answer "yes," to any question posed: Is this right or wrong? *Yes.*

Samantha and I have talked at length about the children here. In sum, there is a very small chance a child will grow to their potential, truly using their mind as it is intended. Village life translates into parents always being too busy to talk to their children, to teach them, encourage them, guide them, play with them. Most mothers I see are expressionless or they are reprimanding the children. Mama is the only mother I have seen that actually smiles at her children. This is evident when all of the children are so eager to show us what they've colored in hopes for some small glint of recognition, satisfaction, praise, attention, and encouragement. They don't receive any of those things other than in our front room. People don't have much— no dictionaries, no books, no toys, no games, no puzzles. Children are left to their own devices for entertainment and affection from the age they can walk. It is next to impossible to foster cognitive development—no chances to encourage ideas, creativity, imagination, problem solving. Adults that grow from children in this type of environment almost seem lackluster about expending any effort on brainstorming ideas, or coming up with creative ways to solve problems. If the solution isn't an obvious one right in front of them, then the problem doesn't get solved and people accept their fate as it is. I can't express how utterly disappointing and discouraging this is. So many children showed up on Monday because they *want* to learn. They *want* to read. They *want* to grow. Show me that same passion in American children, I dare you.

The Anyo Meeting was a relative success, depending on what actually comes from it. I tend to overlook the details that have been frustrating Samantha, mostly because I've accepted that things don't necessarily follow logic or progress here. The meeting ran on African time—starting forty minutes late. It was a slow acceleration into the topics for the meeting. Walter conducted the opening prayer for the meeting. Then Emil read back, very slowly, the minutes recorded from last week's meeting. I thought that was stupid, since it was only a week ago, and the topics for the meeting revolved around Samantha and I, and everyone in Anyo was well aware at this point what we were doing. I sat, stared at the ground, and fought the urge to roll my eyes before we could actually begin.

I explained I was planning on visiting the chief tomorrow to discuss the library. I then went on a slight rant about community responsibility and ownership and investment of a community library. I explained I understood voluntary labor, even in the slightest manner of simply chaperoning the library for a couple hours, is hard to come by when everyone is so poor, and lacks time to devote to something other than work, chores, or their family. I suggested the library be open from 4-6 PM or 5-7 PM on Fridays, Saturdays, and Sundays—three blocks of 2 hours per week. Only 6 volunteers would be needed to each spend 2 hours in the library, twice a month. I thought that was reasonable, but I planned on leaving the specific details up to the chief.

Members of Anyo asked if we should instead turn to the teachers to handle the library, which sent me into a second rant about the teachers. The teachers honestly don't care. They haven't even set foot in the library to see what is readily available to them. The headmaster is just the same. I boldly stated that if they don't care, then they should find another profession, because while they are a teacher they need to conduct themselves properly to foster education and child development (which there are books about, in the library!). Anyo agreed with me, and supported my decision to involve the chief. Walter, the chairman of Anyo, will accompany me and Samantha tomorrow to the chief's compound.

The last order of business was the money from BRIDGE. Apparently, this is the first time Anyo has received money from BRIDGE, which makes me wonder about the last time I was here, when they were also supposed to receive money. I agreed to speak with Bismark about that on Friday when we go to Ho again. Anyo said it will be used for seed money for a farming project (maize). I suggested that 150 cedis be used for seed money, and the other 50 cedis could be used to start a pilot program for emergency medical treatment, using Richard as the first guinea pig for the program. The money is Anyo's money—not the village's, not the chief's, and only Anyo can decide what to do with the money. Emil challenged that 4 people in the village have similar problems to Richard, and what would they think if we used the money for Richard instead of them? This reminded me immediately of the scholarship problem. I explained my position very clearly, that it is better to help one or two people, rather than help none because of petty bickering and jealousy. I used more words and time to make that explanation clear. I said the seed money could yield profits that would contribute to the emergency fund, and the fund would be used on a case-by-case basis, based on urgency and need. It wouldn't pay 100% for anything, but could contribute to the costs of medical treatment. I said that because this would be a pilot program, Richard's candidacy was appropriate since he was a member of Anyo *and* his condition is the only one in the village with as much pain and severity at the moment. Richard agreed to go to the eye center on Wednesday to get a second opinion and a new quote for treatment, and we would go from there.

After the meeting, Hans walked us home, stopping at the mill for us to see how it worked. Inside a shed were two large machines, with belts moving at an incredible speed. It was extremely loud and smelled funny, sweet in a way. Only one mill was running—the one for cassava. The other mill was for corn. Large basins were spread across the floor, four of which were filled with peeled and cut logs of cassava. The other 3 were filled with the white fluff of ground cassava that had already been through the mill. A small girl crouched in front of me with her face next to the machine, and her arm up inside it, constantly pulling out the white fluff. I wondered if this was dangerous.

For dinner, Mama had prepared jollof rice. Apparently, our eating habits in Ho with Sema definitely made an impression. It was delicious, and there was even a small piece of chicken, that I ate happily and recounted the last time I had chicken was on the plane, and it was airplane chicken… Hans was supposed to return for his interview, but didn't, which came as no surprise to me. I settled in to do some writing, after which I planned to finish *New Moon*. Kosi is sitting next to me, reading *Twilight*. He had finished all of the other books we had brought, and looked half-heartedly through the same pile again. Yesterday, I showed him *New Moon* and asked if the print and words were too advanced for him, and he said they weren't. I grabbed *Twilight*, explained the premise and ever since he's been diligently lost in the world of fiction. He doesn't have electricity in his house, so he has to read here. He went home around 9 PM, after reading 20 pages. If he finishes the book before we leave, I'll find someone with a DVD player so he can watch the movie. I told him I would send him the other books if he liked this one. I think I'll let him keep *Twilight* for encouragement. Either way, I'm glad he's enjoying a book that's more at his level.

May 27, 2010
Appointment with the Chief

The night remained cool while we slept, and I even wrapped a shawl around me for warmth. I thought of the world back home where there are top sheets and blankets to cuddle with. This morning, Sema brought the brown groundnut/soy/corn/spices soup for breakfast. She gave us new sets of clean sheets as she took ours with our dirty laundry to wash today. I spent the morning finishing *New Moon*. I had dragged out finishing the book as long as possible, since I still had two weeks left before getting my hands on the third book. The morning stayed relatively cool with plenty of breezes, but by 11 AM the sun was out in full force. The only development of the morning was a persistent wasp who decided to make a home and nest under our table in the front room. This would be a problem. I watched other loudly buzzing insects swirl around the air as if they were drunk, bashing themselves into the walls of the compound with a thud I could clearly hear. Mutant bugs.

Samuel the tro-tro man stopped by briefly to say hello, and agreed to be interviewed. I need to make a schedule and stick to it. Hans never did show up last night and I think Sema is too busy to be interviewed, which leaves me left to track down eight more men and seven more women for interviews. I plan to interview Richard this afternoon after we visit the chief, but all in all I only have four women and four men that have agreed to be interviewed so far. I may need Mama's help recruiting volunteers for this one. Focus groups almost seem impossible, and my lack of motivation is kicking in. I really don't feel like conducting focus groups anymore.

We ate a plate of cassava fries for lunch, and then I took a nap since there was nothing else to do. We visited the chief, very briefly and I stated my case about the library needing volunteers to keep it open and accessible to the community. He liked the idea and said he would bring it to the board, and we should be able to start organizing volunteers on Monday… I think. It's really up to them, I just hope we can see the start of it before we leave. I took another nap until almost 4 PM, when we walked to the library to wait for any JSS kids who wanted a tutoring session. There were about ten kids that showed up, late though because of some intermittent rain. They seemed very interested when Samantha read them a story about a mouse living in a teacup who was friends with a frog. That type of book is really designed for preschoolers or kindergarteners in the States. But these kids were in their early teens, and clinging to every word.

We asked them what were the parts of a story—giving them a hint of beginning, middle, and… waiting for them to answer. This was a challenge. They didn't understand. Their English was…ok… It was ok enough for them to understand the question. They clearly just had no idea that stories had a beginning, middle, and end. They also didn't know what a character was, so we tried to simplify that as much as possible, but it was all too clear the kids hadn't been taught about this. We asked them to write a quick story with a beginning, middle, and end, and to tell us who the characters were, once we explained what one was. They nodded yes, and rather than doing what was asked, they began picking story books off the shelves and read aloud to themselves. A few of them returned to us to summarize what they read. Well, it could have been worse. But again, today was more sad than it was discouraging regarding how much the children didn't know, but could clearly comprehend once it was explained.

After the schoolyard, we interviewed Richard, who was waiting patiently, with two empty chairs for me and Samantha. The interview was quick and went very well—Richard volunteered more information than the other interviewees, including a particular piece about a travelling preacher who visited 18 months ago. The preacher "quoted the Bible" and interpreted it for the community that any method of contraceptive (condoms, birth control, family planning, and even "pulling out") is killing an unborn child, and that would make you a murderer, sending you to hell for eternal damnation for killing a child. He also discouraged masturbation, which is no surprise… that's probably reckless endangerment of an unborn child, definitely frowned upon by the Big Guy Upstairs.

I asked Richard about the sex ed presentations I'd put on before, that he witnessed. I asked if that made a difference, and he replied, "Yes, but the preacher said these things are from the Bible, and so just in case, I decided to believe him." And that, is why Richard now has a baby.

We walked back to our compound, and Samantha crouched down with her arms wide trying to catch a baby goat. I reminded her that she would probably get fleas, again, and that I didn't have a camera to document her little furry friend. She decided to wait until the next day to cuddle with farm animals. Kosi came by around 6:30 PM to read more of *Twilight*. With nothing to do, and not really wanting to read the other books I brought along, I sat and listened to the sounds of the compound. Unfortunately, little Kofi was being punished, beaten with something, and his screaming and the sound of the beating was disturbing and unbearable. Soon it ceased, and Mama brought dinner—rice with canned peas mixed in, and the red sauce. In the middle of dinner, just before 7 PM, the electricity went out. I attached my book light to the top of Twilight so Kosi could still read, and positioned a flashlight so we could see what we were eating. The flashlight burned out after a few minutes. We went to bed early thinking of Market Day tomorrow, because we're almost out of toilet paper and desperately low on water, again.

May 28, 2010
Immersion & Ambitions

This morning we went to Ho, aboard the bus filled with people bound for Market Day. We skipped the market and went straight to the BRIDGE office, but it wasn't open so we settled in for some quality time at the internet café. While we waited for our lunch at White House, I looked up and saw a man pulling an odd-looking dog on a leash. The dog had a funny side-hop instead of a normal gait. Then I realized, it wasn't a dog—it was a monkey. The tro-tro ride home was uneventful, though we did have to stop at a lumber yard to place some sort of metal thing on the roof, and a couple boys rode sitting on top of it. The lumber yard had a few designer coffins sitting out front—a common sight in the market. As we sat there, a couple men carried a brand-new fantasy coffin (designed as a shark) across the road.

Once we were home, the afternoon dragged on with nothing to do. Mama brought us some fresh mango, which we ate way too fast; we should have dragged that out more if we knew what was good for us. After our snack, I lost the fight to keep my heavy eyelids open, crashing before I even knew I was tired. In the early evening, Mama came over to teach us how to "back" a baby (using a single cloth to wrap a baby to your back) using precious and trusting Mawufemor as our prop. Little Cicho came alive; he was excited and animated, which was a new thing for his usually cautious demeanor. It may take a village to raise a child, but it also takes a village to teach a *yavoo* how to *back a baby*. I leaned over to face the ground, with my back parallel, and gently swung Mawufemor under my arm and onto my back. Mama, with Cicho perched on her back, stood behind me situating the cloth, and Sema was in front of me showing me how to fasten the fabric into a tight twist that wouldn't loosen, allowing the baby to fall. After the first try, I was all set! It was so easy! Not so much a strain on the back and you can go anywhere you want and the baby just goes along with it. If they're tired, they sleep, and they get used to you moving around to do your own thing and they're quiet—perfectly content. Not to mention there are *far* less straps and fasteners than are involved with the *BabyBjörn*.

After Mawufemor was safely snuggled onto my back, I was ready for another challenge. I placed a basket on my head and tried to walk, baby on back and thing balanced on my head… I made it about ten feet before the basket began to shift and fall, but I'm still proud. Mawufemor was such a good sport, maybe because she was tired, but I think it's because she's one of the sweetest kids I've ever met. I should note that I find most children somewhat obnoxious unless they're absolute gems. Jessica, Michael, and Mawufemor are definitely in the gem category. Kofi on the other hand, means well but is constantly dirty and way too persistent in his attempts for constant attention, which *is* annoying. But I still feel for him, he gets no attention otherwise.

We had some rice and red sauce for dinner, and we asked Sema to fetch Emil so we could use his phone to call Joy. Emil returned, phone in hand. When he dialed Joy's number, a loud voice came on speaker saying his credits needed to be replenished before he could make a call.

His response was a little funny when he explained, "I just called Joy to tell him I was coming to see you so he should call back. So, it is unfortunate that the percentage is low."

He went home to retrieve another phone, and we did get to speak with Joy long enough to realize travelling to his friend's vacation spot was probably not very feasible. We hung up and Emil hung around for a little bit, which yielded an interesting conversation about the education system. I made a few suggestions, which for better or worse, set several things in motion.

Monday we (Samantha and I) will meet with the JSS head about collaborating with area heads that are doing better, and talk to him about holding teachers accountable for their work. We also plan to show him and the teachers the useful resources at their fingertips in the library and show them how to use the books appropriately. Emil suggested that on Tuesday when Samantha and I go to Ho, we should meet with the manager of the regional education office to discuss more involvement of the Education Director and the Circuit Supervisors who are supposed to be supervising the rural schools. It would also be helpful to ask about implementing an English as a Second Language program as part of the curriculum, reaching out to area NGOs and the Ministry of Education, and possibly send current teachers for extra training on ESL courses. Wednesday will be the weekly Anyo meeting, where we'd like to discuss a petition from the community to the manager at the Education Office regarding these issues. I'm on board with the plan, but I do think it would be more effective if one or two members of Anyo or the community came as well to voice their own opinions. I also don't know how much good this will all do, but I guess an effort can't hurt.

Before he left, Emil said that in August they will be getting a Peace Corps volunteer to be stationed here for two years as a teacher for math and computers. I hope the volunteer can actually do some good… I wonder if they'll continue to teach computer class by a book like it currently is, or if they'll be able to acquire some functioning computers for the students to practice on. Part of me feels some sense of belonging, ownership, and responsibility for this village, but I know that my efforts don't amount to much since I'm not here for very long.

May 29, 2010
Slowest. Day. Ever.

There was a funeral this morning in Saviefe, two villages over from Gbogame. I've been told people dress in red and black, and after the burial and condolences, everyone celebrates with lots of drumming and dancing. We were supposed to go this morning, but Mama forgot about us so we were left behind. While the village was eerily quiet, we napped until 10 AM. Bright, age 19 and in JSS 2 (7th grade), came to visit around noon. He showed us his school book for computer class. Mind you, they don't actually touch a computer. The book is a how-to type of book regarding how to turn a computer off and on, with pictures of screenshots as examples. The book, which was a little smaller than a composition notebook, explained what a computer was, along with its origin and a list in the back of four types of Pentium IV computers, Dell and Gateway among them.

I asked Bright if he would like to be interviewed. Even though he was still in JSS, he was over 18, so I thought it would be ok. The interview went well enough, I did have to stop and rephrase my questions because he didn't understand the English I was using, but all in all it went well. After the interview we were talking and to my livid surprise, Bright explained that Anyo Group had *sold* the four previously donated new Toughbook laptops, and in exchange purchased the three desktop computers (circa 1990s) that were now in the library. I tried to contain myself. The computers in the library are questionable regarding their functionality. The electricity hasn't worked in the library since we've been here, and Hans seems always too busy to fix it. When we arrived, we were asked to test the computers to make sure they worked… I wonder when the last time someone did check, or if they bought the computers without checking. Not to mention, I wonder where the rest of the money went after selling four new laptops. So as to not have a full-on conniption, I ended the conversation and let Bright practice typing on my laptop for a little while.

Sam and I ate our pineapple that we got in Ho yesterday. We tried to eat the fruit slightly slower than we ate the mango, but only stretched it out to maybe one minute. It was really good, warm, fresh and juicy. Sema brought boiled cassava with palava sauce for lunch, which was really good but a little heavy on the palm oil. The palm oil is red when it seeps out from under your food into a pool on your plate. She also surprised us with two cocoa plants, which aren't ripe just yet but we were so glad she brought them. I ate a little bit of the cassava and palava, cautious of what the oil would do to my stomach later. After lunch we sat outside. The air was cooler than usual and the bugs weren't around. I tried to calm the negative feelings I had from the conversation with Bright. I saw Mr. Koju and he agreed to be interviewed at 4 PM, so we took another nap to kill some time.

Koju Asafu reminds me of my late grandfather in so many ways. They're about the same build, they have the same gait, and the same twinkle in their eye. They have the same trousers, grey and creased in the front with an iron, and when you ask one question, they'll talk all day giving you detailed play-by-plays of their life. And if they tell you a story, they pause at the end to raise their eyebrows and smile a little smile, and wait for you to be ready for the punchline. Koju's interview began at 3:30 PM and I think it was fifteen minutes before I could ask the first question because he was telling me the chronology of his accomplishments, each school and training, his first job, his second job offer, how he managed to leave the first job, all with their corresponding months and years. A wise and sweet old man, he will be turning 80 this September. While most interview transcripts have averaged 1,000 words, Koju's transcript rested at 2,500 words, with his interview lasting 90 minutes, twice as long as intended. But I did get some really helpful information from his experiences.

After the interview, Samantha and I decided to take advantage of the cool air and lack of humidity so we took a walk down the road to the big tree. It was really nice, and a few people stopped to say hello. There were several motorbikes and tro-tros that we had to jump out of their way, but I guess more people go out on Saturday evenings.

On our way back, we decided to stop at Mama's house for a visit. We were craving some time outside our compound. There we sat while Mama wrapped tiny bags of groundnuts she'd just finished roasting. The kids had just finished eating, and Michael was in the middle of bathing himself by the edge of the compound, just inside their rock wall. Mawufemor, as little as she is, was taking care of things quite well. She washed Cicho's hands, and after carrying a bucket and basin as big as she was, she carefully washed the dishes one by one.

Michael's job is to round up the goats to put them in their pen at night. He does this with a little food in one hand, waiting very patiently, and then grabs a goat's leg when they close. He leads them as if he's holding the goat's hand. The goats don't seem to mind their leg awkwardly sticking out like it's disconnected from the socket as they continue to calmly walk on the other three legs quite agilely. One goat had a rope tied on it, and it circled Michael twice very quickly, wrapping up Michael's legs and knocking him to the ground.

Cicho is more animated with us now; he recognizes us and plays a Cicho version of peek-a-boo, and hides himself behind a bamboo stick, so inconspicuous. Mama bathed Cicho, covered him in baby powder, put on his jammies and wrapped him up onto her back. Then it was Mawufemor's turn for a bath.

It was comforting to be around Mama's family during their evening routine. It reminded me of appreciating the important things. We took our leave, and found that Sema had left dinner (jollof rice) back at our room. We ate most of it in hopes she'll see the empty bowl and make it again soon.

May 29, 2010
Half Way

It's the half-way mark today; we've been here for 2 weeks, and 2 weeks from today we'll be sitting at the Kotoka Airport in Accra waiting to board our flight home. All in all, I am glad I came, but I definitely have mixed feelings about everything that's happened here. There are some major disappointments, and as much as I want to try, I personally don't have the capacity or manpower to support successful projects. I would like to hope that the few things we are trying to do here will pay off in some way, but I really have no idea whether it will. I would like to say that every little bit helps, but at the same time I see so much going to waste, and so little effort on the part of the community to fix the problems they so easily complain about. I know it takes more than just a few visits to really make a difference, but I do also feel that some people here are willing to just accept how things are, and continue to complain about money. I really hope the new administration in Ghana will step up to the challenge of caring for its rural populations. Many people have said that government policies are implemented only in the urban areas, and never trickle down to reach rural populations.

Samantha and I have a lot to do this week. I have twelve more interviews to complete by Wednesday. Monday, Tuesday, and Wednesday we have more study sessions with the kids from 4-5 PM each day. Monday we will be meeting with the JSS headmaster to discuss the issue of children not comprehending English, and to suggest he collaborates with area JSS heads with better academic records and that he holds his teachers accountable for their work. I also hope to meet again with the chief to see where we stand regarding volunteer chaperones of the library so it can hold evening hours a few days a week. I am also going to talk to the chief about the JSS headmaster and the teachers, we'll see how that goes… Tuesday we will be going to Ho, and I'm going to try to talk to the manager at the regional Education Office about getting the Circuit Supervisors to thoroughly involve themselves in assessing the schools.

We are planning a trip to Cape Coast so Samantha can see it, to leave Thursday, and come back on Sunday. The following week will be our last, and we plan to use one day to *possibly* visit a monkey sanctuary, and also use a couple days to conduct two focus groups. I'll be very surprised if we get more than two focus groups done. As of right now, I'm exhausted from doing nothing all day. I think I'll go to bed early, at 8 PM…

May 30, 2010
Sunday Funday

I slept well last night, despite the 5-inch lizard running up and down the wall next to my bed. We slept late, until 6:45 AM! When I woke up, our shower buckets were already waiting for us in the shower area. We had porridge for breakfast, and I added sugar cubes and the cinnamon I brought along as usual. The morning was somewhat slow, as most people in the village were at church, but in our compound Kofi's mom was busy washing clothes, and Koju Asafu was around as well so the compound wasn't *as* quiet. At 9 AM, Hans finally came for his interview. He is always extremely quiet so I wasn't sure of his English capabilities, but the night before he had assured me that his English was up to par. It wasn't. Because of the language barrier, he answered questions with short responses that didn't make sense. I was sure he didn't understand what I was asking, but my numerous efforts to clarify went without any meaningful result. His interview lasted only 11 minutes, and as soon as it was over he jumped out of the seat and ran off to hang out with Richard.

Soon after, Bright came by to practice typing, but was often sidetracked by curiosity about other games and programs on my laptop. I need to sit next to him to keep him focused, which selfishly is not the extra effort I want to spend on this trip. As much training as I give, it doesn't make a difference since they don't have working computers to practice on. He left after what seemed like a long while, and Samantha and I decided to take a much-needed walk. Our walk was probably about two miles up the road, just past the Big Tree. Fifty minutes later we arrived back at the compound, dripping with sweat, and we decided, *no more noon-time walks*. We discarded our saturated clothing, and lay down in front of the fan for a rest. Sema brought lunch, beans with gary. The beans are the same black-eyed peas in palm oil that is half of the red-red dish with plantains, only this time it was just the beans and a small bag of *gary*, which is ground dry cassava. It looks and has the texture of uncooked dry grits, which you sprinkle on top of the beans… I ate only a tiny bit because the beans had a lot of palm oil in it.

After lunch we packed the laptop and my paperwork and decided to seek out interviewees. Our first stop was Richard's place to assess whether Walter or Sema were home (both are Richard's immediate neighbors). I should note a fun fact: due to a suggestion of mine, Richard now wears a patch of gauze over his cancerous eye to avoid further infection and to pacify my disapproval of the dirty rag previously used to wipe his irritated eye. The *fun fact* part of this is: he has no tape, so he wrapped a white cloth around his head, with one eye hole cut out for his good eye. In a sense, he looks like a ninja turtle with a white eye mask.

Walter wasn't home, but Sema was in her compound washing clothes. We waited a little while until she finished before she could sit down and be interviewed. While we waited, we watched Selom and another boy play soccer with a deflated ball, dodging a large and protective new mother hen with her seven brand new chicks. The chickens and roosters in Sema's yard are significantly larger than any others in the village. The roosters reminded me of that old Looney Toons cartoon with the giant white rooster. They got a little too close for my comfort. Sema's porch is also completed; when I was here last she was in the middle of construction on half of her house. Her compound is shaded and breezy so it was nice to just sit and relax, away from our own. Sema lives here with her nephew, Selom, and a cousin. She surprised us with two small bottles of chilled coke and we began the interview. The interview was also relatively short and lacked some depth because of the language barrier, but it was enough to get by.

Once we finished Sema's interview, we walked to Believe's house to interview her, but were told she had gone to the neighboring village. We went to Peace's store but she was busy, so Mama asked Michael to lead us to another house. After about fifty feet, Michael forgot he was leading the way and started walking next to me, and then slowly started walking behind me. I slowed so he could take the lead, and then he slowed as well. We were crawling through the village and he would stop and pick up a flower or a leaf, and look up and smile. I had to remind him constantly by asking where we were going and asking him to show me. It took forever to reach the house only to find that no one was home. But Michael was a loyal little guide and then showed us to Cassandra's house, where

Cassandra and Jessica came running to greet us. We sat and visited a short while, and Cassandra agreed to come to our compound later in the evening for her interview. As we sat, Cassandra started to nurse Christopher and I forgot how very natural it is here for women to openly nurse. Christopher was paying more attention to us than her so for a little while her breast just hung there. Jessica ran over and grabbed it, shaking it in front of Christopher's face and when he still didn't take the nipple, Jessica pinched the loose skin on her mother's breast and lifted the breast back into her mother's shirt, all while Cassandra engaged in conversation with us. I knew Samantha must have been thinking, *"this is so National Geographic."* But as for me, I guess I just understand that's the way things are here. I should mention that a woman and two other men and one other small child were all sitting with us.

Jessica cheerfully followed us back to Mama's house, where squealing and running and playing commenced between Michael, Jessica, and Mawufemor, with Cicho looking on in wonderment trying to keep up. Samantha and I sat in two plastic chairs facing the chaos, though we were quickly deemed *home base.* The girls would fall into our laps when Michael chased them, giggling and squealing as loud as possible. It was a riot to watch. We sat in the middle of the compound, while Mama prepared fufu in the corner. Between us were three men butchering meat from a newly slaughtered goat on the small wooden table usually designated as the children's eating area. They cut the meat with a dull machete while two other women looked on. The children were running and screaming in circles around all of us. The table was bloody and had many remnants of meat that had already been cut. There must have been forty flies, at least, swarming the men and the meat on the table as the men placed small portions of the cut meat into plastic bags to sell. I couldn't stop staring at the flies on the meat. Mama invited us to eat some fufu with her, five feet away from the butchering table. We accepted and I tried not to look at the fly covered pieces of bloody goat directly to my right. The fufu was really good, and Samantha liked it, to my surprise. We only tried a little bit and decided we should probably go home in case anyone came by for an interview.

We walked back to our compound, hoping that Believe, Peace, and Cassandra would all appear this evening for their interviews. We ran into Samuel on the road and he agreed to be interviewed right then, so we sat on our front steps and got some pretty good information from him. He sat with a friend of his, a girl who appeared to be not in school anymore since her hair had started to grow; all school children through Senior Secondary School are required to keep their hair shaved for uniformity—boys and girls. Samuel is 26 and the girl seemed somewhere between 18 and 24. Their English was good, and they were interested in continuing our conversation until well after the interview was over. They asked if people from the village took time to hang out with us, but we sadly said no, not really. Only Mama really seems to *want* to talk and spend time with us. Even Emil sometimes seems to only do so out of obligation. I'm hoping that Samuel and his friend will visit us more often. It started to rain so we said goodbye and Samantha and I stepped inside just before the rain became heavy.

After a few minutes, Michael, Jessica, and Mawufemor showed up, soaking wet from the rain. I gave them a towel to dry off, sat them on the floor, took out my laptop and started a movie, *Finding Nemo*. It was a success, and before long, Samantha and I were just as engrossed in the film as the kids were. Michael was down in front. Jessica was on the right side of my lap, with

Mawufemor on my left, each cuddled up for most of the movie. It was really cute to watch their reactions. After the movie we ate dinner, which was rice with red sauce, and some type of patty resembling a thin crab cake but made with canned beef, peppers, egg, and spices. It was pretty good. Just after dinner, Cassandra appeared with Kosi, Jessica, and little Christopher on her back. Kosi acted as the interpreter, though I'm pretty sure he answered a few questions as himself rather than his mother's opinions. The interview went relatively quickly, and afterward we visited for a little while. Kosi is ¾ the way through Twilight, reading much faster than I'd expected. Michael, Jessica, Kofi, and Mawufemor were all laying quietly on the floor while the interview was conducted so when it was over I quizzed them on numbers using my UNO cards. They said goodnight, and before long Mama showed up to visit, with a sleeping Cicho on her back.

I really like our conversations with Mama. She is so candid with us, and I feel like she truly enjoys our company. We joke and laugh, and seem to understand each other more so than with anyone else here. We talked about how I've gotten more interviews with men completed than women because the women are always busy. The women work on the farm, watch the kids, prepare the meals, bathe the children and clean the compound, and wash the clothes… while the men work on the farm and then come home and relax for the rest of the day and evening. We talked about her husband, Francis, who currently is in Ho, staying with a friend and looking for work. She hasn't seen him in two months, but they talk every day. He was working with lumber and wood, but whoever had been in charge neglected to obtain the correct permit, which resulted in all of the workers being arrested, and the wood (that they invested in) was confiscated. The investment, the time, and the employment were all lost in one fatal swoop. There's no work still, which puts Mama and her family in a precarious position. There was a very small bonding moment when we talked about having long-distance relationships. Mama listens so well; she remembers things I told her a week ago—names and circumstances of my life back home—things that no one else here seems to care to ask about let alone remember. She brought up Sean by name, which surprised me, but she spoke so easily I forgot that we'd only been friends for two weeks now. It was comforting in a way.

It was late, around 9:30 PM, so she bid goodnight and Samantha and I got ready for bed. Though some were short on length and information, I was pleased we completed four interviews today. I only need three more men and five more women to interview and then I'll be all done with interviews. Of course, then I'll have to start conducting a few focus groups if I can. I so do not want to be a researcher when I grow up. Data collection can be frustrating and full of delays which seem to just drag on. It can feel like a real struggle.

May 31, 2010
Productivity Galore

I did not sleep very well at all last night, tossing and turning from the heat, nausea, cramps, and the thought of having to pee in the dark creepy crawly outhouse did not help either. When faced with a tough situation, I can usually adapt. However, when your stomach is not feeling well and you have to visit the outhouse in the middle of the night, the flashlight is sometimes *not* your friend. As you squat, being sure not to touch the seat, your only light is the flashlight, that you ever so carefully aim at a 6-inch lizard, or cockroach, or giant spider the size of your palm, so you can keep an eye on their whereabouts while you do your business. Inevitably the creepy crawlies will move, and you follow them with your flashlight, obviously pulling all systems to a halt as you have a standoff with the creatures of the night. In the midst of adjusting your weight as your muscles start to ache from staying in the squatting position so long, the creepy crawlies will make their move and disappear momentarily and now you have no idea where they are or if they're about to attack. When you adjust the flashlight, yet another type of creepy crawly has come into view with startling proximity. *Eesh.*

Back to the morning though, I cannot sleep if I think someone will be coming to our door anytime soon; I get anxious. Utterly exhausted, I trudged out of bed and waited for Sema or Mama to bring breakfast or shower buckets. Sema arrived with groundnut soup and fresh pineapple, which I was so pleased about. I was hoping for that as breakfast today, instead of porridge. I meant to go back to sleep after our showers, but Samantha's TIME Magazine caught my eye and I had a sudden urge to jump back into the real world with 2-week-old news. Before I knew it, it was 10 AM and time to go hunt down interviewees again. I rolled my eyes at myself, frustrated that I didn't plan news reading *around* my necessary nap.

We walked over to the roadside stand that acts as a general store to interview Peace (#1). It went fairly well, though quickly since her English wasn't the best. Two of her children translated some for her, but not nearly enough to get in-depth information. Right next door, Peace (#2) the hairdresser sat with no customers, so we decided to spring her for an interview too. Her English was much better but still the interview didn't take long. Samuel (from the tro-tro) had wandered over to Peace #1's store and witnessed part of the interview, and while we interviewed Peace #2, he appeared again to tell us he had arranged for us to conduct a focus group of primary school teachers at the compound! I wasn't expecting his assistance like that, but was very grateful.

The primary school teachers, though educated and spoke English well, were not incredibly forthcoming with details, so again the group went quickly. Afterward, we wanted to visit the JSS headmaster but he wasn't there. Neither was the English teacher so we unsuccessfully tried to talk about the library with the teachers, but they clearly couldn't care less about what we had to say. So, we settled for a relatively uninteresting focus group of the JSS teachers. They seem to think that opening the library for evening hours will make teenage pregnancy worse, because "when the library closes, the kids might not go home." … OK…

We came back home to relax and it only lasted about ten minutes before Sema brought lunch, boiled cassava with pasta mixed with palava sauce. It was really good, and just enough to put me over the edge of exhaustion. I curled up to take a nap, and was surprised by Michael and Mawufemor at the food of my bed, squeals and giggles announcing their presence and expectation of playtime. Samantha was totally out, laying on her bed in complete comfort and satisfaction. With a sigh, I got up to supervise the kids. The kids were dirty, wearing the clothes they wore two nights ago, and flies followed them. Jessica showed up to join us shortly as well, which commenced an hour and a half long coloring session, during which a man named Vincent came by to be interviewed. Emil had set it up, and Vincent is apparently one of the kids' teachers. He asked me why they hadn't been in school, which confused me since I thought their teacher was recovering from a stroke.

After the interview Mama appeared, quite angry with the kids and yelled at them in Ewe to go home and bathe. Apparently, they had told her they were going to the toilet, and instead ran here. If they had told her the truth, she would have made them bathe before visiting. As they left, we realized it was time to head back to the school compound to conduct the reading session for primary 1-3 kids. I was dragging my feet, and really was not in the right mood or mindset to last an hour with a bunch of kids I didn't know very well. Jessica, Michael, and Mawufemor are my favorites, and dirty or not, I love them all the time. Luckily, the children must have forgotten, so we got out of our obligation for the afternoon. We walked back home and closed the door—which is a barrier to all other than Mama and Sema—and settled in for a nap. Not two minutes later we had a knock at the door. It was Believe; she came to show us the skirts she was working on for us. They looked really beautiful, and I was excited to try them on when they were done. She also agreed to be interviewed the next evening. After she left, we shut the door again and I napped for a full hour—it was wonderful.

When I woke up around 5:30 PM, I was hungry, and I noticed the sky was getting dark with another storm coming through. An ancient woman who reminds me of Rafiki from the Lion King (they have the same gait, the same crazy toothy smile, and the same tall walking stick) came by to borrow another children's book. She reads about one book a week, and had just finished reading *Balto*, and was ready for another book. Michael and Kofi arrived to wait out the rain with us—we felt so popular today! As they colored, I sat in the doorway soaking in the breeze that accompanied the night's rain.

Sema and Mama brought sandwiches for dinner! Samantha and I were just talking about sandwiches yesterday. They were small, like sliders, made with thinly sliced sweet bread, and a single meat patty in the middle, similar to the ones we had last night. After dinner we ate our cocoa plant, and planned to relax the rest of the night. I hoped that after an incredibly productive day of three interviews and two focus groups, that we might have the night off to watch a movie by ourselves on my laptop, and go to bed early.

Tomorrow we will go to Ho, and hopefully talk to Bismark about the money that Anyo should have gotten for each volunteer it hosted. We'll go to White House for lunch, and visit the internet café. Emil had wanted us to visit the Education Office as well, but I think it would be best that if it is the solution that everyone at the Anyo meeting agrees on, a representative from Anyo should go to the Education Office themselves, possibly armed with a petition. They know the situation better than we do, and they are less likely to be shrugged off. We'll see.

June 1, 2010
Something Exciting! Just kidding… Same old thing

This morning we had our cocoa puff soup for breakfast again—*yum*! While we were splashing ourselves clean with our buckets of water, Mama exclaimed she had to go to Ho as well, and sure enough, as we rode off on the bus, we saw Mama standing next to a waiting tro-tro at the other end of the village. Once we got off the bus in Ho, we ran into Mama again. She was all dressed up and I wondered if she was going to see her husband today.

We had a fairly leisurely morning in Ho. We walked the mile or two to the intersection where the BRIDGE office is, exchanged money in the air-conditioned bank for our Cape Coast excursion this weekend, and spent some quality time at the internet café. Of course, I always forget one or two things to do on the internet, which is annoying enough but especially today since we won't have internet again for eight days. I did some digging, and after some extraordinary detective work, I came across the phone number for Oasis Beach Resort—the budget hotel in Cape Coast that I was praying we could get a room in. Mama said we could use her phone tonight to call and make a reservation.

After internet, we went to White House as usual for lunch, but it took longer than usual, which meant we were late catching the 1:30 PM tro-tro, which meant we wouldn't get back to the village until probably 3:45 PM. On our walk back to the tro-tro stop we took some candid pictures of Ho. One of these pictures was a severe oxymoron in my opinion. I posed, smiling, in front of the *stream*. The *stream* though is the exact stream you may remember that I described stepping on stones to get to the other side via Emil's infamous short-cut. It was a milky teal-green in color, saturated with sewage and garbage. The oxymoron part is my smile. It is a horrific site, and if you stand down wind, you will feel vomit in the back of your throat. We also took a picture of the house nearby that a quarter of it is missing, burned at the edges from, I can only assume, a fire that swallowed that part of the house. People still live there, and every time we walk by, there are large metal barrels outside the house billowing smoke from whatever they're burning. Perhaps the fate of the house was an occupational hazard of its inhabitants.

A man named Ben saw us on the street, and exited his barbershop to introduce himself to us, which was a bit unexpected since we didn't know him at all. He was friendly enough; for any American I would think this type of behavior is like seeing a fish out of water, or a teacher at the movie theater. Ghanaians are incredibly friendly for the most part, and usually if you walk down the street, a handful will stop to say hello and ask where you're from. Some pride themselves on "having friends in the U.S.," which really means they've met people just like you on the street and said hello. It's a little unnerving at first, but you get used to it, and after a while, you welcome it since many people stare at you with somber expressions which can be slightly intimidating. Most of the time if you smile and wave first, they'll return the gesture with just as many smiles, but some continue to glare.

We got to the tro-tro area just in time to see the 1:30 PM tro-tro pull away, with Mama waving at us from the front seat! Samuel greeted us and told us to wait, since his tro-tro was next to depart. As it backed into position, Samantha snapped a picture, accidentally getting some man selling Fan Ice (sort of an ice cream pop) in the process who became quite irate that his photo was taken. His anger was captured well in the photo, but we did manage to calm him down enough.

The ride home was hot, sweaty, and unbearably crowded as usual. Samantha sat next to the giant window and felt like she would fall out, just like I did originally. She was giving me impromptu agriculture lessons by quizzing me on the kinds of trees we passed. I can now successfully identify banana trees, palm trees, and coconut trees. I mentioned that the view was pretty, which caused Samantha to turn toward me when we went over a bump, which caused her to smack her head against the top of the window just in time for Samuel to look at us from the front and start laughing. Samantha and I were laughing too, but I could tell from the tears in her eyes it must have really hurt.

The tro-tro slowed since there was a tree lying in the middle of the road. A man stood by it, and when the driver asked him to move it, he begrudgingly obliged as he exclaimed, "speed bump!" The rest of the ride was ok I guess if you're going by tro-tro standards. The skinny man on my right sure was taking up a lot of room though. I couldn't rest both shoulders on the back of the seat, only one, squished behind Samantha's shoulder.

Finally, we made it home 15 minutes before we were supposed to meet the Primary 4-6 kids. Luckily no one showed up, so we stopped at Mama's to say hello, but she was lying down on a bench with a headache. I offered her some of my Excedrin, which seemed to help. We went home to take a nap and clean the dirt and sweat from Ho off our skin, but of course it's impossible to simply be left alone. Apparently, the headmaster told the children 5 PM instead of 4 PM, so at 4:50 PM, a young girl showed up to make sure we were going back to the library. We did, and by that time, I had a headache too. The children were pretty well-behaved, and it did last almost an hour. We had them read a story of their choice from their designated shelf in the library, and then draw a picture from the story with some crayons we brought. It went well. Afterward, we came home, closed our door, and lay down to rest, just after I consumed some Excedrin for myself.

We had rice and palava sauce for dinner, which was really good, spicier than usual. I selfishly hoped Bright wouldn't come by for computer training tonight since I just wanted to sleep. My headache wasn't completely gone, and my stomach was aching. He did come though, with his sister so I supervised while they practiced typing. Mama brought her friend by for an interview, and afterward I showed Mama a picture of me and Sean on my laptop. She said "Hello Sean I will say hello to you when I come to the U.S.!" She also said he was very handsome, and noticed his long hair. She said when he comes to visit her in Ghana, she will grow her hair long and shake her head. I asked her if she saw her husband in Ho, but apparently his sister was renting a room to a young woman and her son, about Michael's age (5). The child mysteriously died in the night and Mama's husband went to inform the family. We also talked about Mama's mother who seems to be having severe pain. She was diagnosed with breast cancer and had one mastectomy, so Mama is confused why her mother is still having so much pain.

The water in the barrel used for pouring down (flush) the toilet had run out, and the well in our compound was dangerously low on water. Samantha and I helped carry a few buckets that Mama managed to fill over to the outhouse. We were really scraping the bottom of the well—which isn't pretty. Luckily it was night, so I couldn't see very well what was in the buckets, but Mama's friend did scoop some things out of it before handing me the bucket. It was late so we said goodnight and parted ways for the evening.

June 2, 2010
Last Day of Work before Vacation!

This morning we had porridge for breakfast, and Emil stopped by to say he'd try to get two people for interviews. I appreciated his help, because with only a few left to do, I was losing my motivation. Bismark surprisingly stopped by also. When he greeted us in English, we responded in English, so he exclaimed that we didn't greet him properly (in Ewe). Ugh. I really don't care right now… He wanted to know how we were doing, since we "hadn't come to see him at the office." Well, clearly, when we've been there every Market Day (different days of the week), he's never there because he only works two or three days a week, so obviously we'll never see him…

I inquired about the money that Emil said Anyo didn't get the last time I was here. He explained that since the home office (the two ex-Peace Corps volunteers that founded BRIDGE) in the U.S. stopped supporting the office a year or two ago, BRIDGE found itself in a tough financial position, thereby taking away the obligation to pay the CBOs money, so they could "support the office"… the office that has expensive crappy internet when they're only there two days a week, when you can check email for 20 pesewas downstairs at the internet café… but whatever. I asked him for the breakdown of where the money we paid went, and he said he couldn't be specific since he wasn't at the office. He said on Wednesday he could give me more details. I knew full well that he knew exactly where every penny went.

Emil was standing outside the door listening patiently, which I was pleased about. I didn't really want to have to restate the conversation for the Anyo meeting tonight. Before Bismark left, somehow the topic of our caretakers came up. We said we felt bad that they weren't letting us help with anything. To that he claimed we couldn't wash clothes… I don't know how he thinks Americans go about their daily lives; it's not like we're the Jetsons and have robots doing everything for us… we're perfectly capable. He really irritated me this morning.

We did one interview in the late morning, after which Mawufemor, Jessica and Michael visited us to color. I have to say, it's interesting watching Jessica and Mawufemor together. Jessica is bold, sassy, and bossy. Mawufemor is quiet, sweet, always smiling the biggest most genuine smile you've ever seen. When Michael and Jessica started having issues sharing the crayons with Akiti (Mawufemor), Akiti gathered what she could, put them in the crayon box, walked over to me and placed the box under my chair. That way, she knew she would be able to get more crayons when she needed them. She also goes about and cleans up after everything, and organizes! She's a girl after my own heart. Outside of that though, she really is an amazing little girl. Little, literally—she is 4 years old but could be 2 ½ or 3 by U.S. size standards. Little, as "akiti" describes. I'll really miss her smile when we leave. I wish Mama could move to the U.S. and be my next-door neighbor, and all her kids could go to good schools, and visit real libraries, and get real nutrition.

We held the JSS study session this afternoon, which went really well. Fifteen kids showed up and were so attentive and eager to do the activity. A few were shy about sharing what they read, but several seemed really excited about writing their own story. One girl, Patricia, actually wrote a whole story about *determination* and gave it to us the following Monday. She wrote a different one but lost it, so wrote a replacement. It seems that anything volunteers come to do with children really only gets anywhere with the JSS students. Primary kids are too young, and not as mature to take activities seriously, and part of it is because they don't understand the English you're using. That was something that I found really frustrating the last time I was here, and Samantha is feeling it as well now. They're spoken to in English, taught in English, their exams are in English… yet they are not actually taught English as a language.

We had fufu for dinner; I didn't eat much of it knowing how it sticks to your stomach like the rubber pancakes would in that old Donald Duck cartoon. Afterwards, we headed to Richard's for the Anyo meeting. We updated everyone on Bismark's visit, and the progress with the study sessions and interviews. We decided to do a focus group with Anyo using some new questions I came up with regarding health in general. The focus group went really well and included arguments between people with differing opinions, some really good points were made. I was glad I came up with the new questions. After the meeting, it was a little bit late so we went home to get ready for bed and our journey tomorrow.

Tomorrow we leave for Accra for the night, and then Friday it's off to Cape Coast—I did manage to make a reservation at Oasis Beach Resort, so hopefully it will be a good mini-vacation.

June 3, 2010
Accra

It seemed the bus ride to Ho was the longest ever. It was the first non-market day we travelled to Ho, and because of the lack of tro-tros, the bus stopped *constantly* to let people on and off. From Ho, we caught a tro-tro to Accra. The three-hour journey included scenes of desperately skinny cattle with ribs protruding from their sides, an array of fantasy coffins for sale on the side of the road, and an immigration checkpoint where we (the whites) had to get off the tro-tro with our belongings, show our passports and explain what we were doing in Ghana and why we were travelling, walk ourselves across their checkpoint border, and re-board the tro-tro. A little excessive, but whatever.

Once we were in Accra, we walked maybe a mile to a guesthouse, only to find they had no rooms available. They pointed us in the direction of another, more expensive, guesthouse but at the time it seemed like our best option. We walked, again, to the Avenida Hotel whose rate put us 7 cedis over budget for the trip. But the up-side was we had a ceiling fan and our own bathroom in our room! The toilet flushed, and the sink and shower had running water, and though the sink drained from a hole in the wall where the shower was, it was delightful. We had rice and chicken as a late lunch, a quick rest, and then headed for the STC bus station to purchase our tickets for the next day's travel.

After we bought our bus tickets, we walked around for a bit. Sam bought a little Ghana flag, and I bought a Ghana soccer jersey, though it's a bit small. We had hoped to eat dinner at El Gaucho, a place named in my guidebook for good tapas and game meat. We walked around for what seemed like forever, and even got directions from various people, but the place was well hidden. We never did find it, and settled for something different. We came across *Ryan's Irish Pub*. Obviously since Samantha and I met while both working at an Irish pub back home, we had to go in. Inside, the pub was decorated like any other Irish pub—brown wooden walls, portraits of Irish people, sconces, and real taps for beer. We each had a cider, both were delicious. As promising as menu items may be described, you have to remember that despite the familiar atmosphere, you are still in Ghana. I should have remembered this. Samantha ordered a sandwich, which looked and tasted much better than my spinach and cheese lasagna and salad. I was disappointed by my choice in sustenance, and more so disappointed with the high price of the meal which put us 8 cedis over budget.

We went back to the hotel, and I tried to sleep, worried about how low we were getting on money, and also wondering if any creatures would be coming through the hole in the wall by the window next to my head. I was also paranoid about bed bugs or anything like it, so I wrapped myself in the top sheet and scooted myself toward Samantha for comfort. She probably didn't know that, I think she was already asleep. She had the good mattress anyway.

June 4, 2010
Rain, Rain, Go Away!

We got up at 5:30 AM to leave Avenida Hotel for the STC bus station by 6 AM. It was raining lightly but steadily when we left. I hoped the rain would only last for the journey at most, and the sun would come out when we got to Cape Coast. We waited at the station for what seemed like forever. Apparently, our bus had broken down and was being worked on at a shop. While we sat, I stared at an old boxy television that was sitting in a cage, literally, attached to the wall above the ticket window. The television showed really old dubbed Telemundo, really bad Ghallywood and Nollywood (Ghana and Nigeria film industries) Movie of the Week trailers, low budget music videos with women dancing in the corner of a room, and a Discovery-Channel-wanna-be, which was particularly entertaining.

Our bus, once it arrived and was working again, was air conditioned, and we got our own seats, which made the three-hour journey to Cape Coast much nicer than the usual tro-tro jaunt. We got to Cape Coast and took a quick taxi to Oasis.

The service at Oasis left something to be desired, particularly friendliness. The woman I spoke with when we arrived about my reservation seemed disgusted and annoyed that I had addressed her at all. The room was cute—bungalow style with a tiny sink and mirror in the room. The floor was tiled with broken pieces that made the floor look like a mosaic. There were three twin beds with mattresses situated inside cement frames that were also cemented to the floor. Green mosquito nets hung above the beds, which at first glance looks like you're supposed to sleep in those as hammocks. The outhouse was well lit and clean, and just a short thirty feet from the room. The outdoor shower was a cylinder-shaped structure, painted red, yellow, and green on the outside. The inside was tiled, instead of the usual cement as décor. The spout had running runner, as did our sink. I was excited about how glorious it would be to brush my teeth with running water, and to stand under a showerhead and let the water actually get all the shampoo out of my hair. Though, we couldn't shower yet since it was raining. I mean, I guess we could have, but it was cold.

The rain continued throughout the day and evening, leaving us with nothing to do since our goal was to walk around the castle. Because of the rain, we didn't see any other tourists out. I was wondering if we were the only ones staying at Oasis. The day was pretty boring since we couldn't do anything. We ate lunch, sat by ourselves under a covering while the rain poured down heavily. A good thing about Oasis was that they had dogs. One mama dog with two pups, that looked like shepherd mixes. One pup was all white, so I named him Bruno (for *obruni*). The other was black with tan markings, like the "black tri" markings of some Australian shepherds. The pups were really sweet, and lay by our feet under the table. The ocean surf was really loud, and every now and then there was an explosion of forceful water doubling back over rocks and colliding with each other into an eruption of waves. The rain made it cold, so we were shivering, including the pups. I hadn't prepared for chilly weather, so we took a nap.

We woke up at 8 PM to go have dinner. At that point, it was more crowded in the restaurant area. There were white people everywhere, I wondered where they all came from. But similar to Ryan's Irish Pub, when there's a popular expat spot, usually most *yavoos* were there. We sat with a nice Finnish couple who had been backpacking and staying in hostels throughout Europe, Asia, and Africa since October. She was a part time journalist, sending in a story every now and then. The money could be stretched for a month's living expenses in hostels, and he seemed to be along for the ride. We chatted with them while we listened to a drumming performance going on nearby. We were all too cold to get up and try to actually see the performance. Between sets, the bull frogs continued with their own loud rendition of percussion. I never knew how loud bull frogs were, but good lord they are loud. It was almost 11 PM (we were up late!) and we went back to the bungalow to sleep. I turned off my alarm and fell asleep to the drumming outside, which turned into hip-hop club music until about 1 AM.

June 5, 2010
Cape Coast

The morning was much sunnier than the day before. I saw a delectable item on the menu for breakfast that I just had to order: pancakes! They were delicious. They were like giant crepes, thicker but not as fluffy-dense as American pancakes. There were some sautéed bananas with them, and I ate 3 of the 4 crepes. The last one I gave to Samantha because the bread, jam, and cheese breakfast she ordered looked like what you would get on an airplane—tiny prepackaged individual servings of jam and spreadable cheese substance, and two pieces of untoasted thin wheat bread.

After breakfast we headed to Cape Coast Castle, where the sun really came out in full force. I had been to the castle before with Denise, and everything was just how I remembered it.

Originally a fort, the castle exchanged hands numerous times before landing its infamous reputation as one of the largest slave trading posts on the West African coast. The dungeons were incredibly dark and equally depressing. Five compartments made up the male slave dungeon, holding 250 men in each compartment. The compartments couldn't have been more than 20 feet wide, by 35 feet deep. For 2-3 months, men were held, unable to see daylight which caused temporary blindness when they were escorted out. They sustained with what little food and water was provided, and slept in months' worth of filth—vomit, urine, and feces. When the dungeons were excavated, it was found that the pool of filth that slaves slept in reached a foot and a half off of the floor. Women were kept separately, in two chambers of between 400-500 women in each. Conditions were similar. Both male and female dungeons held slaves roughly between the ages of 13 and 30, though there was a separate entrance in the female dungeon for soldiers to select the most beautiful ones for their nightly pleasures. If a woman refused the advances, she was thrown into a smaller cell, usually holding ten women all for the same reasons. That cell was 2 feet wide by 10 feet long. If women became pregnant from the rape of a soldier, the woman would be sent off to be cared for by a nurse in a home nearby until the delivery of the baby. Once the baby was delivered, the baby was taken to the church to be raised as an orphan and educated in the first formal school of Ghana, in Cape Coast. The mothers were sent back to the dungeons. If anyone tried to escape or fight back, they were sent, as an example, to the *cell for the condemned*. The room had no windows, no opening for light or air. They were given no food or water, and within two or three days, the occupants died. Once transported to the slave ships, people were packed like sardines, with each person sitting between the legs of another for the journey to Europe or the Americas. Many were shackled together, so if one person either fell overboard or committed suicide by jumping off of the ship, the entire line of shackled slaves would follow. If a woman became pregnant from a rape on the ship, she was thrown overboard—no one wanted to buy a pregnant slave. Many people died. Because of the food shortage on ships, dead bodies were mixed in with food to feed to the slaves. For the 25 million or so slaves that survived the ships' voyages, it can be said that upwards of 88 million people had died, either on the ship or within the walls of the Cape Coast Castle. Disturbing, humbling, and heart wrenching, the informative day was well worth it, even the second time around.

After the tour, we stopped at some stands inside the castle walls that were selling various curios as souvenirs. I found some beautiful artwork that I couldn't afford, but settled for some smaller, more simple pieces. We ate lunch at the Castle Restaurant right next door, where I had vegetable coconut curry, which was really good, and a glass of pineapple juice. We watched the waves, and some kids wrestle and play on the sand. Before long we decided to head back to the bungalow for a short nap. Before we walked back though, Samantha stopped to buy a small drum. While she was busily haggling her price down, a woman motioned for my water bottle. I poured some of my water into a baggie she held open, one meant to hold the soy skewers she was selling.

It was so nice out we cut naptime short to sit on the beach. Kids came by selling pure water, oranges, and other things. We watched a group of guys play soccer on the beach, but their game increased in challenge when the tide started to come in. There were some fisherman boats behind them, though I couldn't tell if they were coming or going. The same group of kids appeared, this time to show off in front of other tourists. They did back flips and back handsprings, over and over and over. I ordered a sandwich—a poor decision on my part, I only ate half of it. A boy named Samson approached selling oranges and asked if I remembered him. He gave us guidance earlier that morning as to which way the castle was. Earlier in the day, he had asked me to buy oranges from him and I said "maybe later." Since he found us, I happily bought two oranges for us, and one for him. Three oranges are only 50 pesewas. He looked at the half sandwich that lay on my plate and asked if he could have it, and of course I obliged. Another child brought a turtle over and put it on the table.

Shortly afterward, we moved to a palm covering inside the walls of Oasis since it was getting dark. There was a new group of students who had just arrived. One girl was sitting in front of me, and I could see over her shoulder that she was sketching the scenery. It made me wish I was back in the practice of sketching and drawing. I feel like I used to be pretty good, but lately every time I pick up a pencil, I'm disappointed with my lack of vision, and more so with the end product. There were some evil little children whose parents neglected to see the importance of supervision. While the parents busied themselves with their beers and adult conversation, the children began throwing large stones at the sleeping puppies. I was livid, though I felt if I told the children to stop, it might start a fight. Clearly, animal care is handled differently here. I couldn't stand it so we went back to the bungalow.

I brushed my teeth in our tiny sink with running water. If ever someone doesn't appreciate the little things in life, send them to Africa. I have never been one for religion, but more and more when I'm in Ghana, I find myself praising Jesus for the small graces of the occasional luxury of running water, a fan, or a cold drink of water. There was a toad in the outhouse, which immediately reminded me of the Discovery Channel wanna-be show that was televised at the STC station, particularly the segment about deadly frogs. The entire show was a condensed version of an educational snippet of nature. At the most, four sentences were devoted to describing a particular species, ranging from the wrath of the North American skunk, to the vampire bats of South America, to snakes and frogs, and jellyfish and coral, all of which makes you never want to take a nature walk again in your life. South America is seriously no joke. Not only are you in danger of being shot amid a miscommunication surrounding cocaine possession, but the frogs are out to get you too. And God forbid you play like a monkey in the jungle because Tarzan might shoot you with a poison frog dart. They kept showing the same clip over and over, as if it would have more effect—a naked man in a loin cloth blowing his dart at a monkey, and then the monkey falls to the ground in death... so educational and... uplifting.

June 6, 2010
Long Day of Travel Back to the Village

There's not a whole lot to say for the day. We got up at 6 AM, and I showered before packing up my things. At 7 AM our taxi driver who had dropped us off two days prior was waiting for us. He took us to the STC bus station, where we waited... and waited... Finally, at 8:30 someone came to the window to sell tickets.

I was starting to feel really nauseous, and prayed that I wouldn't get sick on the bus. This time, the bus's air conditioning didn't work very well so the three-hour ride was hot and not well ventilated. I think I slept some, but I'm not sure. I wasn't feeling well at all. When we got to Accra, it had been four hours since we left our room in Cape Coast, and I drank plenty of water trying to aid my aching stomach… so I had to pay 20 pesewas to use a toilet near the bus station.

We took a taxi to the tro-tro station, and boarded a tro-tro bound for Ho. That three-hour journey was better. I sat by the wide-open window, and we had a little more leg room since we were sitting in the front row. I put my backpack under my knees and propped my feet against the driver's seat in front of me. By the time we got to Ho, it was about 2:30 PM, which on a non-market day means you're SOL for finding a tro-tro headed for Saviefe. We walked for a while before we found some taxi drivers that began to fight over who would take us, for an over-priced amount of 18 cedis. It was either that, or walk, and I was not about to embark on that endeavor, especially feeling as awful as I did. Finally, we got back to the village, just before 4 PM. I was starving and nauseous at the same time—we hadn't eaten anything all day, save for one Clif Bar and two granola bars for myself, and 4 Clif Bars for Samantha. We were hoping for jollof rice, and after resting for a short bit, we got our wish. Sema brought jollof rice with a few of those thin meat-like patties. By 8 PM, we were exhausted and ready for bed. I was hoping that I'd feel better in the morning, thinking it was my lack of food that was the problem.

June 7, 2010
Sickness…

I was wrong. Remember when I said that I had brushed my teeth with running water in Cape Coast, instead of brushing with our usual bags of pure water? I also let my guard down and ordered a mango smoothie in Cape Coast, which I'm guessing was not made with ice from a pure water baggie. Enter intestinal parasite... I should mention here that this entry may be slightly graphic regarding bodily functions, so if you're squeamish or don't want to know me that well, feel free to skip to the next entry.

Getting sick sucks. Getting sick when you're not home sucks even worse. But being sick in a remote village in West Africa is awful. These would be the longest 24 hours I'd spent in Ghana. During the night I had to get up four times to visit the outhouse. Number 2s resembled ink. No matter how hard I tried, I couldn't vomit. The nausea and cramping and stomach pains continued through the night, and on throughout the next day. I realized I had a fever. Just for the record in case you were wondering, a fever in Africa is really, really hot.

In the morning I tried to have a tiny bit of groundnut soup, but it came right back up. I felt a little better after I vomited, but it didn't last long. I restlessly lay in bed for most of the day, sweating profusely between my trips to the outhouse. Every time, I was sure there was nothing left in my body, but forty-five minutes later, I would be proven wrong. I felt like death, and according to Samantha, I looked like it too.

Details are fuzzy but I do remember Mama, Hans, and Emil standing in our room speaking in Ewe with concern, and deciding if I should go to the hospital, or medical assistant in the village. Hans and Emil were asking me questions about my bowels, and though I appreciated their concern, I detested having to provide so much embarrassing detail about my number 2s to them. I should mention that during the worst of it, the idea of a hospital with an IV to rehydrate my weak body did cross my mind. Though I wondered how I would get there. I didn't know where it was. I imagined tracking down Samuel and his tro-tro, but then Hans and Emil suggested someone from the next village over had a motorbike. Knowing there was no way I would be able to physically hold on, it was suggested that they could fasten a cart or plank of wood behind the bike that I could lay on. I thought I should have Samantha write a letter to my mother with any last words. I dozed off remembering the numerous interviews I conducted, and how every one of them said there wasn't enough qualified medical personnel in the case of emergencies and sickness... I wondered about the "medical assistant" they spoke of, who was actually a physical therapist, but was in fact also the hairdresser.

Throughout the afternoon I drifted in and out of consciousness, though I remember thinking a lot about Cast Away, and how Tom Hanks was so upset when he lost Wilson to sea. And how can you remove a tooth just by hitting it with a rock? Wouldn't it just break the tooth? I also thought about Free Willy, remembering a dream I had two nights prior that involved me, my boyfriend, and my friend Christina swimming in a pool at night with two orca whales. The orcas were significantly smaller than they are in real life, though in the dream they were still significantly larger than us. I wondered about the trainer who was killed a few months ago in Florida by an orca. So how did they film Free Willy? How could they be sure that whale wasn't going to kill the little boy? Or did they use a mechanical whale?

Mama brought me some pills to take, and a rehydration packet to mix with water. The pills were chewable but tasted disgusting. One of them had aluminum hydroxide and magnesium written on the side. The rehydration packet had the same ingredients as my rehydration tablets, but it also had something to act as a sort of glue... to help stop the "running" of the insides. Samantha took the liberty of filling 25 oz. of water in *my only water bottle* and mixed the rehydration substance in. The resulting product was brownish-green, and resembled brackish pond water. It was supposed to be orange flavored I'm assuming… but the taste was like warm salt water from the ocean, with a hint of orange… I could only sip two or three sips at a time before needing a break when my gag reflexes prompted an unnecessary vomiting episode.

Later, Mama and Sema brought plain rice for me to eat. I managed to eat a banana, and 4 small bites of rice. I knew my stomach wasn't ready for anything yet. But Mama sat there and said I should finish half of the brackish substance before she would leave. I really appreciated her, but I really didn't want to drink it because it would just make me vomit again. The strain of dealing with illness was hard enough, but to keep up my manners and be polite while trying to tell them to leave me alone was impossible. I sipped, steadily, forcing every swallow. While they stared at me, I suggested Samantha show them pictures from Cape Coast, in order to take the attention off of me. They admired the pictures as I stared at the rice in front of me, thinking only one word, "impossible."

Luckily, Mama asked if Believe had finished making the skirts, which gave us an opportunity to show Mama and Sema a couple "finished" garments and ask if the price was unfair. Mama and Sema criticized the work, pointing out details that should have been fixed or completed before giving it to us. They also agreed that the price for my two skirts and dress (35 cedis) and Sam's skirt, dress, and two shirts (45 cedis) was a ridiculous amount. They said that 5 cedis per garment was more than fair, and that tomorrow we should send the items back to Believe and explain clearly that we will not pay that much. The idea of confrontation made me uncomfortable, but I was happy to know they thought it was overly expensive too.

With Samantha's adamant promise that she would make me eat more rice and make sure that I drank all of the brackish grossness, Mama and Sema took their leave and said they would return later. Sometime in the evening I vomited the rehydration substance and the little bit of rice and banana that I had managed to partially digest. At that point, I poured out the rest of the 14 oz. of brackish stuff on the ground when Samantha wasn't looking. I hated to lie to Mama, but I honestly couldn't stomach the thought of drinking any more.

When Mama and Sema did return later that night, I was half asleep. I heard mumbling, and Samantha promising to come get Mama if things got worse in the night. They left a small 200ml bottle of chilled coke on the table for me. I drank a little when I woke up around midnight. I continued to toss and turn; I couldn't get comfortable. The fever was still going strong, though I felt like it had lessened a little bit since the afternoon. I may have vomited again… I'm really not sure. But I did manage to sleep through most of the night, only getting up to pee, which I hoped meant the worst was over.

June 8, 2010
Feeling Better

I woke up feeling much better, not 100%, but still so much better than the day before. I had a little bit of porridge for breakfast, and managed to eat most of a banana (my first meal since breakfast yesterday). Samantha and I dragged ourselves out of the compound to confront Believe about the exorbitant price she was charging for our garments, and to request more alterations. I hate confrontation of any kind, and I didn't want to outright accuse her of cheating us, but part of the problem I thought had been, and was going to be, the language barrier. I think Believe lets on that she understands more English than she actually does. Either way, I wasn't looking forward to this conversation. Mama had said she didn't want to come with us because after we leave, Believe would have it in for Mama, which of course we didn't want… but at the same time I wanted Mama's support.

The meeting with Believe went better than I expected. We sat down, and I explained that the first time I came to Saviefe, she only charged me 2 cedis per skirt, and that 35 cedis for two skirts and a dress was much too expensive. She nodded and smiled, so I continued, trying to find simpler words, just in case. I explained we didn't have that much money left and we could pay her 5 cedis per garment, which was more than fair. She agreed, though I think she was slightly embarrassed. I then went on to specify some alterations: replacing a ribbon as the band of the top of the skirt with a simple piece of leftover fabric; she had cut the dress in two pieces to shorten the length, and hadn't put it back together yet. I seized this opportunity since I didn't like the way she had placed the fabric for the top of the dress differently than the skirt of the dress—I asked her to convert the skirt of the dress into just a skirt just like the others, and I would use the top part of the fabric for my own projects when I get home. The skirts I must say turned out well so far, so I was looking forward to the final product. Samantha went on to specify her alterations, and then we explained that we would need it all by Friday night since we're leaving on Saturday morning. This was the point where surprise crossed Believe's face, putting a time crunch pressure on her work that I'm sure she's never felt before, given the widespread adoption of "Africa time". As we were finishing up our discussion of alterations, Mama walked over, with Cicho following reluctantly behind her. He was sleepy. She had come to see how I was feeling and saw us so she came over, but kept her distance as to not interfere or let on that she supported our ambitions to lower the price.

After we finished at Believe's compound, Mama and Cicho walked with us back to our compound. Cicho was getting cranky while Mama cleaned up after our breakfast and emptied our trash with her hands (had I known they didn't just dump the wastebasket upside down I would have been more neat with the way I threw away banana peels and Q-tips). I showed Cicho a book we had lying on our table, *The Fox and the Hound*. He immediately left his cranky mood aside and became elated as he turned the pages. After every turn of the page, he would squeal and giggle, and clap his hands. Mama finished cleaning up, prompting Cicho to tease her. He would lift the curtain over his head and walk toward her until his face pressed against her face. They were both laughing, and it was really nice to see. As I may have mentioned before, Mama is one of the only adults I ever see playing with and enjoying their child.

Mama said they needed to go, and Cicho rediscovered his cranky side. He walked halfway through the compound, picked up a small stone and walked back... Mama apparently has dealt with this decision before and exclaimed, "If you throw that stone at me I will beat you!" He threw it. Mama just shook her head, and said, "Bye Cicho," as she continued to sit on our step. He picked up a rock this time, bigger than his little fist. Mama reminded him of her previous threat, this time with more conviction. He came to the bottom of the step, arm back holding the rock by his ear, ready to throw it in her direction. He paused, visibly considering his options, and slowly lowered his arm and put the rock down on the step.

After Mama and Cicho left, Samantha and I watched *Marie Antoinette* on my laptop, and then savored our fan for a little while until lunch time. I was hungry, which was a good sign, but also slightly uncomfortable. We were brought French fries for lunch, which I was thankful for. Though, when Samantha gave me a significantly smaller portion than hers, I scoffed in protest. But she was probably right, I shouldn't push it. We relaxed the rest of the afternoon; I caught myself up on writing, and Samantha read a book. Around 2:30 PM, Michael came over after school. We asked if Mama knew where he was and if he'd been home yet. To both questions he answered the usual "yes." He colored for a really short while, sat on a chair next to me, and the next thing I knew, he had fallen fast asleep. At 4 PM, it was time for the Primary 4-6 study session, so I woke him up— drool dripping from his chin, and eyes tired and red, poor thing. We walked him home, and headed for the library and school compound.

I am not meant to handle full on mobs of children. A few well-behaved, sweet ones like Michael, Jessica, Kofi, Mawufemor and Cicho are a breeze. But when there are forty or fifty loud and energetic children, the scene is accompanied by a sense of utter chaos. We gathered the children in the library again, and Samantha was meant to lead the sessions. Though I love Samantha very much, she doesn't really have an ounce of a *disciplinary figure* in her. She asks in a sweet voice if what she had planned is ok. Half of the children don't understand and run amok anyway. The other half behave and do what they're asked and try to explain it to others. But for the most part, even if they do understand, they don't oblige.

Tearing apart the shelves with books, it looks like a tornado blew through the library. You tell them choose one book and we'll do an activity, and they grab one book, look through, throw it on the floor, and go back for another. They surround you like vultures, and pretend they never got a book or a crayon or a piece of paper, when they really have gotten a few. When you only have enough paper and crayons for every child to have one of each, it's frustrating when you recognize some kids have already had their share. You tell them no and tell them why, and they snatch it anyway when you turn your head to look at the mob of children that have backed you literally into a corner. Usually of the two of us, I'm the one who raises my voice loud enough for all the children to hear, and I'm the one who says anything with conviction enough to be respected, and the children usually fall in line. I'm sorry if I sound like a dictator, but seriously... MOBS. At any rate, I gave up. Not feeling 100%, and not being born with enough patience to deal with this situation, I just sat down and waited for it to be over. Granted, I was cranky. The kids were generally happy and excited; it went fairly well despite the chaotic mess they left behind.

Exhausted and hungry, we went back to our compound and rested until dinner. I had just a small scoop of jollof rice, again trying not to push my luck with my stomach. Bright came by to see how I was feeling, as did Mama and Sema. Shortly after dinner I was ready for bed.

June 9, 2010
Last Day in Ho + Ideas

We had groundnut soup for breakfast, which I liked, though I probably ate it too fast. Sema had boiled some water to put in our shower buckets so we actually got to bathe with warm water! We heard the bus's horn as we left our compound, and jogged up the path to catch it before it left for the next village. On the way, we accidentally caught the attention of the resident crazy man. He got excited and ran over to us, blocking our way to the bus. He grabbed Samantha's hand (she was in front of me) and when she passed him, he turned to me. I was not in the mood this morning to be polite. I tried to fake left and go around him, but he grabbed my chest which threw off my plan. I took his arm and threw it to the side. When we got on the bus at 7:50 AM, he hopped on behind us and stood in the doorway staring at me with his creepy smile. It made me shiver.

By 9 AM we had reached the village of Etodome, a mere 6 miles away from Saviefe. I knew it was going to be a long ride. The agenda for Ho, considering our limited funds, was simply to use the internet and talk to Bismark, since he promised he would be in the office. I wasn't really expecting him to be there, but I was still disgusted when we checked both at 10:15 AM, when we got to Ho, and at 12:15 PM, when we left and he still wasn't there. As Samantha so eloquently noted, he has been as useful as two sprained ankles in a 5K race. Since we didn't have enough money for lunch, we headed back to the bus stop and were early enough to catch the bus back to the village, saving us 40 pesewas of our usual combined tro-tro fare. We were not early enough to get seats, however. All were taken, so we perched ourselves on the rear wheel well, something that, combined with the treacherous roads of the rural Volta Region, nearly broke our tail bones.

As the ride began, some woman was throwing an absolute fit because she either got on the wrong bus, or was charged extra because she wanted to get off somewhere unusual. The argument between her, the driver, the attendant, and the other passengers was for the most part in angry Ewe, though one old man did yell out in English, "This is not your personal car!" The rest of the ride was quiet enough, though I wondered if I'd be able to stand afterwards. Luckily, a few people got off and an old woman pointed me to an open seat. Samantha sat, and I on her lap, trying unsuccessfully to "think skinny," since I knew the bumps in the road caused my entire weight to crush down on Samantha's bladder. It's lucky that we did grab that seat because it had started to rain pretty hard. One stop later, ten tiny children, maybe the age of 4, climbed aboard, soaking wet. They clambered about and sat on the floor, exactly where we had just been. They looked at us in awe. Sounding like the baby sea turtles in *Finding Nemo*, two stops later they all squealed "Bus Stop!" in unison. It was cute. Finally, another seat opened up and I snagged it. My back was killing me, as was my neck from tossing and turning all night. I was cranky and hungry and was ready to be home. I couldn't deal with this bus any longer.

We got home and found a new bunch of bananas on the table, a pleasant surprise! We each ate one banana and some crackers as our lunch. Not two minutes after we'd arrived back home, Michael came running up to say good afternoon. I swear he's a spy. Kofi came by too and colored for a little while. Soon it was time for our last JSS study session so we headed for the compound. It went well with some very eager and attentive students who enjoyed the activity. We picked out groups of short stories, had them read at their own pace, and then get into their groups to discuss and write a summary. Though most students cheat and write directly from the book for their summaries, they were reading, and they were enjoying it, which is what mattered most. I have to say, JSS students are so much better behaved than the Primary kids. They're better for my health and I don't feel like I have an ulcer when I leave the JSS students. It was raining, and Bright walked with us back toward our end of the village, talking about the reproductive health interview he'd participated in.

When we got back to the room and after we dried off, I realized I had to pee. I tried to be stealth with the rain, attempting to avoid more wetness as much as possible. It was a feeble attempt, as when I initially jogged to the outhouse, the door was wide open. I asked Kofi's mom if anyone was using it, and the conversation lingered in the rain something like the following:

CB: Oh, is someone using the toilet?

KM: No

CB: So, I can go in?

KM: No

CB: Who's using it?

KM: Kofi

CB: But... Kofi is right there... (standing pant-less beside his mother)

KM: Yes

CB: So, I can use it

KM: Yes

CB: So, no one's in there?

KM: Yes

CB: Ok so I'll go in?

KM: No

CB: uh huh...

And then I just bolted for the door. As often as I seem to walk in on men pooping in the outhouse (for some reason it never occurs to anyone to shut either of the two doors to the outhouse or the stall inside...), I figured one more possibility wouldn't matter.

It was still raining when 5:30 PM rolled around. We were supposed to go to the Anyo meeting but I wondered how punctual everyone would be, or even if the meeting would be cancelled due to the rain. At 5:45 PM we walked over to Richard's. Only Richard was there, with a couple young guys who always hang around his place for shots of whiskey. I tend to forget that Richard acts as the village bartender. A few moments later, Hans appeared in the doorway, and I was tragically hopeful that the meeting would still happen. Soon, the rain picked up and poured down heavily. It was so loud under Richard's tin roof; I had to raise my voice next to his ear to ask him about his eye. The swelling goes down slightly when he takes his pain medication, though the pain continues to agonize him at a fixed rate despite the efforts of Western medicine. He lifted his lid to show me his eye. It looked the same—red, swollen beyond belief, the pupil and coloring around it is almost an exaggerated blob of what used to represent his eye color. It looked as though the eye would explode at any moment. It took all my might not to wince in horror, even though I had seen it a few weeks before.

Two men rode up on their motorbike, soaked to the bone. At first, I mistook the revving of the motorbike's engine as distant thunder. They each took a shot of whiskey, greeted us, and then left. Emil arrived, and soon the other men who frequented Richard's bar left. The rain had died down slightly, and I realized that there wasn't going to be a meeting. Walter wasn't there, and neither was Sema. So, I asked Emil if he would accompany us to visit the chief tomorrow to discuss volunteers to chaperone evening hours at the library, to which he agreed. I also explained that the library still needed benches for the students to sit on, and the lights needed to be fixed, since they would be incredibly necessary for evening operations to work. I also brought up an idea I had come up with earlier in the morning.

The focus group with Anyo was very successful, and noted malnutrition as a very significant health challenge in the rural areas. Because the diet is "one-sided," since most people eat either banku or fufu every day for every meal, essential vitamins from fruits and vegetables are severely absent.

Originally, Anyo's seed money from BRIDGE was to be used to start an income-generating farming project. Of course, the idea of any project that could generate income is a great idea in theory, but as I've had some hard realizations about development throughout this trip, great ideas in practice are much harder to implement successfully. If Anyo did generate some income, there would be disagreements on who should spend the money, on what, how, and why. This was exemplified in Richard's objection to use some of an emergency medical fund for his own eye, when four others in the village also had eye problems. So what project could actually do some good?

A vegetable garden seemed like a good solution to me. It would be run by Anyo Group, and sell vegetables for very affordable prices, not for income or profit, but merely enough to keep the garden growing, to buy more seeds, fertilizer, top soil, etc. I don't know exactly what vegetables would thrive here. If there were any vegetables that could grow here other than cassava, I would have thought someone would have figured that out by now… but then again… maybe not. I drew pictures and described various vegetables—tomatoes, carrots, onions, beets, spinach, peas, green beans, and peppers. We made a list of possible vegetable seeds to buy, as well as materials that would be needed. We decided that chicken wire mesh fencing would be necessary, as well as wood for the fence frame and gate. Lord knows as soon as those vegetables start growing, the goats will be all over it.

Emil, Hans, and Richard seemed very pleased and somewhat excited about the idea. They said they would definitely try it. I suggested that once the garden becomes successful, they could ask a few children at a time to help harvest the vegetables, or tend to the garden. It would present an ideal opportunity to teach the children about vegetables and nutrition.

There's an organization, a bank really, that has been introduced to the region since my last visit—the Agricultural Development Bank. As I understood it, it served to give loans to farmers, and could act as a savings account for farmers as well—a financial option not previously available to farmers with no collateral. Emil, Richard and I discussed the ADB, and I suggested they should contact their regional office to bring a resource person in to teach Anyo about how to farm these vegetables. If the project became very successful, Anyo could expand it with a loan from the ADB. Richard also suggested bringing in a resource person to teach members of the community about nutrition.

Though it wasn't an official Anyo meeting, I thought the visit was very productive. I started to regain some of my original enthusiasm for small scale projects in the village. Richard asked me to write down my postal address, email, and phone number. I couldn't quite remember the correct country code for dialing the US from Ghana, I knew it was either 001 or 011. Richard giggled as he dialed my number into his phone, similar to the way my friends and I did in elementary school when we were getting ready to prank call someone. He tested it first by itself, then with 011, and finally squealed with glee when 001+ my number connected him to my voicemail—something they don't use here. I guess I'll find out when I check my messages at home how long the call was connected, I'm sure I'll be able to hear his squeals and giggles even though he held the phone away in surprise. It was like a child who prank calls someone, and when the person answers, the child forgets what to do, and tries to hand the phone off to someone else, laughing all the while. It was hysterical.

Richard asked when we should have the final Anyo meeting before we head off, and I suggested Friday night. He handed me a familiar book, with "Guest Book," written on the cover. I remembered Denise and I had written messages to Anyo at the end of our last visit, thanking them for the experiences and their friendship. I suddenly realized that this was the first of our last goodbyes. Though I miss home, and was fed up with how things had turned out in the village after my last visit, the people make it memorable and I'll always have a place for them in my heart. Unfortunately, gatherings like tonight don't happen often. Usually Mama is the one to socialize, occasionally Sema will accompany her. I will be sad to say goodbye to Anyo this time. I'm not sure if I'll be back here again. I'd like to transport Richard, Sema and Mama and the kids back to the U.S. though. When I left before, I was sad to say goodbye, but I think deep down I knew I would return. This time… I'm not so sure. I would like to say that I will, perhaps with more experience, more guidance to offer, more projects to start and actually get to oversee… but who knows? It's hard to accomplish anything in less than 6 weeks. It takes a month usually to just get acclimated again to the village, to the culture, to the people, and to understand their needs and challenges. I can't imagine being in a place in my life again where I have the luxury of abandoning responsibility to come live here for any length of time. Though, the last time I said goodbye, Richard did say that whenever I got married, they would send someone from Anyo to attend. Maybe not *that* exactly, but maybe if I get wealthy (unlikely considering my future in non-profit work and my piles of student loans) I can bring Mama and her kids out for a visit. And then maybe they can stay and be my next-door neighbors. And maybe Richard can come too and teach me how to sew. Life in dreams…

June 10, 2010
Coloring and Airplanes

Sema brought us groundnut soup for breakfast, also known as *brown-brown*. We ate the entire bowl, and a banana each. Today was pretty relaxing. After breakfast and our bucket bathing session, we got dressed, got ready for the day, braided our hair, and then took a nap. I slept for a long time, having crazy nap time dreams about sitting in the airport, and seeing random people. When I opened my eyes around 11:30 AM, Jessica was staring at me. I really wasn't that out of it—she was stealth like a ninja entering without making a single sound! I sat with her while she colored for a while. She wrote all of her numbers, which she's gotten better at since we've been here. At first, she would write the mirror images of numbers, but now she wrote them correctly except for the number nine.

Samantha was reading in the other room, and I was glad to have one-on-one time with Jessica. She wasn't in school because her mom couldn't afford the lunch fee. Over the course of the afternoon, I gave Jessica 3 bananas and a bunch of crackers. I started drawing a little bit, two scenes from Oasis, one of which was the turtle sitting on our table. Then I channeled my inner child and replaced my pencil with an array of crayons. I drew a sun, a mango tree, and then Jessica, Michael, Akiti, Cicho, Kofi, Samantha and I all holding hands. Cheesy, I know, but it was cute. Jessica got a kick out of it. After that I instructed Jessica on the fine art of crafting paper airplanes, and the even finer skill of flying them. She would stand on the top of our front steps, and squeal as it went further and further. If it didn't go as far as the one before, she would say, "no," and shake her head and try again.

Mama and Cicho brought us lunch (boiled cassava with pasta in palm oil with onions). Cicho was wearing his usual red shirt that said "six" on it. He and Jessica chased and played. After Mama left, I was tired and asked Jessica if she wanted to go home for a little bit and come back later. She looked as if someone had just murdered her puppy. It was wrong of me to ask that; I should appreciate what little time I have had with her, and what little time is left. I sat with her outside for a while, and soon Kofi appeared with Fafali in tow, both wanting in on the paper airplane action that Jessica was showing off. It was a fun afternoon. All in all, Jessica was with us for six hours.

After Kofi began monopolizing the paper airplanes, Jessica started petting my head and my French braid. I asked her if she wanted to play with my hair and she squealed, "yes!" She went and found my brush (a step up from the flashlight she liked to use on my hair the last time I was here) and began concocting some hairstyle that more and more started to resemble what hair might look like after an electrocution. She was enjoying herself though, and if she pulled too hard, her little raspy voice would say "sorry, sorry sister Christine." Three upper primary girls came by to say hello and took interest. They separated parts of my hair, two of them braided, and Jessica played. Michael appeared and started coloring with Kofi. It was a party! It was almost 5:30 PM so I asked everyone to leave so we could visit the chief. I pulled out the hair ties, along with some of my hair that had been tangled among them, pulled back my hair, and Samantha and I walked with Emil over to the chief's compound.

The meeting with the chief was relatively calm and uneventful. We discussed the logistics (sort of) behind getting volunteers for the library, which would include our presence at a community gathering the following morning… at 6:30 AM. We visited a short while, and then returned to our room for dinner, which was jollof rice with 2 small pieces of chicken. I realized as I finished my piece of chicken that I was eating it more like a hungry monkey rather than my usual pickiness. After dinner, I grabbed my laptop and movies, and we headed over to Mama's compound for a movie night with the kids.

Movie night was a blast. The kids had eaten and had their baths, so cuddling was flea-free! We sat in Mama's living room area on fabric chairs in dark wooden frames. The cushions were covered in purple plastic. I placed the laptop of the coffee table and we gathered on the couch to experience Disney's *Tarzan*. Cicho was asleep on the floor, Akiti was on my lap, and Michael was situated between Samantha and me. Michael would jump at the slightest thing meant to surprise or startle an audience. Akiti bobbed her head to all the background music. Mama joined us soon after the movie started, which added to the fun. She liked to ask questions about what was happening throughout the movie, something I probably do myself too often.

After the movie, we visited for just a little while. I showed some pictures on my laptop that I had downloaded from my phone, including a picture of the White House in Washington D.C. during winter, and a picture of my *Chicken a la CB* dinner I invented (though Sean helped a lot and should be given much of the credit for the recipe). We talked about how long Mama would be living in the village (another year and a half she expects), and so I asked if after that she'll be living in the US. We did talk about visiting though. The last time she checked, about five years ago, Ghanaian passport fees were about 11 cedis each. They can't be much more than that now I assumed, but I knew the airfare would trump any looming passport fee. I would love to have her and the kids come visit though, and preferably stay… I hate the thought of not seeing our favorites again.

June 11, 2010
Last Day in the Village

We woke up expecting to attend the community gathering at 6:30 AM, summoned by a Gong-Gong man. However, since the chief couldn't find the Gong-Gong man, the gathering didn't happen. I assume this is because the chief didn't want to pick up a mallet and hit a gong. After we had showered and had our brown-brown for breakfast, Emil came to inform us of the missing Gong-Gong man, which subsequently meant another attempt would be made the following morning. I was slightly opposed to attending a meeting that would be entirely in Ewe at 6:30 AM, when we needed to be doing last minute packing and saying our goodbyes the next morning. Though I suggested we (Samantha and I) simply not attend the gathering, Emil decided it should be at 5 or 5:30 AM instead to give us time to pack and say goodbyes. Mama later explained that our presence and our words (even if most people could only understand through the chief's interpretation of what we said) would have more effect, more merit, than someone from the community saying the same thing. Mama explained that the community would take us more seriously, and therefore the topic to be discussed (volunteers to chaperone evening hours at the library) would have a better chance at success.

I spent the morning packing most of my things. When I'd finished all but what would be packed the following morning after our showers, I lay down for a short nap. I was restless though, and when I opened my eyes, Jessica was staring at me from the doorway again. She was content to spend a few hours coloring by herself, occasionally asking for a biscuit, which is a cracker, though she pronounces it as *bis-quit*. I rested, and every now and then she would come into the bedroom and say, "Christine, medekuku banana" or just "medekuku," and tapped her head, which I figured out meant she wanted to play with my hair. "Medekuku" means "please." It was a pretty quiet morning, and when Sema brought us French fries, plantain chips, and 2 bottles of coke for lunch (wow!), we shared with Jessica.

Kofi joined us in the afternoon, though Kofi and Jessica started hitting each other and not sharing the crayons. Some random children came over too, and we started to lose our patience. Jessica felt she needed some attention, good or bad, and so decided to eat a crayon. She had little wax particles on her lips and she was spitting bright orange. We kicked them out, and Jessica and one of Emil's sons about the same age parked themselves outside our bedroom window and began peeling off pieces of the screen and chewing on it. I had wondered what animal always seemed to destroy the screens in the village... I found out. Bright came over to practice typing on my laptop, and Kosi soon appeared as well to return the New Moon book I'd leant him. He said he really enjoyed the books so I told him that later tonight we could watch Twilight on my laptop.

Tonight was to be our last Anyo meeting. We arrived at Richard's compound and visited for a short while with everyone. Richard read the comments I'd left in the guest book, most of which were instructive but firm. He asked me what else in the village disappointed me. I explained that my entry in the guest book was only firm because I cared so much about the village, and its people. I explained that the members of the community are fully capable of taking responsibility for their own happiness, and initiative for their own ideas, and that good ideas need constant supervision and effort to become successful projects. I also stated that a library that simply exists does no one any good; it must be used by the community if it will make any positive change for anyone. Emil informed me that the following morning at the community gathering would be a good place for me to "teach the community about why the library is good." I asked him to tell me why he thought the library was good. He and Walter collectively came up with that it would "help the children learn and practice English." I agreed, and also noted that it would be a good opportunity for parents to learn with their children by reading children's books together. Later, Samantha and I discussed how Anyo decided they wanted a library more than nine years ago, and now that it was built and stocked with books, they still wanted an explanation as to why a library should be used by the community.

After our brief Anyo meeting, we walked to the chief's compound, where the chief and Anyo had prepared a presentation of sorts. We didn't know what the presentation would be, and when we walked into the chief's living room, it still wasn't apparent. The room was painted a royal blue, and the blue hue from the light bulb in the ceiling made the entire room glow like a neon sign. There was a very powerful fan oscillating in the corner—the chief must have had the best fan because I could feel it very well from across the room. Next to the fan there sat an old television set, tuned to the opening of the France vs. Uruguay game of the World Cup. Samantha, Sema and I sat on one couch, with the chief to our right in an armchair. Hans, Emil and Walter sat on a couch to our left, flanked by Mama and someone representing the elders, in his elderly robe. A younger man that I didn't recognize sat on the other side of the chief.

They spoke for a long time in Ewe, it must have been twenty minutes. I started to think the *presentation* was watching the World Cup with the chief. I was rooting for France because in the opening anthems, Uruguay players looked like an army of blue robots, and France's players had their arms around each other. I had nothing else on which to base my favoritism, so that would have to do. Plus, France has the Louvre. You could say France started to play dirty, but you could also say that Uruguay just fell down a lot and whined about it. After a while, my concentration on the game was interrupted when Emil started talking in English, which meant he was addressing me and Samantha.

Mama and Sema took us into another room, where there was a second, smaller television set also programmed to the game. They had two nicely wrapped packages under their arms—presents! They presented us each with a fancy African dress (more like a robe with a fancy neckline), a headdress, and bracelets. They were absolutely beautiful. This inspired a photo frenzy when we returned to the room filled with men, and since we're girls and we like our cameras, we took plenty of pictures with everyone while we were all dressed up.

We returned to our compound for dinner, rice with a piece of chicken. Bright and Kosi showed up, and I started the Twilight movie for them on my laptop. The volume isn't the greatest, so it was generally hard to hear, especially after it started pouring down rain on top of our tin roof. But the boys seemed to enjoy it just the same. Half way through, Michael and Akiti came by and settled themselves to watch the movie with us— Michael was on the floor at my feet, and Akiti snuggled on my lap. After a little while they both started to nod off. Akiti's small hand was gripped around my fingers, and the tiny poof of hair on top of her head was smushed against my chin. Mama came by to clean up dinner and asked if she could speak with me outside.

Samantha and I have told Mama on numerous occasions that we'd like her and the kids to come visit us in the United States. I also think that if she decided to live in the States, of all the people in the village, she and her children would be able to make it, not only because of their English skills but also their personalities. When she pulled me outside, she asked if I'd said anything to Sema about our plans for her to come to the US. I said no, and that I wasn't planning to, mainly because for now it was just a nice idea. Mama was worried Sema would be envious of our invitation, though of course we would open up our homes to any of them who came to the U.S. for a visit. Mama said she was calling a friend of hers to get information on Ghanaian passport fees for her and the children. I started to get really excited that she might actually come to the U.S.! We exchanged contact information, and Samantha and I offered to do what we could to help with paperwork (as far as getting a tourist visa for the US… I'm not really sure how that works).

It was late by the time the movie ended, and our room was starting to look bare from all the packing we'd done. I started to think about what I'd like to do in the great U.S. of A. when we got back. Shower, have vegetables, sushi, and tacos, see a movie, and go to the beach. This time tomorrow, we'd be on a plane headed for Germany.

June 12, 2010
Saying Goodbye

We got up just after 5 AM, to be ready for the community gathering, though I expected the Gong-Gong man would go missing again. He was indeed missing again, and there was no gathering, so Anyo and the chief will have to express their need for library volunteers on their own. We had brown-brown for breakfast again, which was awesome because it's my favorite. It was so early that we were able to pack the rest of our things, and spend what little time we had left with Michael, Akiti and Cicho. After a month of hanging out with the little ones, Cicho chose this morning to be the first morning he said anything in English: "Yea!" He exclaimed it whenever he jumped for the most part. It was really cute. He also decided that he would be super affectionate this morning—he kept gesturing for me to pick him up, and if I was sitting he would come over and climb into my lap. I threw him up in the air, which he adored, and he'd giggle and then ask me to do it again. After Cicho and I played chase, Akiti wanted some attention as well. Samantha and Michael were busy trying to catch Samantha's favorite goat for a photo op. It was a really nice morning, and the kids were dressed very nicely. Cicho had on a white polo shirt (how it was still white I have no idea) and Akiti was wearing a pretty silk dress with flowers on it, her hair poof standing tall. I'll really miss these kids. I hope Mama gets a chance to bring them to the US.

When it was time to gather our things, Kosi and Sema helped bring everything to the roadside. We waited a while longer there, at Peace's storefront, while several people came by to bid us a safe journey—Samuel, the chief's wife, Rafiki, Peace the hairdresser… and the resident Crazy. For the most part even at the storefront we were engrossed with Cicho and Akiti. Akiti wouldn't let go of me. She'd stand in front of me, hugging my hands. I think I wasn't as emotional this time around because I so hoped I would see them again, next time in the US. We didn't see Kofi or Jessica to say goodbye, but Kosi hung out with us until we got on the bus. We waved goodbye, and Michael and Akiti were smiling their giant smiles and waving back fervently. Mama didn't want to accompany us to Ho because she didn't want to say goodbye, so Emil and Sema went with us.

They helped us into a tro-tro after going through a mob of tro-tro drivers grabbing our arms and trying to grab our bags to help us to their tro-tro. Finally, we got to the one destined for Accra. Defying the laws of physics, the driver managed to stuff all of our things into the back, and some under seats, and tied the trunk nearly shut with a piece of green string. It didn't look quite strong enough to hold it closed for the entire three-hour ride we were about to embark upon… but then again, the laws of physics don't seem to apply in Ghana. Sure enough, it held. We waved goodbye to Sema and Emil and began the next leg of our journey home.

When we approached the immigration checkpoint on the road, we had to wait for a really long time. Samantha and I went through just fine, but three other men were from Togo and didn't have passports. While they were interrogated, I occupied myself with the scene of a nearby vendor table. Women sat around it, selling cassava and plantains… and snails. BIG snails. At first, I thought they were conch shells, but then I saw the snail heads sticking out and wiggling around. They were piled into three large bowls. I watched as three snails, one at a time, very slowly, attempted escape. They slowly moved from the bowls, dropped down to the table below, slugged to the edge, and dropped again to a lower table. Fascinating.

Finally, we were on the move again. I was starving, and feeling very claustrophobic in the middle of the very back seat of the tro-tro. If I wanted to get out, half the tro-tro would have to exit before I could move since the aisles had seats in them that folded down from the bench seat. I put my head down on the seat in front of me. Before long, Samantha was tapping my arm, a lot. I looked up to see the tro-tro had slowed. I leaned around to try to see what the commotion was about, and then I saw it—a giant baboon was crossing the road. Even crouched, he was still taller than the cars. He walked on his knuckles and waddled his brown naked baboon butt behind him. Once he had crossed, he turned and looked in our direction with a big head, with huge puffy-hairy cheeks. We saw a monkey! We saw an animal that wasn't a goat or chicken!

The tro-tro dropped us at the side of the road, and I thought the driver gestured for us to cross the road to get a taxi to the airport. I looked doubtful at him, hoping that's not what he meant, since carrying my belongings would be a disaster without a proper pack mule. Luckily, a taxi drove up and the transfer was relatively painless.

Once at the airport, I managed to drag myself and my things very slowly to a waiting area that had air conditioning, which was a fair shock to the system. When we finally boarded our flight toward Dulles, I hoped my dad would be there waiting to greet me with some fresh raw vegetables, cucumbers and carrots.

A Summary of Interviews & Focus Groups

My time in Saviefe Gbogame inspired an assessment of sex education in this rural farming community. I am so thankful for their candid conversations that helped me learn about the challenges they face. Seventeen personal interviews and three focus groups (summarized in the appendix) highlighted common themes of problems, needs, wants, and suggestions of a rural community in addressing sex education. Collaborative efforts by local government authorities, rural schools, parents, and community members would help this community a great deal.

Saviefe Gbogame is a Christian community that holds religion as a form of guidance and moral education. Praying is a part of daily life, whether it is for good farming weather, good health, or food to eat. Therefore, it is not surprising that so many participants identified religion as a positive mechanism to encourage good and moral behavior. This guidance is seen as a necessary part of education for adolescents, especially concerning sex education. Combined with comprehensive sex education that can equip children with the information and knowledge necessary to make well-informed decisions about their sexual behavior, religion can encourage both abstinence and respectful behavior in relationships, and help guide children to make thoughtful decisions about their well-being.

It is estimated that half of the JSS students were sexually active. Several interview participants felt that sex education may encourage children to practice sexual behavior and therefore felt it should be taught when the child is older, between the ages of 14 and 20. However, in light of an increasing number of teenage pregnancies and subsequent school dropouts, some considered the earlier sex education could be introduced, the better. Roughly half of the interview participants felt that sex education should begin at or before age 10. It is clear that the gravity of the current situation is forcing some parents to believe that waiting to educate children when they are 14 or 15 would be in vain, as by that time many adolescents are already sexually active. A 9-year-old girl was the youngest child they were aware of who had been sexually active, though the age of the older boy was not revealed. Because of this, it is not surprising that even though all participants were advocates of abstinence, many perceived the introduction of contraption methods as a necessary component of any sex education effort for both adolescents and adults in the community.

Many cited the lack of parental initiative in teaching children about sex and reproductive health as the main reason children are resorting to peers for often-inaccurate information. It was mentioned in an interview that peer information could do more harm than good when they share inaccurate knowledge of contraceptives and how to use them. A few participants explained that the parents are also uneducated regarding reproductive health and are therefore unable to impart information to their child.

Many people living in Saviefe Gbogame rely on farming as their main source of income. Rural women are often charged with most if not all of the domestic chores. They are up before dawn, preparing food, washing clothes, and caring for the small children. They spend all day at the farm, return home, cook supper, bathe the children, and are exhausted. There is no leisure time for a parent to help a child with their homework, let alone educate them and provide guidance regarding reproductive health.

Because women are continually perceived to be the only gender affected by pregnancy, and who care for children day and night, it is no wonder that many reproductive health education efforts have failed to reach males in the community. This perception transcends to whom the sex education should or should not be targeted, and also affects the dynamics between a man and woman in a sexual relationship.

One woman described her perception of necessary check-ups for sexually transmitted infections while engaged in unfaithful sexual activity:

> "If you keep to one person you can examine yourself and know what you are. If you run from here to there, you need to go. If you keep to your spouse there is no need [for check-ups]. It is common for men to get check-ups if they are unfaithful. But men will get upset if you ask them to wear a condom in marriage."

This demonstrated that even though some may understand that sexually transmitted infections are a risk, many perceive it to only be a problem if you are the one with multiple partners. If you are faithful to one partner, it is not necessary for you to get checked, even if your spouse has multiple partners. Individual behavior is not connected to who is actually at risk.

Poverty is a part of life in Saviefe Gbogame. It affects one's nutrition, education, and can impose limitations on how to occupy one's leisure time. It was mentioned often among the interview participants that adolescents resort to prostitution when their parents cannot provide food or clothing. The children were not necessarily choosing career prostitution along with the inherent implications of a criminal lifestyle, but rather engaging in individual discrete acts in exchange for soup or an article of clothing. Poverty was also cited as a reason why most people only seek medical care in emergent cases, and why some choose to treatment ailments with traditional methods, rather than seeking professional medical care. With the introduction of the country's health insurance plan, those registered are able to access affordable care. However, accessibility becomes an issue when dealing with rural communities. Transportation costs can hinder one's ability to get to a medical facility. Even if one can afford the transportation fees, many farmers cannot afford to lose a day's worth of work and wages to travel for medical care.

An overwhelming majority of interview participants expressed a desire for the Ghanaian government to help implement a sex education program in the rural schools, as it has done for urban schools, and to provide sources of reproductive health education for the community as a whole. Whether due to a lack of resources, or a lack of manpower, it was evident that government policies and projects were not reaching the rural area of Saviefe Gbogame. The community received sporadic health education efforts from various NGOs in the past, but failed to see any sustainable efforts or results. The groups asserted that any effort of reproductive health education would be more credible when facilitated by a trained, government-appointed representative, and should be a collective effort between the Ghanaian government, the school system, and parents within the community.

Adolescent reproductive health and the services and education that are inherently involved have been the subjects of much research, and increasingly so over the past few decades. However, as we further our understanding of the situation facing many rural adolescents, our responsibility is to ensure they are equipped with the knowledge and skills necessary to make smart decisions as they attempt to balance relationships, young adulthood, and sexuality. The implementation of effective rural reproductive health education is vital in achieving this goal.

APPENDIX A: Interviews

I asked participants at what age they thought children should be exposed to sex education, and nearly half expressed a desire for sex education to start at or before age 10. Two people thought ages 12 to 13 would be more appropriate, while five others didn't want children to learn about it until 14 or 16. Three felt sex education would not be appropriate until the child was between the ages of 18 and 20, as they expressed concern that upon exposing the children to this type of education would encourage sexual behavior.

> "It should be earlier than puberty, from 10 on. These days at the age of 13, they are pregnant. In our time it wasn't like that. The earlier sex education starts, the better."

> "Even at 6 or 8 years, kids know what sex is. At 12 years [sex education] is fine. By 14 or 15, it is too late."

> "Last year, three girls from Primary 6 were pregnant and dropped out of school. They were 13, 14, and 15 years old. Because in this financial system being tough, everything is quite unbearable. So to protect yourself, don't become involved in unwanted pregnancy. So you want to educate in sex education."

Gender bias was identified within current views of sex education, where females would obtain information about reproductive health more easily than males because females were the ones to experience pregnancy, child birth, and family care.

> "Girls cannot go to school because of pregnancy and finish school, and the boys are still able to go. It's upsetting."

> "It's the women who suffer a lot. I'm a man. I can impregnate you. After the delivery of the baby I can run away, so you the woman will suffer and need the sex education more than I do. She needs to understand sex education, because if pregnant you will become a school drop out."

Eleven of the seventeen participants perceived religion as a positive mechanism for encouraging moral behavior, and an asset to reproductive health education.

> "Kids in JSS, half are sexually active. It is very common. But when we go to a church service and hear the word of God, we are able to control ourselves. Church encourages people to wait. Some fall from peer pressure. Church helps you fight peer pressure."

> "One thing about us is that we believe in Christ. So you cannot do anything without praying and preaching the good news to them. Talking to them, giving them examples, and seeing themselves in those examples. And when you have sex you have transmitted diseases that damage you. You cannot go forward with education. if you the boy are handling the baby you cannot go to school or get a job because you take care

of a child. All these things involved praying and education."

Four participants identified some churches to be against sex education, contraception, and family planning:

"Some churches don't teach about condoms and the family planning I know about. They don't want anyone to have sex until they are married. Some churches don't like family planning or child spacing."

"Some churches preach that you don't have to go to hospital and pray instead. They always believe God is there. It is a sin for you to go to hospital--think it's a miracle, if there is a problem you can come to God. It's a problem, some churches don't even allow them to go to hospital, God will provide. It's not very common, but they are there. We have one like that in town called Faithful Lamb Church."

The travelling religious figure was described as follows:

"My mistake is contraceptives. If I had known, things would be different. A church brought someone to talk to us about sex about someone who didn't want to have a child. So in time of their love making, he spit his sperm outside which is killing the unborn child. He said also God didn't like masturbation. It is against His law. It's doing more harm than good. That's part of my dilemma. He came two years ago. He taught that you were a murderer. He was quoting from the Bible, and we are Christians. We thought he was telling us the right thing as we believe in the Bible. I am not convinced about what he was teaching because I know he's not a medical expert. But I also don't want to be a murderer. It is a problem. The church is ok with teaching contraceptive use. The traveling preacher taught this on his own agenda."

Poverty was mentioned often in the interviews as a contributing factor to teenage pregnancy. Prostitution as a means of survival was identified, and several people cited the lack of financial resources as a barrier to being able to afford medical care: transportation costs, long distances, and the loss of wages. Three participants perceived the poverty-induced lack of entertainment as a reason that adolescents engage in sexual behavior.

> "Hospitals are not near, and clinics are not common. If someone were to travel, the roads are bad and you will not feel like going. Work hinders as well."

> "If you don't have the money you cannot go including travel and doctor fees. The rural areas, you may have the money but lack transportation because of the route."

> "They don't have anyone to educate them on sex. Because of that, there is too much teenage pregnancy. With no sex education, there is peer pressure. Some parents let their kids to their own devices. Either listen to friends for advice or turn to prostitution for food. Also there is a lack of entertainment after supper. Married couples sleep at this point and the kids have no

entertainment, three or four hours outside before bed. Some sneak out to another person's house just for sex."

Nearly everyone expressed a desire for government implementation of sex education in rural schools as well as for the community. Many agreed as well that it would be taken more seriously if facilitated by a government appointed person. Some noted that government policies that involved sex education in public schools had only been implemented fully in urban areas, leaving the rural areas still at risk.

> "If the government passed a bill or any information, it goes from urban, then to rural. So you can see that they are already in the system so they have to take the forefront before the rural area gets the information."

It was also perceived that NGO involvement was inconsistent and unsustainable, and another factor in discrepancies between services and education offered to urban versus rural areas.

> "The government should be responsible but at times the government leaves it up to the NGOs to handle it. They should put [sex education] in rural schools. Three years ago, my church went to Ho about this sex education. A pastor directed us to a lawyer who is a woman for advice. Set a time to come but couldn't, so taught class at a nearby village instead. They took a banana and gave it to a girl and passed it around to ten people. The example was going from boy to boy you can see your life being destroyed like the banana going soft. The response was very good but it didn't stick at all. It should be an ongoing thing."

"As the rural areas, we have more production of babies. We don't have the education on how to prevent pregnancy. Urban areas have NGOs, resource specialists educating people. Rural areas, we don't have that."

"Five years ago an NGO came here called Jeremiah Mission. They have taken four people here and another community. We were trained for three days to talk to the community about sex education."

The lack of parental involvement in sex education was identified as a contributing factor to teenage pregnancy as well.

"Families don't teach them. In this area we are not trained in such a way, your mother, father, will not call you down and tell you about it. And kids feel shy about asking. The best place is at school and the community sessions. Parents don't discuss in rural area. NGO, school or church should have information that teaches about sex education. It depends on the family, but they probably don't teach it."

"Many parents are not performing their duties as parents. It is a failure on their part to educate their kids. There is not time. Parents just have no time with their kids. Parents go to farm and are tired when coming back, prepare fufu and then go to bed while kids are out."

In three interviews, it was said that most people only seek professional medical care in the case of an emergency. Four people mentioned the use of traditional methods of treatment, such as herbs and leaves to be ingested. Six people asserted that children obtain most of their knowledge of sex from their peers, rather than adults or other more accurate sources of information. It was unclear whether those who had been trained by the Jeremiah Mission were involved in any current efforts to educate the community on reproductive health. Participants mentioned the radio and festivals, like the Women's Rally or the Young Festival, as reliable sources of reproductive health information:

> "The Young festival is organized by chiefs. Churches are involved. It teaches women in the marriage sector how to go about sex, and keep your husband. These bring a lot of education to the women. Different churches have different programs. We have health education people we use to weigh babies and educate the mothers. Once a month a health official will come to weigh babies and teach prenatal and postnatal care. We also have a national women's rally once a year. Locally the district also has one twice a year. Women's Rally is a gathered parade to educate women on how to take care of the house and themselves so their husbands will be pleased, how to care for visitors, and keep husband from going out. It teaches local trades. Some mothers are about learn such as beads, silk making. Child health is a main topic because it is only for women, no men. The better you take care of them, the better life will be. These programs benefit teenagers and

women because you will know how to space children
and how to talk to your
husband and help your family grow better."

The majority of participants thought it appropriate for
adolescent sex education to include information on
contraception as well as encouraging abstinence. In fact, a few
specifically expressed a desire for more information on methods
of contraception.

> "They may not stay away for abstinence and use a
> condom thinking he is then 100 percent protected and
> then the harm is done. Talk about it, but make sure they
> know everything. One thing about the kids is they learn
> most things from their peers. Someone may introduce
> a contraceptive to a sister or friend, but they may not
> teach them how to use it. That's what's wrong with it."

Two participants expressed the desire for sex education to be
ongoing:

> "It is important in rural areas. Education should
> continually happen. To change from one way to
> another is difficult. Once you are used to a situation, it's
> difficult to change. Health education should be here
> every day. It will take time to get used to it, but it will
> be good. Change will work."

APPENDIX B: Focus Groups

Participants expressed a desire for the Ghanaian government to help implement and facilitate health education programs in rural schools, as the government has done for urban schools. When asked if there were members of the community who would want to volunteer to run some sort of health education program in the village, participants suggested that may require compensation. They agreed that bringing in a representative from the Ministry of Health would be more effective, and taken more seriously than just a member of the community.

The focus groups agreed that sex education should include: basic biology of puberty and sexual intercourse; abstinence; contraceptives; risks of sexual behavior (sexually transmitted infections, teenage pregnancy); and the importance of visiting a doctor for regular check-ups. JSS teachers stressed the teachings of contraceptive use as a means to reduce the number of unwanted pregnancies among students as young as those enrolled in Primary 4 or Primary 5 (ages 9-10). They believed many JSS students were sexually active, and noted that most children obtain information about sex from peers rather than parents or other more credible sources.

Poverty and ignorance were identified as barriers to accessing medical treatment, claiming some women to resort to local herbal treatments rather than attending prenatal clinics, as many people struggle with transportation fees to and from clinics.

> "If someone is sick, you tell them to go to the hospital but they think they will be ok, or use herbs and local

medicines. If the person doesn't have money, it sometimes even trumps the ignorance."

What limited information that is available on reproductive health is perceived to be obtained primarily from television and radio. One group asserted that nothing was in place in the rural areas to help address women's health concerns, and expressed a desire for more education on contraceptives.

> "If a woman should know that having sex without protection can have plenty of kids, which may cause a problem in the future. Though the husband may not like to protect, she should still try. Someone should come and talk to the women of the community and talk to them about all these things, and talk to the men about protection as well. Now we have a female [condom] and a male condom. If a man doesn't want to use it, the woman can protect herself with a condom."

AFTERWORD

Every so often, I receive a text message with updates or a holiday greeting from Emil on behalf of the Anyo Group. I smile every time, and I applaud the Anyo Group as they continue efforts for development within the Saviefe community which includes a healthy abundance of okra from their community vegetable garden!

Though at times I was frustrated by a few actions made by Anyo Group, it was helpful to see how they came to certain decisions. It's hard to imagine that someone without any guidance would instinctively know how to run a library, or the value of desktop computers versus laptops, or how to develop problem-solving skills to navigate through difficult situations. It lends support to the importance of project continuity and continued guidance for members of the community. I took for granted being raised in a country where kids are taught to speak their mind, or raising voices for change, or just general problem-solving activities.

The people of Saviefe shared their world with me. They are generous, warm, and welcoming. I am fortunate to have had this experience, and I'm grateful that their friendship has made such an impact on my life. I think of them fondly, and will always cherish the time we spent together.

www.ingramcontent.com/pod-product-compliance
Lightning Source LLC
Chambersburg PA
CBHW031054250726
48655CB00004B/1438